The Master Trader

The Master Trader

Birinyi's Secrets to Understanding the Market

LASZLO BIRINYI

WILEY

Published by John Wiley & Sons, Inc., Hoboken, New Jersey.
Published simultaneously in Canada.

For general information on our other products and services or for technical support, please contact our Customer Care Department within the United States at (800) 762-2974, outside the United States at (317) 572-3993 or fax (317) 572-4002.

Wiley publishes in a variety of print and electronic formats and by print-on-demand. Some material included with standard print versions of this book may not be included in e-books or in print-on-demand. If this book refers to media such as a CD or DVD that is not included in the version you purchased, you may download this material at http://booksupport.wiley .com. For more information about Wiley products, visit www.wiley.com.

Library of Congress Cataloging-in-Publication Data:

Birinyi, Laszlo.
   The master trader : Birinyi's secrets to understanding the market / Laszlo Birinyi.
      pages cm.—(Wiley trading series)
   Includes bibliographical references and index.
   ISBN 978-1-118-77473-1 (cloth); ISBN 978-1-118-77486-1 (ebk);
ISBN 978-1-118-77478-6 (ebk)
   1. Investment analysis. 2. Technical analysis (Investment analysis)
3. Speculation. 4. Investments. I. Title.
   HG4529.B55 2014
   332.6—dc23

                                                                    2013027503

Printed in the United States of America
10 9 8 7 6 5 4 3 2

*This is for the women in my life; Natalie, Anna, and my wife
Jill Costelloe who knows better than most the true meaning
of "for better or for worse, through sickness and in health."
For that I am, and will always be, grateful.*

Contents

Acknowledgments

A large number of individuals contributed to this book: hundreds of clients and accounts who provided me an opportunity to learn and develop an understanding of the market. I hope that they have directly benefitted from the education and will continue to do so.

More specifically, Frank Basile gave me an opportunity to trade when my only attribute was enthusiasm. Jay Mangan encouraged me to develop ideas and aids for traders. At "The Brothers," MRB allowed me unprecedented latitude in product development, while EO and SS understood the value-added component of what we developed.

More recently, the staff at Birinyi Associates contributed to this writing with a special thanks to Jeff Rubin, my long-time associate, whose prodigious memory and organizational skills were critical to this effort and without whom it would not have happened.

While I am grateful to all of the above, the issues and content are mine alone and any failings or shortcomings are those of the author.

Preface

This is not a book about making money in your spare time, nor does it contain formulas that will allow you to retire early or double your money over the next two weeks. There are no guaranteed recipes for success or easy roads to riches.

Warren Buffett once said about life, or maybe it was the market, that the key was to make a large snowball and find a steep hill. For investors today, both professionals and individuals, the reality is not only that the hill is getting steeper but that it is increasingly *uphill*.

For a variety of reasons, including technology, communications, regulatory changes, and the like, investing is getting more complex and with complexity comes increased difficulty. Regulators and legislatures would like you to believe that rule changes, new instruments, and other developments have made life easier for the individual. I've disputed that from day one and our research and experience regularly highlight the failings of their conclusions.

Exchanges are no longer quasi-public institutions, but are now businesses. And like all businesses, they have to compete with one another. Brokerage firms' primary focus is on their own, not customers' activity. Stockbrokers have been replaced by financial advisors whose focus is on funds and instruments that provide continuous income to themselves—as opposed to buying a stock that you may hold for five years and that would therefore never generate commissions after day one.

Funds engage in marketing rather than markets, and while I do believe that some of the criticism of professional managers is unwarranted, their failing to adapt and adjust will continue to result in mediocre performance, which is still rewarded with seven-figure compensation.

At the same time, the individual can no longer count on employee pension plans. Now IRAs and 401ks have shifted the burden to the employee and very few individuals have the wherewithal, the education, or even the time to run the financial maze.

This book details many of these issues. It should make you aware of some of the issues every investor faces (including professionals who are sadly unaware of many of them as well). Among our recommendations is education, including reading both current and historical articles and writings. *The Money Game* by Adam Smith, the 1967 bestseller, must be at the top of your reading list.

If money is a game, then like all games there are winners and losers. Hopefully, you will emerge a winner by understanding the reality of today's markets and being aware of the landmines and pitfalls. It is not necessarily a guide to making money but should illustrate what you must do and consider to avoid *losing* money.

It is also intended for the sophisticated or professional investor. Sadly, one of the characteristics of money managers today is their disregard for the market itself. No longer are ticker tapes a critical input, trading feedback is nonexistent, and history is seldom incorporated or interrogated.

Peter Lynch once suggested that poker was a useful ingredient in the investment process and I would argue that it has been more useful to me than my graduate studies. I have addressed some of the issues that should be incorporated in the investment process:

- If futures are down 1 percent, what is the market likely to do that day?
- A stock reports good news after the close and trades up 10 percent; what will happen tomorrow?
- What is the best measure of investment sentiment?

Unfortunately, going forward is going to be even more difficult. Issues such as computerized trading, fragmented markets, unregulated blogs, and commentary will continue to obfuscate the investing landscape and investors' lives will become even more difficult.

Having lived in New York City for many years, I never got into golf. Nevertheless, I think that game and the market have some parallels. Very, very few golfers become scratch or even one-handicap players. But someone with a 10 or 12 handicap can enjoy the game, hope to break 80 one day, and play at various courses around the world.

Very few individuals will ever beat the market. Remember that in June 2013 the very best golfers in the world played the Open at Merion and no one beat the benchmark! Most individuals must play the financial game, and hopefully we have outlined and highlighted some of the rules. One which you should tape to your computer was a banner in the *Financial Times* in the summer of 2012:

Wall Street Always Wins

The Master Trader

CHAPTER 1

Technical Analysis: Fuhgeddaboudit

*I realized technical analysis didn't work when I turned
the charts upside down and didn't get a different answer.*
—Warren Buffett

*There are three roads to ruin: women, gambling, and
technicians. The most pleasant is with women, the quick-
est is with gambling, but the surest is with technicians.*
—Georges Pompidou

Admit it. You were as surprised as I was to find that the former President
of France said something about technical analysis. Perhaps it illustrates that individuals who have even a casual interest in the stock
market are more likely using a technical approach of some sort. Usually it
comes via charts because charts, tables, and graphics are, after all, part and
parcel of our daily life. It is easier to show a chart on *CNBC*, *Bloomberg*, or
in *BusinessWeek* than GM's balance sheet or income statement. Most market
letters are technical in nature, claiming to provide guidance and clarity by
reducing all required inputs to a simple, concise graph or table.

Unfortunately, neither life nor the stock market is that simple. We contend
after years of analysis and experience that *technical analysis* does not work.

It is not predictive, it is not consistent, and it is not analysis. While we
may not go so far as to compare it to a snake oil salesperson or three-card
Monte players, in the ultimate test—making money—it fails.

It fails for a variety of reasons. To begin, it is not a discipline. Unlike
the more traditional, fundamental analysts who begin with the economy,
examine industries, and eventually look at individual stocks, the technical
tool kit is a vast array of approaches and ingredients.

At one recent seminar, the speaker provided a list of technical elements:

Charts: Line & Ratio	Technical Studies: Oscillators
Bar Charts	Trending
Candle Patterns	Price Pattern Analysis
Point & Figure	Psychology
Market Picture	Fibonacci
Kase Charts	Dow Theory
TBL Charts	Cycle Theory
	Elliott Wave Theory
	Sector Rotation
	Sentiment
	Breadth

This list is by no means complete. Over the years, the stock market has been "forecast" by astronomy, musical lyrics, any number of statistical/mathematic approaches, and, lest we forget, the Super Bowl. We would be remiss not to mention an article in *Playboy*: "How to Beat the Stock Market by Watching Girls, Counting Aspirin, Checking Sunspots, and Wondering Where the Yellow Went" (July 1973).

In mid-2010, investors were warned about the ominous signals coming from the Hindenburg Omen:[1]

> *Over the past week, the amount of media coverage given to a rather obscure conglomerate of technical signals called "The Hindenburg Omen" has been extensive . . . it is supposed to be a very bad sign for the stock market.*
>
> *The word "crash" is frequently found in the Omen forecast.*

A *Wall Street Journal* blog later reported "Yep, it was a dud", and the market, rather than crashing, cracking, or correcting, gained 22 percent through year end (see Figure 1.1).

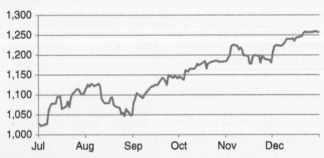

FIGURE 1.1 S&P 500: 2H 2010

Source: Birinyi Associates, Inc., Bloomberg.

INDICATORS: PICK ONE, ANY ONE

The technical analyst/chartist has therefore an abundance of options. Our contention is that too often the facts or indicators support a conclusion; if the indicator changes, no problem, another approach (bearish or bullish) or indicator is inserted.

One approach that we would endorse is to have a consistent process, perhaps beginning with an analysis of the 30 stocks in the Dow Jones Industrial Average (DJIA). A manageable sample that could be regularly analyzed and then supported by some of the other elements listed previously.

Unfortunately, one such exercise only reinforces our argument that technical efforts are of little value. Some years back, *Barron's* asked three chartists to review the 30 individual stocks that comprise the DJIA:

> *The first reported that it was indeed "a classic long-term bull" and expected 2,410–2,825 for the rest of the year with an upside target of 3,400–3,425 "possible" over the next twelve months.*
>
> *The second was a bit more cautious: "supporting one more move into new high ground" with the possibility of a "more serious down" turn in the Spring.*
>
> *The third felt that eighteen names were bullish with six others neutral. "During the current quarter . . . test the Dow's intraday high of 2,745." After that "could rise above 3,000" in the first quarter of the next year.*

Unfortunately, for investors and analysts alike they were woefully wrong.

October 12, 1987
Analyzing the Dow
Three Top Technicians Size Up the 30 Industrials

Figure 1.2 illustrates and articulates one of our concerns regarding the approach: *Technicians have a disappointing record at critical junctures.* This applied not only in 1987 but regularly and, sadly, increasingly so.

The 1987 Crash marked the end of the great Volcker rally, which began August 12, 1982 and saw the S&P gain 229 percent. At its birth, at another critical juncture, the technical community was also AWOL. It is interesting to review the mood of those times, while the stock market was technically, in a bear market, it was to be a relatively mild decline (losing 24 percent). But the economy was in a recession (which ended in November 1982) and a number of economists suggested that *depression* might better describe

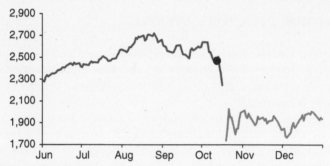

FIGURE 1.2   DJIA: 1987
Source: Birinyi Associates, Inc., Bloomberg.

the landscape. Inflation made investors wary of bonds, even as the 30-year Treasury was yielding 14 percent.

The inflation concern was dramatized in the infamous *BusinessWeek* cover, "The Death of Equities," shown in Figure 1.3.

Ironically, the magazine was not an inflection point or buy signal, as it was actually published during a bull market (see Figure 1.4).

FIGURE 1.3   *BusinessWeek* Cover (August 13, 1979)

FIGURE 1.4   S&P 500: 1974 Bull Market
Source: Birinyi Associates, Inc., Bloomberg.

Less notorious was *Forbes'* response with their cover "Back from the Dead?" (September 17, 1979).

While the rally's catalyst was Dr. Henry Kaufman's comments on August 17, 1982, the market had actually bottomed the previous Thursday. Over the intervening weekend, a lengthy *New York Times* article detailed the views of several technical analysts:

Dark Days on Wall Street
The long bear market seems to be entering its final phase. The end could be violent but also cathartic.

A prominent technician argued that the market must first capitulate "... a time when everybody simply gives up." He suggested a final sell-off could come by November, maybe sooner, and the next six months would be critical.

Joe Granville, the most visible member of the community, suggested 550 to 650 by January.

On Tuesday, August 17, the DJIA rose 38.79 or 4.9 percent and traded 92 million shares (the average of the previous 50 days had been 53 million shares). On August 18, a new record, and the first 100-million share day saw volume rise to 131.6 million shares. Despite the gains and activity, chartists were generally unimpressed:

... the Dow could well break its '82 low.
    ... an even lower Dow reading, about 680, is anticipated by the end of the month by Justin Mamis, a well-regarded technical analyst.[2]

One month later, John Schulz wrote a piece for *Barron's* on September 13, 1982:

Messing Up the Tea Leaves, Where Technical Analysis Went Wrong

Why did so many pros fail to see it coming? Technical analysis must shoulder much of the blame . . . [technical analysis] offered monumentally bad advice just when—for perhaps the first time in modern history—it finally proved decisively instrumental in shaping majority opinion.

Schulz wrote that the technicians were unanimous in their view that a bottom would be accompanied by "waves of massive selling." Cash was not at expected bear market levels, and sentiment readings likewise failed to reflect an overwhelmingly negative view. He also suggested that the bearish indicators had become too popular and accepted and therefore discounted.

1990: ANOTHER OPPORTUNITY MISSED

If the chartists were negative in 1982, their attitude in 1990 was even more pronounced (see Figure 1.5). Following Saddam Hussein's foray into Kuwait on August 2, 1990, the market took a sharp, concentrated dive that many expected to be protracted and painful.

Since the decline was event-driven and abrupt, one cannot fault analysts—technical or otherwise—for failing to anticipate the drop. But

FIGURE 1.5   S&P 500: 2H 1990

Source: Birinyi Associates, Inc., Bloomberg.

their reaction afterward is further evidence of our concern that at critical instances, the approach is unsatisfactory:

Analysts Are Reading Their Charts—And Weeping
With virtually every major indicator pointing south, the market slump may stretch well into next year. . . .

How low is low? Some see the Dow touching bottom at 2,200 . . . or 1,700 . . . or 1,444.

BusinessWeek, **October 8, 1990**

A Bear-Market Rally? It Sure Looks Like One
. . . watches for three signals that would indicate more than just a bear-market rally. Right now he can't detect evidence of even one. . .

Jack Solomon, technical analyst at Bear Stearns, puts things bluntly. The first rallies don't hold. Sell them . . . it's a trap.

Wall Street Journal, **November 21, 1990**

Analysts: Shades of Nostradamus
On December 24, 1990, after the market had gained 11 percent off the bottom, *Barron's* interviewed four analysts.

The first expected a "slide toward 2,400 and then a modest recovery to 2,700–2,800." The second was looking for gains late in 1991 after trading to the 2,100–2,200 level. Analyst number three also thought 2,100 was the next stop followed by a rally to 2,700.

The fourth was the most bearish (2,000, "maybe 1,900") and then trade in the range of 2,000 to 3,000 over the next four or five years (see Figure 1.6).

At the end of the year, the best we can say about these calls is that they tried (see Figure 1.7).

The Market May Be About to "Start Acting Ugly"
. . . technicians are widely predicting grim tidings for the market . . . some analysts are warning of a possible reprise of the events of 1987.

The market traded a bit lower in November/December (–6.9 percent) so once again the bears were in full cry:[3]

Watch Out for Falling Bulls
Wall Street's technicians are trumpeting a horrible crash—again.[4]

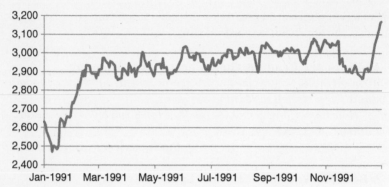

FIGURE 1.6   DJIA: 1991

Source: Birinyi Associates, Inc., Bloomberg.

(These articles were full-page features, not small, insignificant stories relegated to the bottom corner of a page.)

We cited Mr. Buffett earlier. One indicator that is often cited is the weekly sentiment of the American Association of Individual Investors (AAII). Figure 1.8 shows the chart for the 2009 bull market.

Figure 1.9 is the same chart but inverted. As the gentleman from Omaha said . . .

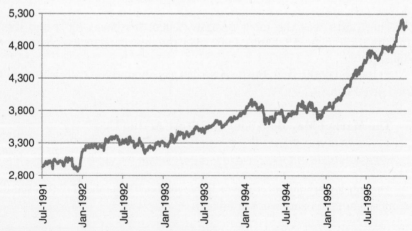

FIGURE 1.7   DJIA: 2H 1991 through 1995

Source: Birinyi Associates, Inc., Bloomberg.

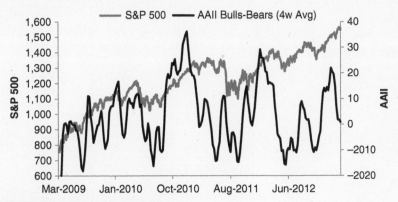

FIGURE 1.8 AAII versus S&P 500

Source: AAII, Birinyi Associates, Inc., Bloomberg.

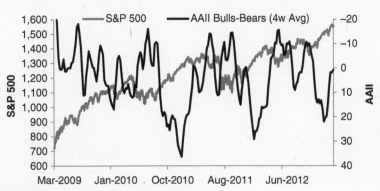

FIGURE 1.9 AAII versus S&P 500 (Inverted)

Source: AAII, Birinyi Associates, Inc., Bloomberg.

NOTES

1. Michael Kahn, "Taking Stock of a Scary Market Signal," *Barron's*, August 8, 2010.
2. Dan Dorfman, "Stock Rally Washed Away," *Daily News*, August 27, 1982.
3. Gary Weiss, "The Market May Be About to 'Start Acting Ugly,'" *BusinessWeek*, August 4, 1991.
4. Gary Weiss, "Watch Out for Falling Bulls," *BusinessWeek*, December 15, 1991.

CHAPTER 2

The Failure of Technical Efforts

*Economists set themselves too easy, too useless a task if
in tempestuous seasons they can only tell us that when
the storm is long past the ocean is flat again.*
— John Maynard Keynes

The obvious question is why, given the resources and talents of so many, does the technical approach (in all its manifestations) apparently fail to provide guidance and illumination. As we suggested earlier, the abundance of approaches under the technical umbrella provide a "salad bar" of indicators and tools from which an analyst can choose to support a conclusion.

In addition to a lack of discipline and coherence, technical analysis—in our view—fails for reasons that include:

- Amazingly, a lack of *analysis.*
- Most analysts didn't, and don't, *understand* the market.
- Not recognizing the changing nature of the market, the industry, or the environment.
- Commentary rather than tangible advice.

It is both surprising and disappointing to find that little analysis and rigorous testing have been undertaken on the various indicators that analysts incorporate in their efforts. Earlier we cited John Schultz's concern that the prevailing opinion at the 1982 bottom required a massive sell-off or, as it was later termed, capitulation.

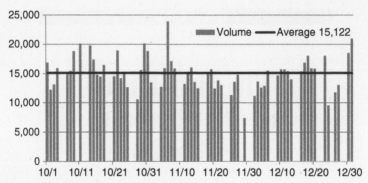

FIGURE 2.1   DJIA Volume 4Q 1974 (Shares)

Source: Birinyi Associates, Inc., Bloomberg.

But why? The previous significant bottom, December 1974, was not accompanied or characterized by investor flight (see Figure 2.1). There was no discernible increase in activity as volume remained about average throughout the entire quarter. Did no one consider that in their strategy?

Or, we might examine the popular and oft-quoted weekly survey of advisory services, which is tracked and provided by *Investors Intelligence*.

This indicator is considered a *contrary* one arguing that if too many individuals are positive, who is left to buy? Also, it suggests that there is the madness of crowds and this is one method to identify when that tipping point has been reached. Like many theories, the logic is impeccable but this is, after all, the stock market.

Historically (back to 1963), the most positive readings of the survey were January 16, 1976 and January 23, 1976, with 81 percent of the respondents bullish, a year the S&P was to gain 19 percent (see Figures 2.2 and 2.3).

FIGURE 2.2   S&P 500

Source: Birinyi Associates, Inc., Bloomberg.

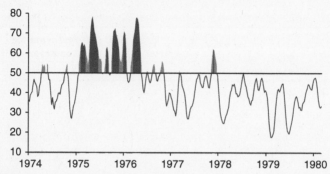

FIGURE 2.3   Investors Intelligence Bullish Sentiment (Four-Week Moving Average)
Source: Investors Intelligence, Birinyi Associates, Inc.

Later in that same market it was more useful. At the beginning of 1979, investors were bearish as the S&P traded to 100 before staging a rally that was to take it to 130. But as the market rallied, so did investors. We might also note that the volatility of the results is unsettling.

A LACK OF ANALYSIS . . . (AGAIN)

Another favored indicator is the number of stocks above their average price of the last 200 days, or roughly ten months. This indicator occurs as the result of many stocks having had a substantial move. The assumption is that it is more likely that the market will pause or slow down than continue higher. It, like other indicators, creates what is commonly termed an "overbought" condition. Conversely, when relatively few stocks have done well, a rally is more likely, creating an "oversold" condition.

The latter is actually true; when relatively few stocks (by this definition) have done well, it suggests that most stocks are doing poorly. Indeed this is the case. As shown in Table 2.1, there have been (in the past 20 years) six instances when only 20 percent of the S&P names are higher than they were—on average—200 days ago. If we measure from when we first breach that measure, in five of the six instances, the market, as we might expect, rallies. It rallies despite the fact that the readings may go lower. In January 2008, at the low, only 1 percent of the S&P 500 names were above their 200-day average.

As shown, buying when this indicator is oversold is not only profitable, it is very profitable. To illustrate how much so, we might at this point interject our 5 percent rule. Over the past 100 years, the DJIA has had an average annual price appreciation approximating 5.5 percent. In Table 2.1,

TABLE 2.1 S&P 500 Performance After It First Crosses Below 20 Percent

First Below 20%	Min Reading	S&P 500 Performance After It First Crosses Below 20 Percent		
		1M	3M	6M
Dec-1994	20%	3.42%	8.46%	20.23%
Aug-1998	15%	0.21	13.84	21.93
Sep-2001	18%	11.15	18.03	19.26
Jul-2002	16%	15.80	7.87	9.99
Jan-2008	1%	−1.69	−2.82	−10.55
Aug-2011	7%	−2.17	3.15	9.36
	Average	**4.45%**	**8.09%**	**11.70%**
	Median	**1.81%**	**8.17%**	**14.63%**
	Percent Positive	**67%**	**83%**	**83%**

Source: Birinyi Associates, Inc.

buying in August 1998 led to an almost 22 percent return in six months or what would have taken, on a historical basis, four years to achieve. As the cliché goes, that works for me.

What then happens when a large number of stocks are overbought? Using 80 percent as a threshold or indicator of an overbought market, we might expect a correction or consolidation as shown in Table 2.2. In fact, the market becomes even more overbought and six months out has gained well over 6 percent.

Thus, buying when the market becomes oversold is, not surprisingly, a profitable strategy. On the other hand, buying when the market is overbought is similarly profitable.

TABLE 2.2 S&P 500 Performance After It First Crosses Above 80 Percent

First Above 80%	Max Reading	S&P 500 Performance After It First Crosses Above 80 Percent		
		1M	3M	6M
Jul-1997	83%	3.53%	5.87%	6.13%
May-2003	91%	1.31	4.07	9.84
Dec-2004	81%	−3.49	−3.11	0.29
Feb-2007	84%	−4.23	3.73	1.20
Jul-2009	94%	5.11	10.77	17.82
Jan-2011	83%	2.53	4.76	5.33
	Average	**0.79%**	**4.35%**	**6.77%**
	Median	**1.92%**	**4.42%**	**5.73%**
	Percent Positive	**67%**	**83%**	**100%**

Source: Birinyi Associates, Inc.

FIGURE 2.4   S&P 500: 1986

Source: Birinyi Associates, Inc., Bloomberg.

At this point, we might introduce a market axiom:

The market is not symmetrical.

If an indicator suggests higher prices, the reverse of that indicator does not necessarily suggest lower prices.

Our analysis is limited to the past 20 years but other evidence suggests its merit. In 1986, a *New York Times* article cited the indicator:[1]

Technical Data Signal Danger
A chart in a recent issue of the Merrill Lynch Market Letter shows that 85 percent of stocks on the NYSE are above their 200 day moving averages of price. . . . Such a high reading can precede a market top or consolidation.

Six months later, the market was basically unchanged, but had presented some trading opportunities and neither topped nor consolidated (see Figure 2.4).

Our analysis of these and other indicators, technical and otherwise, has led us to endorse President Kennedy's comment: "The enemy of the truth is not the lie but the myth." We will argue that many market conventions and rules are more a function of myth than analysis.

THE ADVANCE/DECLINE LINE: A FAVORITE TOOL, BUT WHY?

Another failing of the technical community results from a lack of understanding. It may appear incomprehensible that individuals who spend many waking, as well as restless, hours dealing with markets, numbers, charts, and tables truly often do not understand them. We might begin with probably the simplest of all technical indicators, the advance/decline line (A/D).

The A/D calculation is a simple one: advancing stocks minus declining stocks (unchanged issues are ignored). As shown in Table 2.3, on July 1, 2011, 466 more S&P names went up than down (the market was up over 1 percent that day). The next day there were 163 more declining names, than advancing, so the two-day total becomes +303 (466 – 163). The process continues and by month's end, the sum of the 20 days was –1,317. Not surprisingly the market was down 2.2 percent over the same period.

Two notes of caution: First, the results are *unweighted*, meaning there is no consideration as to the significance, or market value, of the companies. General Electric, for example, is a much bigger and more important issue than Gannett or People's United Bank but it is counted equally. Second, no allowance is made for the size of the move. Ten stocks going up $1 should not be offset by 10 stocks each losing a dime, but in this calculation they are.

TABLE 2.3 The Advance Decline Line (A/D) 10-Day Formula

		Daily A/D	Cumulative A/D	10-Day A/D Oscillator	10-Day Formula
Day 1	7/1/2011	466	466		
Day 2	7/5/2011	−163	303		
Day 3	7/6/2011	73	376		
Day 4	7/7/2011	379	755		
Day 5	7/8/2011	−366	389		
Day 6	7/11/2011	−484	−95		
Day 7	7/12/2011	−129	−224		
Day 8	7/13/2011	132	−92		
Day 9	7/14/2011	−382	−474		
Day 10	7/15/2011	114	−360	−360	Day 1 to Day 10
Day 11	7/18/2011	−433	−793	−1,259	Day 2 to Day 11
Day 12	7/19/2011	444	−349	−652	Day 3 to Day 12
Day 13	7/20/2011	−40	−389	−765	Day 4 to Day 13
Day 14	7/21/2011	384	−5	−760	Day 5 to Day 14
Day 15	7/22/2011	−6	−11	−400	Day 6 to Day 15
Day 16	7/25/2011	−290	−301	−206	Day 7 to Day 16
Day 17	7/26/2011	−196	−497	−273	Day 8 to Day 17
Day 18	7/27/2011	−459	−956	−864	Day 9 to Day 18
Day 19	7/28/2011	−142	−1,098	−624	Day 10 to Day 19
Day 20	7/29/2011	−219	−1,317	−957	Day 11 to Day 20

Source: Birinyi Associates, Inc.

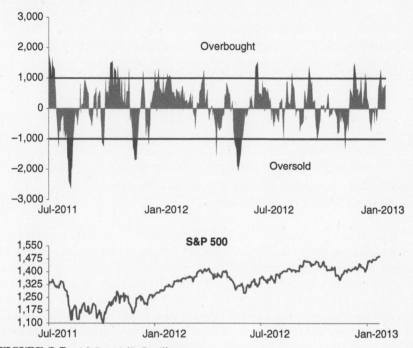

FIGURE 2.5 10-Day A/D Oscillator
Source: Birinyi Associates, Inc., Bloomberg.

Technicians also use the data to create a 10-day oscillator. As shown in Table 2.3 (10-Day Formula), every tenth day is plotted, which creates the chart shown in Figure 2.5. We have extended the data from mid-July 2011 through January 2013. When the 10-day results exceed 1,000, the market is considered extended, or another case of *overbought*. While the concept has some moderate merit, it is inconsistent. Granted, the overbought condition of mid-July was followed by a decline. And there was some recovery from the grossly oversold reading of early August (–2,500), but the market was to go even lower and traded to 1,100 on October 3. At the time, the indicator's reading was barely negative.

On July 19, 2012, there was a strong overbought condition, but the market actually went up 1.4 percent the next month and 7.6 percent over the next three months.

Its lack of predictive value might also be illustrated by the 1970 bull market shown in Figure 2.6. That market's cumulative result peaked well before the market did. In fact, the market rose another 14.8 percent after the high on April 28, 1971.

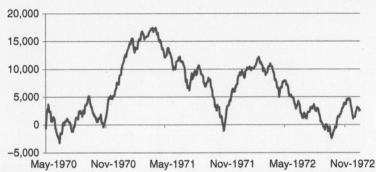

FIGURE 2.6   Cumulative A/D Line: Bull Market 1970 through 1972
Source: Birinyi Associates, Inc., Bloomberg.

This is more usual than unusual. In only two bull markets has the market peaked somewhat in line with its net advances. Yet this is a staple of technical analysis (see Figure 2.7).

The critical issue when it comes to the A/D line, new highs/lows, most active, and many other measures is not how many, but which ones. And the A/D has another characteristic that makes it less useful, which is true of almost every technical indicator endorsed by the chartist community:

Technical indicators are almost universally descriptive, not indicative.

The fact that more stocks went up today than went down tells us that and little more. It does not in any way suggest what will happen *tomorrow.* That is not to suggest it doesn't have any value, but its value is in understanding, not forecasting.

A market with very broad participation (strong net advances) is difficult to outperform because everything is rising. One must therefore pick the best of the best. In 1999, the A/D line was declining, which most participants viewed as a negative. Strategists and technicians alike were alarmed by the fact that so few stocks were rising and the A/D line was falling, surely indicating an upcoming decline.

In early October of that year, *BusinessWeek* reported: "Seventy percent of the gain in the S&P 500 year-to-date came from increases in the

FIGURE 2.7   Cumulative A/D Line Peak During Bull Markets Since 1962
Source: Birinyi Associates, Inc.

prices of just 10 stocks." Other stories also reflected the somewhat unique circumstance:

Nasdaq's Climb: The Air Is Getting Thinner
. . . according to Salomon Smith Barney, almost 40% of the gain in the Nasdaq Composite Index since Oct. 1 can be attributed to only five stocks (Cisco, MCI, Qualcom, Oracle, and Sun Micro).
BusinessWeek, **November 29, 1999**

Nasdaq's Gains Mask a House Divided, Stocks Show Equal Split of Rich and Poor
71% gain . . . nearly half of all Nasdaq's stocks have actually fallen in price this year.
Wall Street Journal, **December 20, 1999**

The Bear-Bull Market: As Indexes Soar, Most Stocks Fall
New York Times, **December 24, 1999**

While any measure of market breadth was disappointing, some managers and analysts recognized the reality and the opportunity: if only 10 or 15 stocks are buoying the market, *buy those 10!*

Lastly, we would note that the A/D is, at best, coincidental. We have regularly tried to construct a model with the hope of finding some relationship between the number of stocks going up and the change in the index going forward. We were unable to do so. In fact, if we analyze the historical results it is clear that the change in index prices is only tangentially related to the absolute number of stocks that went up or down, as shown in Table 2.4.

TABLE 2.4 Bull Markets—Net Gain versus Net Advances

Market	DJIA Change (%)	Net Advances	Net Advances per 1% Gain in DJIA
1949–1961	355	42,051	119
1962–1966	86	15,315	179
1966–1968	32	13,348	412
1970–1973	67	3,333	50
1974–1976	76	25,267	334
1978–1981	38	10,081	265
1982–1987	250	50,939	203
1987–1990	73	76,064	1,048
1990–2000	396	−38,784	−98
2002–2007	94	175,714	1,861
2009–2013	111	162,173	1,459

Source: Birinyi Associates, Inc.

VOLUME? ANOTHER IMPORTANT INDICATOR? REALLY?

A somewhat similar circumstance exists for another alleged technical indicator—volume. We have collected a large number of books and publications on the subject of markets, analysis, indicators, and the like. Nevertheless, we have never found a definition of what constitutes good or heavy volume. Clichés such as "volume is the weapon of the bull" have little pragmatic value.

In the markets of the twenty-first century, where shares are measured in the billions and 2 or 3 billion shares is considered a "light" day, it is even more difficult to ascertain what might be critical. But even a superficial analysis of volume in the "good old days" suggests that it was never a critical factor in market forecasting (see Figure 2.8).

> **Fall in Stock Trading in Past 6 Months Worries Analysts**
> *Wall Street Journal*, October 20, 1986

> **Slowdown in Trading Volume on Big Board Is Causing Some Concern**
> *Wall Street Journal*, March 24, 1988

In this case, shown in Figure 2.9, the market rallied, traded lower, but six months later was higher.

We suggested earlier that volume is another of the issues that many analysts fail to understand. Specifically, there is the contention that volume in a rising market or stock is good. To illustrate: Assume two stocks have similar characteristics in terms of price, activity, and volatility. One day each stock is up $1 on 100,000 shares. One, however, traded 50,000 shares at a $2 discount before rallying on light volume, while the other name had

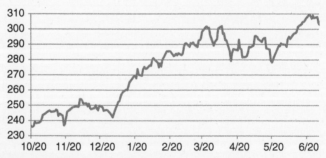

FIGURE 2.8   S&P 500: 10/20/1986 through 6/30/1987
Source: Birinyi Associates, Inc., Bloomberg.

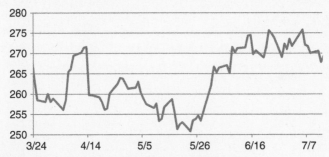

FIGURE 2.9   S&P 500: 3/24/1988 through 7/12/1988

Source: Birinyi Associates, Inc., Bloomberg.

a slow steady rise throughout the day. The net result for each was the same but there was a marked difference between the two.

Take a classic example American Cynamid (ACY) on December 10, 1979. The stock was the subject of takeover rumors and traded 920,800 shares (five times the norm) and closed up $2.125 to $31.625. By every measure this was a significant, positive development as reflected in ACY's January 30 call options, which rose 32 percent that day.

Upon a more detailed analysis, it was noted that there were 36 block trades (10,000 shares), which accounted for 45 percent of the trading. As shown in Table 2.5, *not a single block was affected on an uptick.* In effect, institutions *sold* into the rally, which is also reflected in the fact

TABLE 2.5   NYSE Block Trader Monitor

TKR	Issuer	Total Volume	Close	Change
ACY	AMERICAN CYANAMID	920,800	31.625	2.125
	Date of Run	12/11/1979	Tuesday	
	Date of Trades	12/10/1979	Monday	

	Block Trades		
Time	Volume	Price	Change from Last Sale
1004	14,200	27.500	0.000
1050	15,000	30.125	0.000
1106	15,200	30.125	−0.125
1114	10,000	30.250	−0.125
1123	10,000	30.375	−0.125

(continued)

TABLE 2.5 (continued)

		Block Trades	
Time	Volume	Price	Change from Last Sale
1128	20,000	30.375	−0.125
1152	10,000	30.375	−0.125
1210	10,000	30.375	−0.125
1213	10,000	30.375	−0.125
1246	10,000	30.250	−0.125
1248	10,000	30.375	0.000
1303	30,000	30.375	0.000
1311	10,000	30.375	0.000
1315	16,400	30.250	0.000
1315	10,000	30.500	0.000
1316	20,200	30.500	0.000
1322	15,000	30.500	0.000
1326	15,000	30.500	−0.125
1331	18,600	30.625	−0.250
1358	10,000	30.750	−0.250
1412	10,000	30.875	−0.125
1416	10,000	30.875	0.000
1422	10,000	31.000	0.000
1424	10,000	31.000	0.000
1443	15,000	31.125	0.000
1445	10,000	31.125	−0.250
1452	10,000	31.125	−0.125
1524	25,000	31.000	−0.250
1539	10,000	31.125	−0.125
1545	15,000	31.125	−0.125
1545	10,000	31.125	0.000

Source: Salomon Brothers.

that there were no especially large trades. Traders were parceling stock into the market, but without completely satisfying the demand. Had they been more aggressive, that is, selling larger blocks, the rally would have been arrested.

Thus, while price and volume on the surface appeared to support a bullish conclusion, more detailed analysis did not. (American Cyanamid was eventually acquired by American Home Products in 1994.)

One technical metric for volume is the 90 percent up or down day. This, we contend, is somewhat flawed as it assumes that the closing price reflects the entire day and that all the volume in a rising stock was positive.

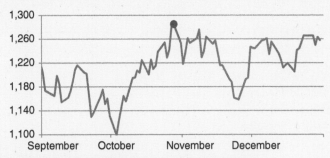

FIGURE 2.10   S&P 500: 9/20/2011 through 12/30/2011
Source: Birinyi Associates, Inc., Bloomberg.

More critical is that is doesn't seem to work. One chartist noted the 90 percent positive as well as increased volume on October 28, 2011 (see Figure 2.10):

> *Yesterday's 3.4% rally was a 90% up day on higher volume. Higher volume on a rally is typically bullish.*

The charting community also fails because it is slow to incorporate change. Markets, participants, processes, and instruments change. "It's not your grandfather's (or father's) market" is not just a cliché or slogan, but is in fact reality. Concepts such as "stock broker," "board room," or even "ticker tape" are history, often ancient history. The introduction of options, futures, derivatives, global markets, ETFs, and even MBAs have revolutionized the business. Add to these increased and faster communications, cheaper technology, and more awareness.

NEWSLETTERS—ONCE UPON A TIME . . .

Some time ago we were asked by *Barron's* to review the ads for the funds in the paper. In doing so, we were struck by the number of those ads, and by the fact that there were no ads for other services. As a simple test we bought the March 20, 1967 issue at random. There were 47 ads for newsletters including:

- Chartcraft
- Dow Theory Forecasts
- George Lindsay's Opinion
- Granville Letter

- Jan's WS Irregular
- Lowry's Reports
- Technical Stock
- Buck Investment Letter
- The Dines Letter
- The Haller Theory
- Tillman Trader
- Wyckoff Associates

Many of these were prominent, including several full-page ads. On the fund management side there were 12 ads.

In the January 26, 1981 edition, we found 50 newsletter ads and 22 for funds or managers.

Clearly, this reflects the fact that the newsletter advisory business has undergone an upheaval over time. More importantly, it causes us to wonder about the validity of the sentiment survey that tracked their thinking. While it continues to exist and is still published, we have reservations about its validity, relative to decades earlier.

We might also consider the mutual fund cash measure illustrated in Figure 2.11. Historically, when cash was 10 percent of the portfolio, it was considered a contrary indicator. Whether it was or was not indicative of a rally is not important at this juncture. At one time, a billion-dollar fund was a behemoth, and when Gerald Tsai raised almost $500 million it was worthy of the front page. He and others could maintain large cash positions (relative to assets) as a market decision. But with multibillion-dollar funds, having 10 percent cash is a *business* risk. A dramatic market move

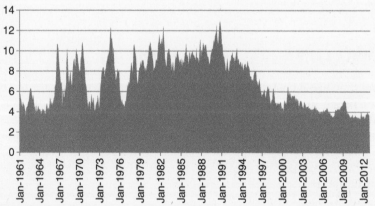

FIGURE 2.11 Mutual Fund Liquidity Ratio (%)
Source: Birinyi Associates, Inc.

(as in March 2009 where it rallied 19 percent off the bottom in less than two weeks) could (and did) leave a portfolio well adrift of the market.

Nevertheless, analysts regularly discuss the low levels of fund cash as being a concern.

PREDICTING RAIN DOESN'T COUNT; BUILDING ARKS DOES

An old, bad story: A balloonist lost control and landed in a cornfield, 25 yards from a gas station, about a quarter mile from an interstate, and across the street from a school.

He asked a passerby as to where he was. "You are at the edge of a cornfield, across from the local high school, and approximately 25 yards from an Exxon station."

The passerby was surprised and stunned when told that he was a technical analyst and responded, "However did you know?"

"Because," the balloonist replied, "everything you told me was accurate but totally useless."

I said it was bad, but I first heard this many years ago. Perhaps, because I spent many years on a trading desk, I—and my employers—had little tolerance for possibilities, probabilities, and potential. Some time ago, I read somewhere that investors should be weary of "weasel words." While we might have disagreed with the terminology, the point was that terms such as *could, may, average, usual,* and *typical* were of little real value to an investor.

As we have often said, there are no *average* markets. And the comment that the market *could* trade higher also suggests with equal conviction that it could trade lower. Investors should therefore dismiss the greater majority of pronouncements from analysis, technical or otherwise, that are in effect speculating on possibilities without supporting evidence.

In the same vein, we find that comments such as *support* and *resistance* are generally useless. To articulate that support exists at 1,400 and then again at 1,375 hardly justifies a multi-digit salary. [In my personal experience at Salomon, advising the traders that $85 was a strong support level for Exxon, when it was trading at $89, was even more detrimental to our future well-being than the cigarette warning.]

We are reminded of the story about Ben Hogan who asked his caddy about the yardage. When told it was 145/146 yards, Hogan responded curtly, "Make up your mind." Over the years, we have often been told that some individuals enjoyed reading about my experience in *Wall Street Week.* While that was often pleasant, and occasionally led to a free drink, it was considerably more satisfying to be told that someone had actually bought or sold a recommendation.

In October 1992, a *Wall Street Journal* story asked the rhetorical question, "Who Are the New Oracles on Wall Street?" Several strategists and economists were listed, but no technicians. One prominent chartist was an obvious candidate. But the paper wrote that he was passed over because:

> . . . *usually writes reports that are dense with hedges, conditional clauses and predictions going in several directions at once.*

As we showed earlier, the approach has an uninspiring record at market turns. Just as a doctor's true value is at times of illness, anticipating market turns is always more profitable than reinforcing trends. Equally disappointing is the history of technical approaches to stock picking and specific, actionable recommendations.

We first became acutely aware of this deficiency in the 1980s. A major firm published a quarterly analysis of various chart patterns, including cup and handle, rounding bottom, and so on. In an effort to see which characteristics were most reliable, we tracked the six positive groupings—five of which not only underperformed but actually lost money; of the five negative groups, three were up sharply. Buying the positive names and shorting negative ideas, in just one quarter, resulted in a 10 percent loss even as the market gained 2 percent (see Figure 2.12).

After tracking the publication for another quarter, we discontinued the exercise for obvious reasons.

Nothing we have subsequently seen, catalogued, or tracked has given us any confidence, or desire, to emulate the stock-picking approaches of this community.

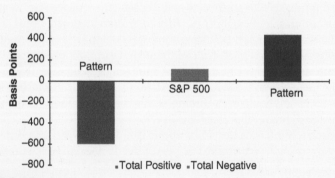

FIGURE 2.12   Totals
Source: Birinyi Associates, Inc.

One of our exercises is to monitor recommendations from a variety of sources. We are especially sensitive to ideas that appear in several disciplines. Thus, if a strategist recommends a company and it is also upgraded by an analyst, we consider it. While we are confident that technical approaches do not result in outsized gains, we do not dismiss them willy-nilly because it can be helpful if someone is bringing an idea to the marketplace.

We could present any number of technical lists, recommendations, and comments—all of which fail to meet, or even approach, market results. Several examples should highlight our conviction:

- An article in *Bloomberg Markets* (November 2012) highlighted one analyst who clearly had a successful business and lifestyle. His comments are almost always confined to markets. One exception was in August 2011 " . . . European banks all bottoming right now . . . Société Générale, BNP, they all look like buys."
- The *Bloomberg* Europe Bank and Financial Service Index lost 11 percent through the end of December while BNP Paribas was to go from €37.50 to €28.19 a month later, before closing at €32.37 in December. Société Générale was to go from €25.27 to €19.00 a month later, and end the year at €17.20.
- During the same period the MSCI Europe index was virtually flat, losing 0.66 percent.
- At the end of 1998 a major firm published its "Technical Top Picks for 1999." The list of 10 names lost 7.93 percent while the S&P was up 8.83 percent.
- Also in the 1990s, we were briefly exposed to the Lowry Timing Fund, one of the few blatantly claiming a technical pedigree. *Morningstar* reported the fund had a unique approach: They bought at the top and sold at the bottom.

Two analysts sound alarm on IBM: $75 days ahead
There's just no two ways about it. IBM is clearly a wrong stock to own right now.

***New York Daily News*, June 14, 1984**

You just can't make this stuff up! (See Figure 2.13.)
In 1962 *Fortune* ran two lengthy pieces on the subject:

The charting of stocks, once a recondite art practiced only by a few Wall Streeters, is becoming the recondite preoccupation of masses of investors.[2]

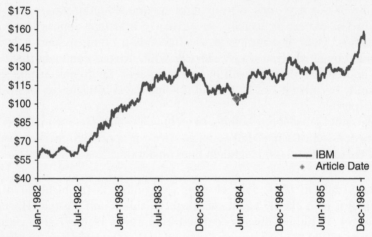

FIGURE 2.13 IBM

Source: Birinyi Associates, Inc., Bloomberg.

The second, a month later, provided some results:[3]

> *To test the claim,* Fortune *examined every buy and sell signal given on every one of the 700 NYSE stocks that Chartcraft routinely covers. For the first six months of 1961, Chartcraft's record may be called disappointing, to say the least.*

It was disappointing because 855 trades were generated. Forty percent were gains averaging 10 percent while 60 percent were losses with the same 10 percent result, but on the downside.

TECHNICAL ANALYSIS FAILS A RIGOROUS TEST

It might be argued that we have reinforced a bias and selected especially egregious situations. Perhaps, but signaling an "all clear" on the DJIA 30 names barely a week before the Crash is not just a "random" selection.

Our *Bloomberg* terminal provides a number of technical indicators. At one time there were 11 (since expanded) including the familiar Moving Average Convergence/Divergence (MACD) and Relative Strength Index (RSI). They also allow analysis, using *Bloomberg's* BTST (back-test) function, whereby one can determine the value of the individual indicators on stocks, groups, sectors, or indices at previous points.

FIGURE 2.14   S&P 500 MACD: March 9, 2009 through April 23, 2010
Source: Bloomberg.

We analyzed both the market and individual stocks over a period from March 9, 2009 through April 23, 2010 for the 11 indicators. Over this period the S&P 500 rose 79 percent (see Figure 2.14).

Given its apparent popularity, we began with the MACD function, which generated a net gain of 5.5 percent, hugely underperforming the market.

None of the 11 indicators even approximated the market's return: 4 lost money; 5 had single digit results.

The results of all 11 indicators are detailed in Table 2.6.

TABLE 2.6   S&P 500 Index 3/9/2009 through 4/23/2010

	Trades			
Strategy	**Long**	**Short**	**Total**	**Total**
Buy and Hold	1	0	1	79.09k
Bollinger Bands	1	1	2	1.52k
Cmdty Channel	7	7	14	3.29k
CMI	11	10	21	8.05k
MACD	12	12	24	5.53k
RSI	2	2	4	2.38k
Stochastics	6	6	12	23.84k
William's %R	6	6	12	−10.78k
Parabolic	16	16	32	−2.63k
Ichimoku	5	4	9	17.40k
MAE	0	1	1	−46.63k
TE	2	3	5	−19.68k

Source: Birinyi Associates, Inc., Bloomberg.

TABLE 2.7 Bloomberg BTST Results: Thirty DJIA Stocks Technical Indicators: 3/9/2009 through 4/23/2010

Strategy	Change (%)
Bollinger Bands (BOLL)	−11.30
Commodity Channel Index (CMCI)	−3.12
Directional Movement Indicator (DMI)	15.02
Ichimoku (GOC)	9.03
Moving Average Convergence-Divergence (MACD)	8.36
Moving Average Envelopes (MAE)	−9.72
Parabolic (PTPS)	6.91
Relative Strength Index (RSI)	−16.71
Stochastics (TAS)	3.66
Trade Envelope (TE)	−8.11
William's %R (Wm)	−6.97
DJIA	**71.13**
S&P 500	**79.93**

Source: Birinyi Associates, Inc.

We then looked at the individual 30 names that make up the DJIA. Thirty stocks by 11 indicators resulted in 330 possibilities. Only 17 of the 330 (1.2 percent) generated "trades" that outperformed the stock over the given period. Six of the 17 were in Exxon, which was the worst performing stock in the index. Verizon was the second worst performer and had six "winners." The best performer was Bank of America (up 391 percent), netting out to −29.8 percent on the various measures. Tracking BAC's buys/sells from RSI would have cost investors 90 percent of their investment.

The results are summarized in Table 2.7. The best results are for DMI, which generated a 15.02 percent return, if all its recommendations were followed for each of the 30 names. Even more disappointing is that these are without commissions or market impact. MACD generated 341 trades or more than 10 percent in a period just over a year.

NOTES

1. Daniel Cuff, "Technical Data Signal Danger," *New York Times*, April 14, 1986.

2. Daniel Seligman, "Playing the Market with Charts," *Fortune*, February 1962.

3. Daniel Seligman, "The Mystique of Point and Figure," *Fortune*, March 1962.

CHAPTER 3

Technicals: The Last Word

*Scientific is not—as many management scientists naïvely
seem to think—synonymous with quantification. If it
were true, astrology would be the queen of sciences.*

—Peter Drucker

A notable but subtle conclusion with critical implications comes from our analysis of technicals: *Corrections are not a function of technical circumstances.* Most technical measures have an apex and nadir, which are allegedly the market's version of the familiar red/green stoplight. They are usually referenced as *overbought* and *oversold*.

One popular approach is the difference between a stock (or index) price and its 50-day average price. Years ago, brokers would take a new pencil and place its eraser on a chart. If there was space between the eraser's edge and two lines (current price and 50-day average), the stock was considered overbought or oversold, depending on the direction.

We use a somewhat simpler approach and measure the difference. In the 1982 bull market, that spread exceeded 5 percent on nine occasions, none of which was coincident with a correction. In fact, the only correction (−14.38 percent) in that five-year market took place one year and 59 days into the rally. At that time, most technical measures were indifferent (see Figures 3.1 and 3.2 and Table 3.1).

Despite our concerns and criticisms, monitoring certain indicators is an approach we have found useful to *understanding* the market. While this may seem a bit hypocritical, our concern regarding charts and other measures is not so much with technical *analysis* as it is with technical *analysts*.

To us, many indicators might be compared to a blood pressure gauge or cholesterol reading. If the former is 190/80, it does not indicate that one should go home and prepare for some dramatic event in six months and

31

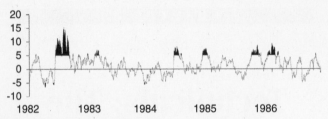

FIGURE 3.1   S&P 500 50-Day Moving Average Spread (%)
Source: Birinyi Associates, Inc.

four days. It does *suggest* that steak with béarnaise sauce, followed by an ice cream sundae and a cigarette, might not be prudent.

Our chart, when overbought, likewise suggests that some softness or lack of forward progress is likely while an oversold circumstance provides more positive potential than negative. Unlike chartists, we do not demand or project that this or that will happen. We might also liken this to the familiar streetlight.

In New York City, crossing with the light does not ensure safe passage, but the odds are in your favor. Likewise, crossing against the light will not endear you to your life insurance agent, as most individuals only hesitate briefly if no cars are coming.

So despite our disdain for technical, we would monitor several indicators, beginning with the cumulative advance/decline line. Over the past 15 years, the best years for portfolios were probably 1999 and 2009. In those years, the market was a function of relatively few stocks. Some aggressive mutual funds, as well as hedge funds, recognized that if 10 or 18 stocks were responsible for the greater portion of the market's gain, buy those 10! Their gains were not necessarily a function of astute stock selection, but were more just a realization of the environment.

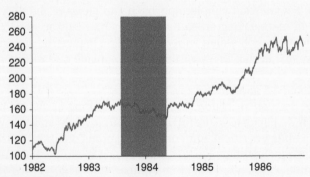

FIGURE 3.2   S&P 500
Source: Birinyi Associates, Inc., Bloomberg.

TABLE 3.1 Technical Indicators, October 10, 1983

Technical Indicator	October 10, 1983
10 Most Active Stocks of NYSE Volume (%)	3.0
OEX Put/Call Ratio	0.95
NYSE Highs/Lows	67
NYSE Daily A/D	241
NYSE 10-Day A/D Line	171
50-Day Spread (%)	4.55
200-Day Spread (%)	−7.82
Bull/Bear Sentiment (%)	39.7/21.6

Source: Birinyi Associates, Inc.

In 2009, a number of funds piled into financials. They doubled in two months and again had superior performance. In the first quarter of 2013, the S&P A/D line was extraordinary, perhaps the strongest in history for any one quarter, as shown in Table 3.2 (unfortunately, the data begins only in 1991).

In actuality, this was not necessarily a positive development for investors. While strategists recommended various sectors or classifications (dividend names, stocks with or without international exposure), the reality was that everything was participating and managers could no longer select by first eliminating broad swatches. Then it became a case of discriminating between the good and the very good, and there was an abundance of "good" names to choose from.

TABLE 3.2 S&P 500 Change and Breadth: Selected Quarters

	Percent Change	Cumulative A/D
2Q09	15.22%	1,521
3Q09	14.98	3,211
3Q10	10.72	2,158
4Q10	10.20	2,265
4Q11	11.15	1,878
1Q12	12.00	2,539
1Q13	10.03%	4,255

Source: Birinyi Associates, Inc.

TOPICAL STUDIES: AN INTRODUCTION

Before we put our concerns and comments on technical analysis to rest, we should discuss the widely used Volatility Index (VIX). It is used by technical and other analysts as well, and was the subject of our 2010 publication: *VIX—Much Ado About. . . .*[1]

This publication was one in a series of topical studies that we began some years ago. Topical studies are an exercise where we look at an issue objectively with a view toward understanding. We gather all available source data, historical records, and original documents, which we present in an almost academic effort (without Greek letters and applied mathematics). One money manager once told us that ours was the only example of *basic research* on the Street. And one of my prouder moments was when Sydney Homer, who basically invented bond market and interest rate analysis, came into my office at Salomon Brothers and said that if he had had the time, he would have done with equities exactly what I was doing.

Our first study analyzed pension plan flows. The conventional view was that they were seasonal and heavily funded in January. We wondered why AT&T or Kmart would pay their annual bills in just one month. After requesting Form 5500 from the IRS, we reviewed more than 50 of the nation's largest corporations and found that the telephone company, for one, funded their plans on a monthly basis.

In addition to the VIX study our publications have included:

- *The Buyback Paradox* (Topical Study #6)
- *Why Institutions Underperform* (Topical Study #7)
- *The Case Against Indexing* (Topical Study #9)
- *Money Flows: Mr. Market Speaks* (Topical Study #12)
- *Pension Reform and Global Equity Markets* (Topical Study #17)
- *Global Equity Markets* (Topical Study #24)
- *Market Records* (Topical Study #29)
- *Volume* (Topical Study #43)

And most ambitious of all is our three-volume, several-thousand-page study of cycles, which we detail in Chapter 14.

Our VIX publication was an effort to determine the investment implications of this measure of volatility (. . . expected return volatility of the S&P 500 index over the next 30 days).

We found that not to be the case:

Low volatility is followed by little or no movement over the next month and two months, but by higher prices in three and six months.

Periods of high volatility precede positive markets over the next month, three months but six months out the market is down.

Extreme readings—both up and down—are followed by a market which is higher 90 days later.

Our view was not a solitary one, as a number of articles questioned its value:

Date	Source	Headline
9/8/2008	Reuters	VIX pops even as stocks climb.
3/6/2009	*Wall Street Journal*	VIX seems to be failing as signal.
4/3/2009	*Wall Street Journal*	Fear gauge out of flux with turbulent markets.
7/15/2009	Reuters	Volatility index is out of sync with market rise.
12/26/2009	*Wall Street Journal*	VIX is no crystal ball.
3/4/2010	*Wall Street Journal*	Volatility index's decline baffles some strategists.

We might also detail other stories we discussed in that publication:

Date	Source	Headline
3/2/2009	Bloomberg	VIX premium shows stocks bear market lasting two years.
3/17/2009	*Wall Street Journal*	Rise by the "fear gauge" foretells the S&P's fall.
4/2/2009	Bloomberg	VIX falls as options traders brace for stock rally to end.
5/8/2009	Bloomberg	VIX futures show traders betting stock rally to end.
12/11/2009	Bloomberg	Options show S&P 500 rally in peril.

After surveying the landscape, one might reasonably ask: Why bother? Given the apparent dismal and lack of compelling results, how do chartists survive?

We appreciate that technicals are enticing, as they provide the *illusion of certainty*. Many years ago, we were asked by the Market Technicians Association to debate the people from Elliott Wave. Our conclusion was that the market was rising, was likely to continue rising, and we expected that, on a historical basis, it had at least 15 or 24 months to go.

The other guest provided all sorts of forecasts, and did so with precision and confidence. He was besieged with questions and more interest. While we had been more correct, his willingness to provide precision was of greater interest.

We might also cite an article in the *New Yorker* by Robert Heilbroner. While he was specifically talking about economists, it holds true for other forecasters as well:

> . . . *they have a profound human need to hear utterances about the future, plausible or not. . . . The human psyche can tolerate a great deal of prospective misery, but it cannot bear the thought that the future is beyond all power of anticipation.*[2]

NOTES

1. *VIX: Much Ado About* . . . Birinyi Associates, Inc., March 2010.

2. Robert Heilbroner, "Reflections," *New Yorker*, July 8, 1991.

CHAPTER 4

Wall Street: Games People Play

The buyer needs a hundred eyes, the seller not one.
—George Herbert

S ome years ago, Michael Lewis began a career as a successful writer with *Liar's Poker*. While we might dispute some portions of his days at Salomon Brothers, we heartily agree with at least one assessment:

. . . Laszlo Birinyi made a valiant and often brilliant pitch . . .

Michael was less charitable toward his clients and his attitude—reflecting Salomon's—is well documented, although exaggerated and embellished. More recently a former Goldman Sachs employee wrote a *New York Times* op-ed regarding his former employer:[1]

To put the problem in the simplest terms, the interest of the client continued to be sidelined in the way the firm operates and thinks about making money.

We cannot, after 40 years in the business, declare the business innocent. Hubris might be the most common denominator (at least in the institutional business), with the majority of bankers and traders considering themselves masters of the universe acting as exhibit A. While this has been subsiding (significant layoffs and cutbacks can be deflating), customer service is almost an oxymoron on Wall Street.

One of the manifestations of this attitude is an inability to admit failings or recognize shortcomings. Analysts are seldom wrong, although they are sometimes "early." Portfolio managers may not perform better than their benchmarks, but they do have good "relative" performance, while technicians will bury their old forecast with a new one. One academic effort uncovered significant inefficiencies which failed in the 1990 bull market because investors were *"irrational."*

It has been suggested that the business at Broad and Wall is not so much one of markets as it is one of *marketing*, with its focus on brands and product placement. Truth is too often the victim, although we recall the comments of Paul Tudor Jones. When congratulated for forecasting the decline of the Japanese market in 1989, he remarked that it was the fourth straight year he had done so.

In 1995, I was addressing a meeting in Singapore and was questioned regarding our 1996 forecast. I was positive for a number of reasons including a somewhat subdued attitude, which was similar to the cautious view investors had going into 1995. A representative of a large institutional buy-side firm took objection to my view, as that firm had a recommended exposure of 80 percent at the beginning of 1995.

It was neither the time nor the place. But I knew that while the firm did indeed have a recommended equity weighting of 80 percent, it had been cut to 60 percent in January and cut again in May.

In the best year of the past 50 years, the firm's exposure was relatively light, although they continued to be "bullish" and "consistently positive."

In 2000, the firm's exposure had risen to 70 percent equities but was cut to 65 percent in March. On the same day, the 1,575 year-end target was reiterated and a 12-month target of 1,625 was presented (see Figure 4.1).

Unfortunately for investors, the market never approached those levels and closed at 1,320. At year's end a spokesperson for that firm reminded investors that the firm had advised clients to lower their exposure. We find it somewhat incongruous to be positive with a 55 percent exposure in a

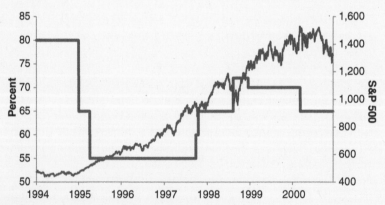

FIGURE 4.1   Large Buyside Firms' Equity Allocation
Source: Birinyi Associates, Inc., Bloomberg.

good year (1995) and 65 percent in a declining year. Yet somehow they claim to have been helpful in both cases.

Even the professional investor is unlikely to recognize many of the shortcomings regarding market commentary and advice. One, which is well established and common practice, is the concept of average return where a recommended list or a portfolio is calculated on a price-weighted basis. Simply put, it assumes that an investor buys one unit, or 100 shares, of all the recommendations. These results regularly do well because there will be a $4 stock that goes to $8 and a 100 percent gain will largely offset the $74 stock that loses $4. Again, this is the norm, but investors should be aware of their potential underperformance.

The gamesmanship, marketing, and lack of candor are illustrated in the case of one technician's recommendation of IBM in 1999:

> *Back on July 19, we upgraded back to our technical Buy list the Computer Hardware sector . . . [we have stressed IBM]. The group had been rated a Buy from November 9, 1998 through April 20, 1999. [Excerpt] . . . for a short period, April 20 to July 19 (emphasis added).*

While the analyst "stressed" IBM, the results were less than scintillating during the period (November 1998 to September 1999 when the S&P was +15 percent and the technology sector gained 66 percent). In fact, tracking these recommendations would have resulted in limited gains. From the initial recommendation (11/9/98) to the downgrade (4/20/99) the stock gained $9.19 (12.1 percent). But during the "short period" where it was not recommended, it went from $84.88 to $135.63 for a gain of over $50.

From the July 19, 1999 upgrade to the date of the report (September 3rd), the stock lost $5.77 to $128.86. It closed the year at $107.87.[2] See Figure 4.2 and Table 4.1.

FIGURE 4.2   IBM: September 1998 through September 1999

Source: Birinyi Associates, Inc., Bloomberg.

TABLE 4.1 IBM: September 1998 – September 1999

Action	Price	Change (%)	Notes	Change ($)
11/9/98	75.69			
4/20/99	84.88	12.14	Gain	9.19
7/19/99	134.63	58.62	Miss	49.75
9/3/99	128.86	−4.28	Gain	−5.77
	Net Gain	**7.86**		
	Actual Performance	**70.25**		

Source: Birinyi Associates, Inc.

A BROKERAGE FIRM CAN'T CALCULATE PERFORMANCE?

Perhaps the most egregious example of our concern was a report recommending the purchase of Nasdaq (see Figure 4.3). The approach generated a buy signal, which is important because . . . *the average duration of the previous seven buy signals was 30 months, for an average gain of 94.73 percent.*

The first buy occurred in 1975 and the results were exceptional in the ensuing 28 years. In our view, they were too exceptional.

The report provided the details on the trades, which seemed to confirm the results (see Table 4.2).

There was also a second table (see Table 4.3) that was probably redundant given that the purchases and sales were listed in Table 4.2. Or were they?

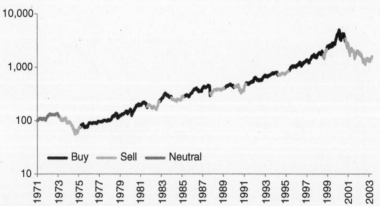

FIGURE 4.3 Nasdaq Composite with Long-Term Buy/Sell Signals
Source: Birinyi Associates, Inc., Bloomberg.

TABLE 4.2 Long-Term Buy Signals: Nasdaq Composite

Signal		High Reached		Length	Point	Percent
Month	Close	Month	High	(Months)	Gain	Gain
March-1975	75.66	May-1981	223.47	74	147.81	195.36%
November-1982	232.31	June-1983	328.91	7	96.60	41.58%
March-1985	**279.20**	**August-1987**	**455.26**	**29**	**176.06**	**63.06%**
February-1989	399.71	October-1989	487.53	8	87.82	21.97%
March-1991	482.30	March-1994	804.43	36	322.13	66.79%
April-1995	843.98	July-1998	2,028.06	39	1,184.08	140.30%
December-1998	2,192.69	March-2000	5,132.52	15	2,939.83	134.07%
May-2003	1,595.91					
AVERAGE				**30**	**707.76**	**94.73%**

Source: Birinyi Associates, Inc.

Upon more inspection we found that the High Reached in Table 4.2 was actually the monthly high-water mark of the period. *In effect, the report was claiming results assuming that one had sold at the absolute, subsequent high.* In 1987, for example, the sale occurred just before the Crash:

> *"March 1985 produced the third Buy signal, two months after the 1985 lift off, producing a gain of 63.06 percent and lasting 29 months."*

Unfortunately, that gain was realized only if one sold at the absolute top, just before the Crash. Table 4.3 shows the actual recommendations of the analysts where they recommended selling. In 1987, the analysts indicated their sell was issued in October at 323 producing a gain of 15.8 percent (323.30 vs. 279.20), not 63 percent.

TABLE 4.3 Long-Term Sell Signals: Nasdaq Composite

Signal		Low Reached		Length	Point	Percent
Month	Close	Month	Low	(Months)	Drop	Drop
February-1973	120.41	October-1974	54.87	20	65.54	54.43%
September-1981	180.03	August-1982	159.14	11	20.89	11.60%
January-1984	268.43	July-1984	225.30	6	43.13	16.07%
October-1987	**323.30**	**December-1987**	**292.92**	**2**	**30.38**	**9.40%**
February-1990	425.83	October-1990	322.98	8	102.85	24.15%
April-1994	733.84	June-1994	690.95	2	42.89	5.84%
August-1998	1,499.25	October-1998	1,357.09	2	142.16	9.48%
October-2000	3,369.63	October-2003	1,108.49	24	2,261.14	67.10%
AVERAGE				**9**	**338.62**	**24.76%**

Source: Birinyi Associates, Inc.

TABLE 4.4 Long-Term Buy Signals: With Actual Prices

Action	Start	End	Price (Start)	Price (End)	Point Change	Change (%)
Buy	March-1975	September-1981	75.66	180.03	104.37	137.95
Buy	November-1982	January-1984	232.31	268.43	36.12	15.55
Buy	**March-1985**	**October-1987**	**279.20**	**323.30**	**44.10**	**15.80**
Buy	February-1989	February-1990	399.71	425.83	26.12	6.53
Buy	March-1991	April-1994	482.30	733.84	251.54	52.15
Buy	April-1995	August-1998	843.98	1,499.25	655.27	77.64
Buy	December-1998	October-2000	2,192.69	3,369.63	1,176.94	53.68
					Program Change (%)	**1,408.82**
					Nasdaq Change (%)	**4,353.65**

Source: Birinyi Associates, Inc.

We constructed a table based on the actual purchase and sale recommendations that underperformed the index over the 25 years (see Table 4.4).

We brought this to the attention of management, but amazingly, a week later the process was repeated for both the S&P and the DJIA. Once again they had terrific results but this time they provided only the first, hypothetical results, and did not share their detailed recommendations.

The group also maintained a portfolio, or a list of recommendations. Later that year they reported in bold, uppercase (as shown):

DUE TO THE DISCOVERY OF SOME STATISTICAL ABBERATIONS, THE PUBLICATION OF THE PORTFOLIO'S VALUES HAS BEEN SUSPENDED FOR THE TIME BEING. WE EXPECT THE REVIEW OF THE DATA WILL BE COMPLETED SHORTLY.

MR. PRECHTER

Then there was the issue of Robert Prechter in 1987. In the mid-1980s, he received fame (and fortune) for his market calls based primarily on the Elliott Wave. We tracked his efforts for some time and never found them to be especially persuasive. It was subject to interpretation, which might well have been our failing.

We readily admit that his early 1987 *Barron's* interview was an important ingredient in that year's January rally (see Figure 4.4):

3600 on the Dow?
That, Says Bob Prechter, Is Where We're Going

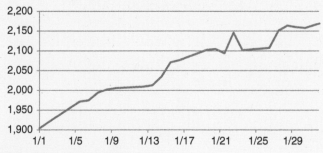

FIGURE 4.4   DJIA: January 1987
Source: Birinyi Associates, Inc., Bloomberg.

Interviews and stories (as well as subscriptions) continued and he stayed with his 3,686 target. As the year developed, we were less impressed as his predictions were often vague and, from a trading perspective, confusing and off target.

In early March:

> *. . . Expects the Dow to fall as low as 2,050 by late March but recover to 2,700 by year end and zoom to 3,600 by late 1988.*
>
> *. . . Breadth, volume and rate of change statistics all suggest that a correction is approaching in the stock market.*
>
> *New York Times,* **March 11, 1987**

Through the second quarter, the market did not correct, did not approach 2,050, and actually provided some significant trading opportunities on the buy side. The press and traders glossed over the issue and Prechter continued to be a staple of the media (see Figure 4.5).

Through September, he continued to generally reflect optimism (see Figure 4.6).

Early in October of 1987, controversy developed regarding his stance:

> *. . . Traders said he had sent out a bulletin indicating that a decline below 2,500 might presage a 300 point fall in the DJIA . . . there was nothing to indicate that Mr. Prechter had changed his long-term forecast that the average would surpass 3,600.*[3]

Then the analyst did or did not send out a special bulletin, advising clients to buy or sell and did so via a recording or mailing. Allegedly, clients who subscribed to the dial-in service were warned, while those who waited for the mail were not.

Unfortunately, accounts and details were controversial and even today it is hard to determine exactly what, when, and how Prechter stood.

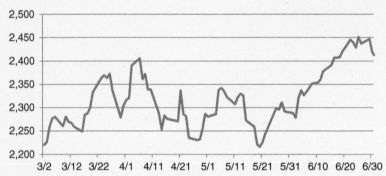

FIGURE 4.5   DJIA: March 1987 through June 1987
Source: Birinyi Associates, Inc., Bloomberg.

Several months later, on *Wall Street Week* (February 19, 1988) Louis Rukeyser was less than gracious:

> *The old . . . Super Cycle . . . ended in 1987, he now learnedly contends. And the new cycle . . . won't end until the Dow is below 400.*[4]

Prechter continued to forecast and we have been told that his views on commodities and other markets have been helpful. With regard to the stock market, he has had some markedly negative comments as evidenced in an interview with the *New York Times:*

> *. . . convinced that we have entered a market decline of staggering proportions—perhaps the biggest of the last 300 years.*
> *. . . go all the way back to . . . South Sea Bubble in 1720 . . . Dow is likely to fall well below 1,000 over perhaps the next five or six years.*[5]

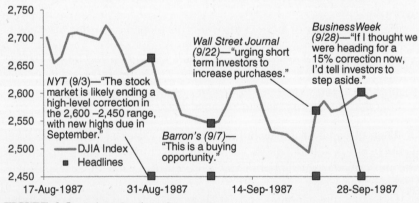

FIGURE 4.6   Robert Prechter Commentary
Source: Birinyi Associates, Inc., Bloomberg.

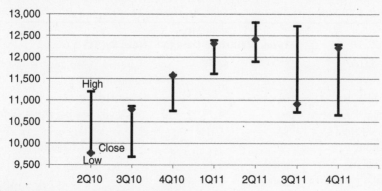

FIGURE 4.7 DJIA: 2Q10 through 4Q11
Source: Birinyi Associates, Inc., Bloomberg.

Alas, the comments were published Sunday, July 4, 2010, with the market at 9,686.48. The next week, although holiday-shortened, saw a 500+ rally as the market breached 10,000 and never looked back (see Figure 4.7).

While these are extreme instances, they are not uncommon:

- Suze Orman, a frequent and knowledgeable commentator, especially on personal finance, has an association with a money manager, Mark Grimaldi of Navigator Money Management. His Sector Rotation mutual fund strongly outperformed the S&P from 8/31/2002 through 10/31/2011.

  The fact that the fund was not introduced until 12/31/2009 seems to be incidental. And the fund claimed to have outperformed the market in 2009: 24.58 percent vs. 19.79 percent. Alas, 2009 the S&P was up 26.46 percent, not 19+, an inconvenient fact that was attributed to a "typographical error."[6]

- *Morningstar* regularly reviews their picks and does so over a one-year period. The four names from the February/March 2011 edition of *MorningstarAdvisor* had three good results and one that was "liquidated."

  Okay, but if it was liquidated should they not have a price? Actually it wasn't, as it was morphed into the S&P Banks Select Industry Index (SPSIBK) and was down 16.78 percent[7] (see Table 4.5).

- The January 3, 2013 issue of *Investors Business Daily* lists their top 10 stocks as of the beginning of the year, ". . . names that would go on to perform well."[8] In fact they barely outperformed the market. The paper might have noted that assuming one was a devotee of their process, an investor would no longer have owned all the stocks.

TABLE 4.5 *MorningstarAdvisor:* February/March 2011

Pick	Type	Cumulative Return to Date (%)	Now, We Say . . .
Pfizer AMD	S	14.38	"Can withstand generic competition."
SPDR KBW Bank	ETF	—	Liquidated
Meridian Value MVALX	MF	4.73	"Suddenly has big shoes to fill."
Diamond Hill Large Cap Equity	SA	5.04	"Proven management, excellent results, great stewardship."
S&P 500 TR	Index	5.12	
S&P MidCap 400 TR	Index	2.55	

The February/March 2011 issue was mailed to subscribers in February 2011. Return data is from February 1, 2011, through March 1, 2012.

Source: Morningstar Inc., Birinyi Associates Inc.

At various points, some names went off the *Investors Business Daily* 50 list (3D Systems, for example, was the highest ranked name not only on January 7th but also on February 19th. The next week, it was dropped completely). Furthermore, the paper regularly advises that investors sell on 7 to 8 percent declines. As shown in Table 4.6, 3 of the 10 names had at least one 10 percent setback.

TABLE 4.6 *IBD* Top Ten from Start of 2013

Ticker	Name	IBD Rank Jan 7	Price OP 1/7/2013	Price CL 5/31/2013	Percent Chg	Amount of Decline
DDD	3D Systems Corp	1	41.11	48.52	18.0%	−38.7%
FLT	FleetCor Technologies Inc.	2	55.01	86.14	56.6%	
CVLT	CommVault Systems Inc.	3	71.09	70.40	−1.0%	
SWI	SolarWinds Inc.	4	54.87	41.57	−24.2%	−34.4%
SODA	SodaStream International Ltd.	5	49.91	69.06	38.4%	
SSYS	Stratasys Ltd.	6	83.35	80.15	−3.8%	−36.0%
KORS	Michael Kors Holdings Ltd.	7	51.98	62.24	19.7%	
RMD	ResMed Inc.	8	42.80	47.22	10.3%	
ARMH	ARM Holdings PLC	9	38.19	42.50	11.3%	
OCN	Ocwen Financial Corp.	10	34.46	42.99	24.8%	

Source: Investors Business Daily, Birinyi Associates, Inc.

NOTES

1. Greg Smith, "Why I am Leaving Goldman Sachs," *New York Times*, March 14, 2012.

2. The report prices IBM at $123 that day while the high/low was $128.735 – $129.75.

3. Randall Smith and Beatrice E. Garcia, "Stocks Plunge, Partly in Reaction to Sell Signals from Forecasters," *Wall Street Journal*, October 8, 1987.

4. N. R. Kleinfield. "Enduring Not Always Endearing 'Wall Street Week,'" *New York Times*, November 11, 1990.

5. Jeff Sommer, "A Market Forecast That Says 'Take Cover,'" *New York Times*, July 4, 2010.

6. Jason Zweig, "Meet Suze Orman's Newsletter Guru," *Wall Street Journal*, January 21, 2012.

7. "February/March 2011." *Morningstar Inc*. February/March 2011.

8. Donald Gold, "IBD's Recipe for Stock-Picking: Buy the Best in a Rising Market," *Investors Business Daily*, June 3, 2013.

CHAPTER 5

Money Flows: The Ultimate Indicator

In short, the two players with powerful hands have not bet in order to disguise their strength, then they both raised in order to claim it. In other words, money has its own language in poker. The way you use it supplements and qualifies the information your opponents glean from your cards.

—Herbert Yardley

As we detailed earlier, any number of approaches have been attempted in order to analyze and predict the future course of stock prices. While some are compelling, detailed, and occasionally (but inconsistently) useful, vigorous analysis and experience shows that they ultimately fail.

Several years ago, a Harvard professor wrote "How Doctors Think"[*] and concluded that the most critical ingredient in the diagnosis was the patient. Unfortunately, the trend is to "encourage the doctor to focus on the disease, not the patient." Physicians, he felt, spent too little time questioning and listening to the patient and too much time examining, probing, and prescribing.

From our experience, we recognize that there is an abundance of information within the stock market itself. Sometimes even noise is information. Years ago when the NYSE expanded into a third trading area, the Blue Room, traders were uncomfortable with the lack of noise. As a result, noise literally had to be imported from the main room and the Garage. Years later, Salomon Brothers opened a new trading floor. Within a month, an overhaul was undertaken, as the ticker tape was too short and the acoustics worked

---

[*]Jerome Groopman, M.D., "How Doctors Think," Houghton Mifflin. 2007.

too well. Traders could no longer sense the increased activity that often accompanied a change in trend.

Traders have long understood the importance of the market itself, not as a place or point of execution but as a source of intelligence. Jesse Livermore told the story of, what we would call today, a *hedge fund manager*. A waiter had overheard a conversation that a pool had been formed to buy shares of American Sugar. The intent was to drive up the price, drawing attention to the stock, and then unload it to unsuspecting buyers. The manager entered an order to sell the stock.

Sometime later, he sold more and the waiter could not understand the manager's ignorance. The stock, he reiterated, is going to go up. After receiving reports and watching the price, the trader finally entered an order to *buy* a large amount, as well as a few shares for his friend, the waiter.

As he later explained, the story sounded good but the only way to determine if someone was actually buying was to offer stock and see how aggressive the alleged buyers were. He was unsure with the first sale, but the second convinced him that indeed someone was buying and doing so aggressively.

Traders historically closely tracked the ticker tape as it, more than any other form of research, provided them with information. This was detailed not only in the well-known *Reminiscences of a Stock Operator*, by Edwin Lefèvre, but other books as well:

Tape Reading and Market Tactics, by Humphrey B. Neill
Studies in Tape Reading, by Richard Wyckoff
Truth of the Stock Tape, by William Gann

Brokerage firms provided accommodations for clients to come and discuss the dancing numbers. Many trading rooms also had paper tapes so one could review the activity of the last hour or two. Eberlin's, a restaurant steps from the Exchange, provided a tape so their customers could keep up with prices as they ate.

Traders relied on the tape, not only for a sense of the market, but also trends. The following, for example, reflects a market order to buy 500 shares of Ford. Apparently 200 shares were offered at 37 1/2 and then 300 at a slightly higher price, which defines it as a buy:

200 F 37 1/2 . . . 300 F 37 5/8

A market order to sell 500 Ford might appear as:

200 F 37 1/2 . . . 300 F 37 3/8

If one saw a series of buys (or sells) in key stocks, such as Ford, it was usually a suggestion that the market was beginning to rally or decline.

Another example might be a series of trades in Boeing:

100 BA 45 3/4 ... 15,000 BA 45 ... 500 BA 45 1/8 ... 800 BA 45 ... 1,200 BA 45 1/8

Here we would suggest that an institution wanted to sell Boeing and was willing to accept a 75-cent discount. But the subsequent small trades told a trader that, in all likelihood, the broker had not been able to find buyers for its entire block. So the firm itself bought the excess shares and was trying to unwind (sell) the stock as quickly as possible. And perhaps even pick up an odd eighth for their efforts.

It also told potential sellers that since the brokerage firm had not been able to find buyers for all 15,000 shares, today might not be a good time to sell Boeing.

PLAYING WITH BLOCKS

In addition to monitoring the tape itself, some investors regularly reviewed the block trades, which appeared in *Barron's* every weekend. Table 5.1 shows some of the blocks from the March 10, 1967 paper (unfortunately, after 1982 block trades became too numerous to detail and the feature was discontinued).

TABLE 5.1 Large Block Transactions

New York Stock Exchange			
March 10	Price	Volume	Previous Sale(a)
Dan River	22	15,000	22
Sperry Rand	35 7/8	46,100	34 7/8
Sperry Rand	35 7/8	10,000	35 7/8
Fansteel Met.-c	38 7/8	47,000	38 3/4
Allied Prod.	38 1/2	11,200	38 1/2
Miehle-Gross Dex.	29 1/2	12,600	29 7/8
Beckman Inst.	71	14,200	70 1/2
Benguet-c	4	10,000	4
Max Factor-c	52 1/4	50,000	52 3/8
Cox Bdcsty-c	48	19,000	48 1/4

Source: Barron's.

(After a presentation in Chicago some years ago, a gentleman introduced himself and said that he had been Mr. Buffett's broker in Omaha and that Buffett paid careful attention to the weekly list.)

In the late 1970s, Salomon Brothers automated tape analysis. Initially we focused on only block (10,000 share transactions), which proved its value almost immediately with Woolworth.

Until 1978, Woolworth (whose ticker symbol was Z) was averaging less than two block trades per month. In the last two weeks of October, six such trades were done, an additional four in December, and five more in January 1979. In addition, March and April saw a total of 25. Equally important, most of them were done at the last sale or at a higher price, including two trades in excess of 100,000 shares, both $0.375 higher than the existing price.

On April 9, 1979 Brascan, a Canadian retailer, announced a hostile takeover for Z and admitted that they had *already* purchased 4.9 percent of the company's shares. It could be argued that other approaches might have detected the buying as well. We think not as the stock was generally flat (in price) and there was no appreciation in volume leading up to the announcement (see Figure 5.1).

Salomon realized that to segregate block trades, the program had to analyze each trade, which was then done. The dollar volume of each trade was calculated and classified by size, as well as sector or group. Trades done at higher prices (upticks) were considered buys, while those at lower prices were sells. And those trades at the last sale, or no change, were considered only for volume and the other classifications.

A simple example might illustrate the concept. Your brother Jack goes to Las Vegas and plays blackjack. He plays blackjack for $10 a hand and

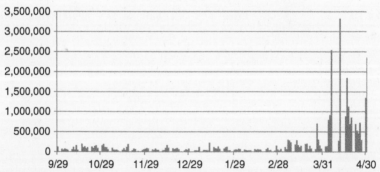

FIGURE 5.1   Woolworth Total Volume: 9/29/1978 through 4/30/1979
Source: Birinyi Associates, Inc., Bloomberg.

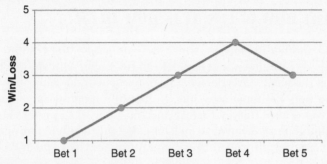

FIGURE 5.2   Money Flow Example: Win/Loss
Source: Birinyi Associates, Inc.

wins the first four hands, netting $40. Thinking that he has found a way to instant riches, he increases his bet to $50 but now loses:

	Amount Bet	Result	Cumulative Record
Bet 1	$10	W	$10
Bet 2	$10	W	$20
Bet 3	$10	W	$30
Bet 4	$10	W	$40
Bet 5	$50	L	−$10

He and the casino will tell you that he is a great gambler and wins 80 percent of the time as reflected in our charts of wins vs. losses (see Figures 5.2 and 5.3).

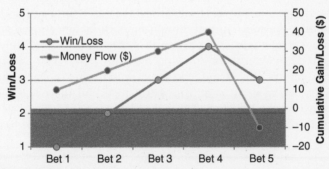

FIGURE 5.3   Money Flow Example: Win/Loss versus $
Source: Birinyi Associates, Inc.

IT IS NOT HOW OFTEN; IT IS HOW *MUCH*

If we add another dimension, which we call *money flows*, a different picture evolves. (An interesting parallel can be drawn with sports. The team that gains the most yards does not necessarily win the game, nor does the team that gets the most base hits. In fact, the greatest single game ever pitched was a loss. Harvey Haddix, in 1959, pitched 12 perfect innings for the Pittsburgh Pirates but gave up a hit in the thirteenth inning and lost the game. Or as someone said in 1975, "Jimmy Conners had a great Wimbledon, he lost only three sets, all in the final.")

By analyzing every single trade in every single stock, money flows are able to determine the amount and degree of interest in a stock, group, or index.

At this point we might digress and suggest that money flows is a generic term. Our definition applies to actual purchases and sales *within* the stock market. This is different than flow of funds, which should be considered as monies going to intermediaries. A purchase of mutual funds shares, or a deposit in a savings account, is a flow of funds. When a mutual fund manager buys or sells stocks we consider that as money flows in, or out, of the market.

The difference is critical, as many analysts will suggest that large flows into mutual funds are a positive for stocks. In reality this is the case only if the fund uses those proceeds to buy stocks. A large pile of cash does not necessarily translate into higher stock prices.

Money flows also differ from other related approaches. When we introduced the idea, Joe Granville's publicist wrote and accused us of usurping his idea of "On Balance Volume," which was a useful concept in its day. That approach assumed that all the volume on a good day was buying and all the volume on a bad day was selling, which of course is never the case.

Several surviving charts from 1982 illustrate the concept and its value. GM began the year at $40 and traded to $34 in mid-February, but there was no real selling pressure. In fact, in mid-January money started going into the stock even as it was going lower. From the bottom ($34) buying continued and did so even as the stock occasionally faltered (see Figure 5.4).

Exxon, on the other hand, was being sold during the same period. In mid-January, as the stock went from $29.50 to $31.50, there was selling and again in early March ($28 to $29.50) (see Figure 5.5).

At this point, we might highlight some key points regarding money flows:

- The critical issue is divergence. Money flows, if useful, lead prices. If money and price are coincidental, they provide no added insight.

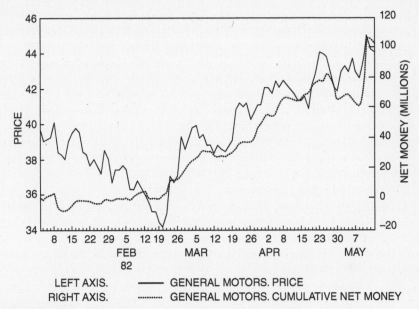

LEFT AXIS. ——— GENERAL MOTORS. PRICE
RIGHT AXIS. ·········· GENERAL MOTORS. CUMULATIVE NET MONEY

FIGURE 5.4 General Motors, January 4, 1982 through May 14, 1982
Source: Salomon Brothers Inc.

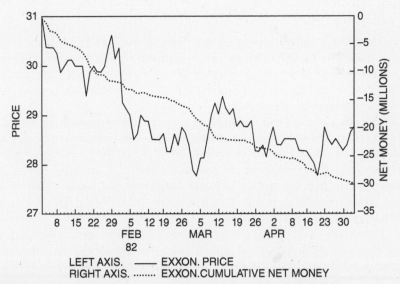

LEFT AXIS. ——— EXXON. PRICE
RIGHT AXIS. ········ EXXON.CUMULATIVE NET MONEY

FIGURE 5.5 Exxon, January 4, 1982 through May 5, 1982
Source: Salomon Brothers Inc.

- Other market measures are one-dimensional and show price or price and volume. Here we show *weighted* price so that a 1,000-share trade carries 10 times the weight of a 100-share trade.
- Each trade in every stock is incorporated. Unlike graphs, which are mostly influenced by the last trade of the day, the money flow calculation is as much a function of 10 A.M. as it is of the close. One does not, after all, value or judge a portfolio on the basis of how Whirlpool or Xerox performed, for example.
- Manifestation of the clichés: It's in the stock, the stock has anticipated, or some version thereof. That can be determined only by this approach. Our experience is that only 20 percent of the market is discounting some event [at any given point].
- Buying on weakness, such as seen in General Motors, reflects significant buyers. Here, an institution or a series of institutions, is attempting to accumulate large positions as they anticipate positive developments. If it were only retail orders, or a small institution, they would just have bought the stock.

Instead, someone is trying to buy thousands of shares and, like a good poker player who has been dealt three aces, they gingerly accumulate stock lest it run up. And as is often the case, if one firm has come to a positive conclusion, others have as well. Rather than upset the balance, they unwittingly cooperate. They allow the stock to trade lower on small, scattered trades and display their interest only when there is a large amount available for purchase.

The money flow tool was later refined as institutional trading began to increase. We realized that there were, in effect, two markets. One was the institutional, or wholesale, market where trades were effectively transacted on the trading desks at Salomon, or Merrill, before being posted on the ticker tape at the Exchange.

The other market was the Exchange itself, and we came to understand that this was probably *the only market in the world where retail could set wholesale prices*. While traders at Merrill might be negotiating a block of Standard Oil of NJ, assuming the last sale was $96, Aunt Mae's sale of 200 shares might drop the stock to $95 3/4. Buyers would demand that as the now going price. As a result, Merrill's sales and trading personnel might have to begin negotiations anew.

Given that there are two markets, our approach was to monitor both and require that they were in agreement with one another. As shown in Figure 5.6, this was the case for MCI Communications (MCIC).

MCIC shareholders were not enjoying 1986. The stock, which started the year in the low teens, was trading lower and was going into the single digits by year end. Institutions, however, were generally buyers.

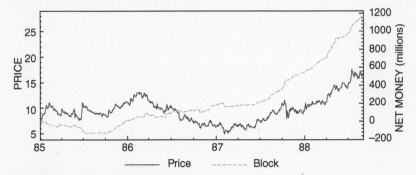

FIGURE 5.6 MCIC: Block Trades
Source: Salomon Brothers Inc.

Individuals were indecisive until the beginning of the third quarter, when they too began accumulating the stock. Unfortunately, as countless clients reminded us, the stock was to lose almost 50 percent of its value in the second half of the year, thereby highlighting that *money flows told you what but not when* (see Figure 5.7).

Beginning in 1987, the stock turned and over the next 11 years gained over 1,000 percent (see Figure 5.8).

Almost from the beginning, institutions rejected the idea (although all readily admitted to having and reading Livermore's *Reminiscences)*. The initial objection was that for every buyer there had to be a seller, and how then could we determine that one was more important than the other? The temptation was to respond flippantly and suggest a few hands of high stakes poker, but the answer really begins with trading experience.

In one of our first publications using money flows, we highlighted the selling in Waste Management, even as the stock was trading higher. A portfolio manager at a fund called us and detailed his experience. He

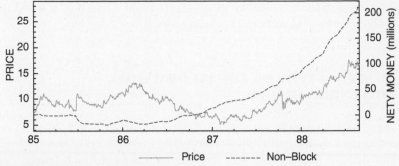

FIGURE 5.7 MCIC: Non-Block Trades
Source: Salomon Brothers Inc.

FIGURE 5.8   MCIC: 1982 through September 14, 1998
Source: Birinyi Associates, Inc., Bloomberg.

decided to buy the stock when it was trading around $51. After giving the order to his trader, he got a cup of coffee and as he was returning, his phone rang.

His trader told him, in a somewhat congratulatory tone, that he had been able to buy all 50,000 shares at $50.50, or a half-point discount. As he told it, in somewhat more colorful tones, he knew that he had just been passed the spade queen. Our chart only confirmed what his gut and experience had already concluded.

A week or two later, Waste Management was accused of dumping toxic waste illegally, and lost 18 percent in one day.

I might also recount the story about an analyst friend who was interested in buying a house in Greenwich. His realtor called one evening regarding a listing that had just come on the market, and which met my friend's specifications.

The next morning he took the first train out of Grand Central and, while the owners of the house were still sleeping, he bought the house. One buyer, one seller, but was that house bought or sold? One can only speculate on what the owners must have thought when they learned that their house was sold without ever being listed!

THE SEC'S STUDY ON THE INFORMATION FROM LARGE TRADES

A more concrete response was provided by the SEC. In 1971, the Commission published a multivolume effort, *The Institutional Investor Study*, which had 300 pages devoted to the "Price Impacts of Block Trades." The study had the authority to analyze the original order and found conclusively that block trades that traded on upticks originated as purchase transactions, while those trades that traded lower were initiated as sells.

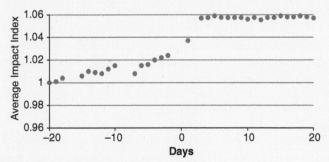

FIGURE 5.9 Price Impact of Uptick Block Trades
Source: SEC.

With regard to their forecasting, the Commission found that uptick trades continued higher. After 10 days they tended to outperform by 5 percent. (Downticks tended to underperform on the order of 3 percent; see Figure 5.9.)

In 2001, several academics, unknown to us, engaged in "rigorous empirical evidence" and concluded:

> *Most important of our findings is that money flow appears to provide investors with information regarding future returns.*[1]

A graphic of their conclusions not only provided support, but was interesting in the lead time. This suggests that the concept, as we always suggested, was valuable for investors as it provided ample opportunity to investigate and analyze (see Figure 5.10).

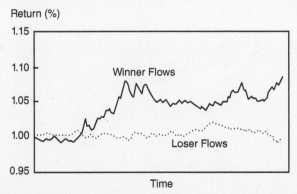

FIGURE 5.10 Cumulative Market-Adjusted Returns: Portfolios Based on 30-Day-Lag Money Flow with 30-Day Holding Period[2]
Source: CFA Institute

Investors then demanded to know what the market was discounting. While the market was never so accommodating, we find it intriguing because the very question—What is the market saying?—is a tacit admission that the market is saying something. And perhaps the real job of the manager or the analyst is to uncover the market's secret. What we could say, with some confidence, was that the market does not anticipate quarterly earnings, analyst revisions, accounting fraud, or downgrades.

The market, as we repeatedly illustrated, discounts significant fundamental developments, which lead to equally significant opportunities:

- **We like the oils.** On February 22, 1983, OPEC cut oil prices. The effect on the oil stocks was dramatic, as investors sold. A large state fund asked us to review the trading, as the manager felt that net, net the news was positive. Our chart showed that the oils had been under accumulation. More importantly, we found that after the initial trade, investors had *bought* the stocks. Mobil, as an example, was down $1.375 on the opening trade, with net selling of $668 million. From that point, there was an inflow of $1.2 million on the day.

  The fund was an aggressive buyer and was overweight the sector, which was to gain 160 percent over the next four years vs. the S&P's 90 percent (see Figure 5.11).

- **Rates—the real consensus.** Going into 1995, the mood on Wall Street was somber. Issues in Mexico and the fear of rising rates, following a

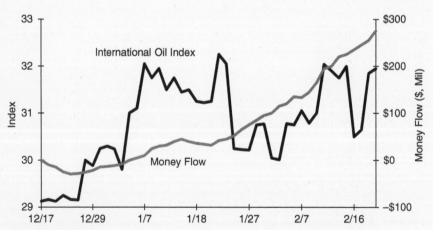

FIGURE 5.11 International Oils Money Flow: December 1982 through February 1983

Source: Salomon Brothers Inc.

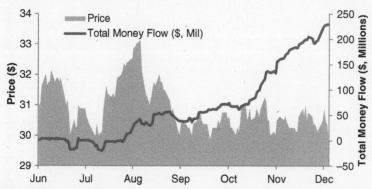

FIGURE 5.12 GTE Total Money Flow: June 1994 through December 1994
Source: Birinyi Associates, Inc., Bloomberg.

non-event year, unsettled investors. Our end-of-year *Wall Street Week* forecast was for a market that would open at its lows and trend higher all year. I would be the closest of all panelists in our high, low, and close forecast. We have never aspired to forecast bonds, but we noted that while the world was expecting higher rates, the market had a different outlook.

GTE in the fourth quarter of 1994 was to go from $30 to $30, attracting no attention whatsoever. We noted, however, that there had been over $170 million in net buying, or approximately 5.6 million shares (see Figure 5.12).

Why were investors piling into an interest sensitive stock if rates were going appreciably higher? Our conclusion was that the *market* was suggesting *lower* rates. The long U.S. Treasury, which began the year at 7 3/4 percent, with expectations of going higher, actually traded below 6 percent.

- **The only *lead* market indicator.** As we wrote earlier, there are no technical indicators that forecast higher prices. Oscillators have to oscillate, trends have to develop, and net advances or declines have to occur. Money flows tell us something is going to happen.

  When looking at the market, we had always used the DJIA non-block results. Traders would be more acute to changing market trends than investors and more likely to buy key Dow names like IBM and GE. In 1990, for example, money flows turned higher *before* the market bottomed. They forecasted higher prices and the ensuing bull market. Technicians, as we noted earlier, were negative and strategists were cautious, suggesting investors were waiting until the 1991 Gulf War actually developed (see Figure 5.13).

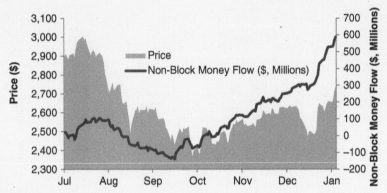

FIGURE 5.13 DJIA Non-Block Money Flow: July 1990 through January 1991
Source: Birinyi Associates, Inc., Bloomberg.

One recalls that the conventional view of January 1991 was that the conflict would begin with a 200-point decline, which would clear the air. In fact, the market opened sharply higher (helped by IBM's results) and while the market churned for most of the year, it never accommodated the bears.

Throughout most of the decade, we were accused of being a redundant bull, which only reflected the fact that there was a continual inflow through most of the decade, including the corrections associated with Long-Term Capital and the Russian Ruble crisis (see Figure 5.14).

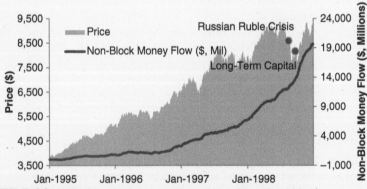

FIGURE 5.14 DJIA Non-Block Money Flow: 1995 through 1998
Source: Birinyi Associates, Inc., Bloomberg.

WALL STREET WEEK: THE RECORD

Not only did money flows produce market direction, they might have been the ultimate approach for stock selection. In Table 5.2 we cite our results on *Wall Street Week* from 1992 through 1999.

In addition, we regularly produced recommended lists and portfolios, which outperformed the market by significant margins (see Table 5.3). I was interviewed by *Barron's* in the March 22, 1999 edition and provided a table of stocks with the "strongest money flows" as well as one with the "weakest."

Over the next month the strongest list gained 13 percent vs. 1 percent for the market, and 5 percent for the weakest. The three-month results were +16 percent (strongest), +3 percent (market), and +10 percent (weakest). But a year after the article the strongest names were up 94.7 percent, crushing the market's 12.8 percent gain, while the other list was actually down 2 percent (see Figure 5.15).

The record of flows on the other side—selling—is also compelling. In 1993, one of the more favored stocks was Philip Morris, which was in most portfolios as a top five holding. We noted selling as early as the fourth quarter of the previous year. Our calls were not well received. On April 2, 1993, or "Marlboro Friday," the company announced that it was cutting prices on its best-selling product (see Figure 5.16). Clearly this was "in the stock" had anyone cared to ask.

Exhibit two on the sell side might be a recommendation made by our then-colleague, Gregg Schoenleber, on March 16, 2000:

Birinyi Money Flows
First Weak Money Flows in Telecoms and Warning Signs for Technology

TABLE 5.2 Laszlo Birinyi's Record W$W Eight-Year Record: 1992 through 1999

	Laszlo Birinyi	Panel Average	DJIA	S&P 500
1999	54.9%	18.5%	25.2%	19.5%
1998	23.2	18.5	16.1	26.7
1997	74.8	24.4	22.7	30.3
1996	54.8	16.9	26.9	22.7
1995	42.0	37.2	34.5	37.1
1994	17.7	2.2	3.6	1.3
1993	32.3	16.8	15.1	10.0
1992	49.2	12.7	5.7	7.6
Average Return	43.6%	18.4%	18.7%	19.4%
Cumulative Return	1,604.2%	272.2%	283.6%	297.8%

Source: Birinyi Associates, Inc.

TABLE 5.3 In the Money

These Companies Have the Strongest Money Flows in the Market

Strongest	Symbol	Recent Price
America Online	AOL	109 1/16
American Express	AXP	120 15/16
Apple Computer	AAPL	34 1/16
Charles Schwab	SCH	86 7/16
Ford Motor	F	57 3/8
IBM	IBM	178 1/16
JP Morgan	JPM	121 1/2
LSI Logic	LSI	27 1/16
Merrill Lynch	MER	88 3/8
Motorola	MOT	68 1/2

These Companies Have the Weakest Money Flows in the Market

Weakest	Symbol	Recent Price
Allstate	ALL	38 15/16
Atlantic Richfield	ARC	63 1/4
Best Foods	BFO	48 15/16
Campbell Soup	CPB	41 9/16
Harris	HRS	30 3/4
May Department Stores	MAY	58 5/8
National City	NCC	68 5/16
New York Times	NYT	28 15/16
Occidental Petroleum	OXY	16 15/16
Walgreen	WAG	29 7/8

Source: Birinyi Associates, Inc.

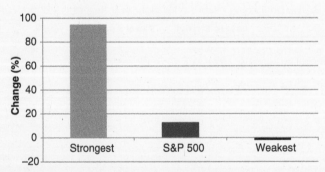

FIGURE 5.15 Results of *Barron's* March 22, 1999 Lists
Source: Birinyi Associates, Inc.

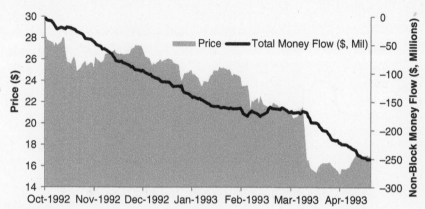

FIGURE 5.16 Philip Morris Non-Block Money Flow: October 1992 – May 20, 1993
Source: Birinyi Associates, Inc., Bloomberg.

The first signs of Money Flows weakening in the high performing Telecoms and Technology sectors. In 1999 Telecoms and Technology had money in-flows of $4,066m and $1,894m respectively. In the last 4 weeks this has reversed to outflows of $1,671m and $907m respectively.

APPLE IS A BUY AT $3?

Many investors will remember our recommendation of Apple (then Apple Computer) in 1997 on the year-end *Wall Street Week* show. As shown in Figure 5.17, it was to be, in the parlance of Wall Street, a home run.

It would probably be useful to further detail the stock and provide a scenario that likely transpired.

Sometime in the second quarter of 1997, the attitude toward Apple changed (see Figure 5.18). Even though the stock was trading lower, some managers saw the proverbial light. A hypothetical portfolio manager might have given his trader, Joe, an order to buy the stock.

The trader in turn called the trader/salesman at Zeta Securities (let's call her Jane) and told her to buy some Apple stock using the instruction, "participate, don't initiate." Basically, this suggested that the institution wanted to buy the stock, but not aggressively. Jane then approached her trader, Bill, who was making a market in the stock and said it was $4 to $4 1/8, 10,000 up. In effect, the customer could buy 10,000 shares immediately at $4.125.

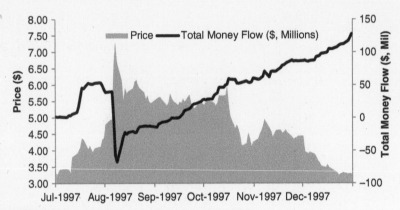

FIGURE 5.17   Apple Total Money Flow: 2H 1997
Source: Birinyi Associates, Inc., Bloomberg.

Jane, knowing the customer, passed. She realized that the institution didn't own the stock and that their usual commitment was never less than 10 million dollars or, in this case, 2.5 million shares. And buying stock at a higher price, even just 12 cents, was not what the customer wanted.

Bill, who was willing to buy stock at $4, for himself, now had a customer. So he might have increased the size of his bid to 20,000 shares, and over the course of the next few hours bought 100,000 shares there with the stock closing at $4.

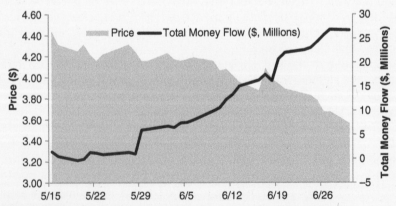

FIGURE 5.18   Apple Total Money Flow: May 1997 through June 1997
Source: Birinyi Associates, Inc., Bloomberg.

The next morning there were some negative economic developments and Apple was quoted lower at $3 3/4 to $3 7/8. This was actually good news as the buyer was now able to buy more stock at a lower price. Once again: participate, don't initiate. Bill continued to "work" the order, buying stock at $3 3/4 when a Boston fund called and indicated some interest in selling the stock. Bill bid $3 3/4 for 50,000 shares but the seller was "at" $4 for size.

After further dialogue, it was determined that 250,000 shares were available at $4, and the market was doing a little better. Some dealers raised their bids to $3 7/8. Jane called the trader, Joe, and told him that 250 were available at $4. His response was: "Does it work at 7/8"? Jane didn't think so and was told to try, but if not, buy the stock.

Joe had stepped up, in part because he was hearing that there was developing interest in Apple. If 250,000 shares traded and he didn't buy any of it, he would have to explain why not. After all, the original order didn't happen in a vacuum. Whatever prompted the portfolio manager to buy the stock was likely to have been seen or discussed at other firms as well.

Two hundred and fifty thousand shares traded at $4. Everyone was happy except other traders, who were trying to buy the stock, missed it, and were now paying $4 1/8, or a quarter. Everyone now knows that Zeta Securities has a large buyer so they are inundated with offerings:

"10,000 Apple at a quarter."
"Apple, can your buyer use more?"
"Apple, in touch with size to go."

Jane and Bill realize that they are looking at more stock to buy, but they could lose the rest of the order if they tipped their hand. So even when they see 10,000 shares offered at the last sale, Bill passes. He's hoping that the seller goes into the market place and sells the shares lower so he can buy stock cheaper. Or he might actually sell a little stock out of his inventory and take a slight loss. He certainly will not buy the market orders that come in to sell 1,000 or 2,500 shares at the market. They will trade on the bid side and establish lower prices.

Given that the institution has readily bought so much stock already, the broker wants to exhibit the full range of his skills. Within the next month, a total of 1 million shares are bought at prices as low as $3.50. Now buyers, sensing a really cheap stock, become aggressive and drive the stock up to almost $5.

On August 7, 1997, a positive development catapults Apple, briefly, above $7 (see Figure 5.19). Our manager, who did such a great job of identifying Apple at the low, concludes that this move is ridiculous and that the news, whatever it is, must be insignificant. In addition, he has close to a 100 percent profit in a matter of weeks.

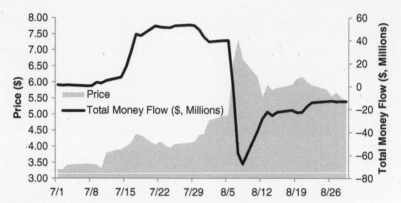

FIGURE 5.19   Apple Total Money Flow: July 1997 through August 1997
Source: Birinyi Associates, Inc., Bloomberg.

Now the situation is reversed and stock is sold, but again, only when large amounts can be fed into the market and not enough to satisfy all the buyers. The stock is not sold near the end of the day when it might depress the stock.

The stock trades in the $5.50 area for several months but slides in the fourth quarter (see Figure 5.20). When it gets to $4 in early December, Jane gets a phone call. . . .

With the introduction of decimal trading, fractured exchanges, dark pools, aggressive hedge funds, and other structural changes, the value of money flows has been greatly diminished. But discussion and details regarding them still provide useful insights into the market as well as the psychology of investors.

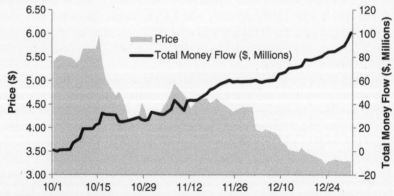

FIGURE 5.20   Apple Total Money Flow: October 1997 through December 1997
Source: Birinyi Associates, Inc., Bloomberg.

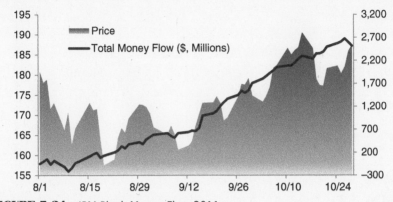

FIGURE 5.21 IBM Block Money Flow 2011

Source: Birinyi Associates, Inc., Bloomberg.

Therefore, we think it is worth reviewing the process, calculation, and implementation of money flows today for several reasons:

• They can still, on occasion, be useful especially with large trades that are not likely to be traded electronically.

In mid-2011 we noticed an almost classic accumulation pattern in IBM (see Figure 5.21). On November 14, we learned that Mr. Buffett had taken an $11 billion position!

In the first quarter of 2013, the company's earnings and revenue apparently missed estimates, but the market looked upon the decline as an opportunity to *buy* (see Figure 5.22).

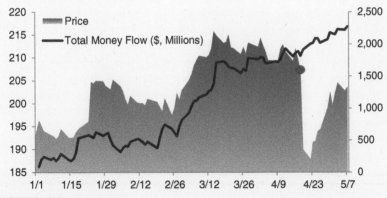

FIGURE 5.22 IBM: 2013

Source: Birinyi Associates, Inc., Bloomberg.

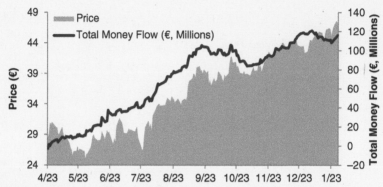

FIGURE 5.23   BNP Paribas Total Money Flow: 4/23/2012 through 1/29/2013
Source: Birinyi Associates, Inc., Bloomberg.

- Despite the woes of Europe for much of this decade, in mid-2012 several European banks were under accumulation at their lows. France's BNP Paribas was to go from €25 to €45 in just over a month (see Figure 5.23).
- There is an increase of interest in social networks and other "big data" approaches which might be thought of as money flows once removed. A *Financial Times* article (4/26/13) discussed research being done ". . . . to predict the direction of the stock market, according to an analysis of search engine behavior." Obviously we have no idea how this will develop. We read articles about Twitter feeds and other approaches, which might approximate money flows.
- Money flows have highlighted the importance of the *market* itself.

  As Mr. Berra once said, in reference to another context, "you can observe a lot by just watching." In the markets of the twenty-first century, investors and even traders are increasingly divorced from the markets with the market often being the end result of a process rather than an integral part thereof.

  One of our favorite trading stories involves Bill Simon, the former Secretary of the Treasury who was responsible for government and municipal trading at Salomon Brothers. He sent a trainee to buy $10 million of short term paper at $4.00. The young man came back and said that it traded away.

  Simon told him to go bid $4.10 but that too failed. "So bid $4.20." After the trainee sheepishly came back, Simon said:

  "Young man you couldn't buy it at $4.00 you couldn't buy it at $4.20, and you couldn't buy it at $4.30. So sell!"

  After selling at $4.40 the instrument came back in, the trader covered his short at $4.10, and also bought the original $10 million he wanted in the first place at $4.00.

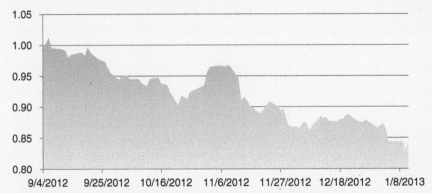

FIGURE 5.24   Relative Strength: Microsoft versus S&P 500
Source: Birinyi Associates, Inc.

In early May 2011, the world focused on an election in Greece with concerns that some radical parties might gain more seats. We have no claims to understanding Greek politics but we did note that the Greek Index was up seven days in a row:

Date	Price	Change (%)
6/13/12	499.56	2.09
6/14/12	550.10	10.12
6/15/12	560.26	1.85
6/18/12	580.67	3.64
6/19/12	600.07	3.34
6/20/12	603.04	0.49
6/21/12	614.09	1.83
Total		25.49

Microsoft introduced a variety of products at the end of 2012 including a new tablet, new versions of Windows, and rumors of a new phone. While there were some favorable reviews (as well as unfavorable) the market was unimpressed (see Figure 5.24).

MR. MARKET'S VOICE

Perhaps the most critical take away from money flows is that it highlights a critical flaw in the professional investment process: *Analysts and commentators really don't understand the market.* That may be a strong indictment, but over the years we have been dismayed at the failure of money managers and analysts to understand the underlying insights of money flows.

They are not, as some would believe, a technical indicator. Nor are they a model, a sample, or anything of the sort. They are *the ultimate fundamental input*. Many investors talk about Mr. Market. Flows are Mr. Market sharing with us where developments are likely to occur in the future.

It is the market's own articulation discounting some upcoming fundamental development. Sadly, for most investors that is not enough, they demand to know *what* is being discounted.

Historically, as noted earlier, at any point in time, only 20 percent of stocks are showing accumulation or distribution. We have always suggested that rather than selling advice, we were also selling time, so that managers and clients could focus on those few stocks that would ultimately affect their portfolios.

Peter Lynch once gave a reporter investing advice: "Learn how to play poker." Poker players recognize the information content of a transaction, even if there is only one buyer and one seller. They realize too that an anxious seller is not doing you a favor.

We might at this point reiterate why money flows "work" and the rationale behind the process is. First, they are multidimensional. Unlike other measures that provide closing (or average) price and are biased as a result, flows incorporate every trade and the last one is no more important than any other. Secondly, prices are weighted so that 200 shares are twice as important as 100 shares. It is not as much how many, but how much.

Bill Gross spent some time after college playing blackjack and I once asked him (although I already knew the answer) what his winning percentage was. As I recall, it was 48.5 or 49 percent, which meant he lost more than he won. When asked how he did with the $100 or larger bets, his percentage was around 52 percent.

It is not how often but how much that matters.

The concept, in effect, captures smart money. A manager determines that such and such a stock has a good prospect despite a lagging price and general lack of interest. He decides to buy 500,000 shares, which could create an imbalance in the market. The trader gives his broker an order to buy Colgate or Boeing and accumulate the stock. This means stay on the bid side, let the stock come to you, and buy the odd 600 or 1,100 shares.

A good trader, knowing his customer, will quietly do so and will sometimes fade out of the market if he fears that sellers are sensing buy interest. Over the course of the morning, he might buy 8,500 shares. The brokerage firm might find an institution that wants to sell 50,000 shares at the offering side, which might be three-quarters with the last sale one-half. The buyer might suggest one-quarter would be an equitable price, but the seller is in no hurry and remains committed to three-quarters.

The broker and the institutional buyer acknowledge that ultimately they will have to buy a lot of stock (even though neither may know the final number) and they "take it" at three-quarters. Other sellers come in offering 800 or 1,500 shares, and the like. The buyer does not want to appear anxious, claims no further interest, goes back to a quarter picking up odds and ends at that price until another block is available several hours later or the next day.

In reality, if one manager made the decision, it was more than likely that others did as well and while they may not acknowledge one another, no one wants to create a situation that exposes their interest.

Money flows are seen in the other "markets" as well. Years ago, we applied the approach to Off Track Betting (OTB). Another underemployed colleague and I would compare the odds at OTB versus the out of town tracks. If a horse was 4 to 1 in New York but 2 to 1 at Pimlico, we contended that the Maryland money was likely to be better informed and over time we took out our original stake several times.

Unfortunately, for the punter and the trader the opportunities did not regularly present themselves and we often went days between transactions.

Yet another example: Several years ago Hollywood released a movie that was millions over budget, well past its expected date, the subject of mixed reviews, four hours long, and one in which everyone died.

The market, however, endorsed *Titanic*.

NOTES

1. James Bennett and Richard Sias, "Can Money Flows Predict Stock Market Returns?" *Financial Analysts Journal*, November/December 2001.
2. Ibid.

CHAPTER 6

Anecdotal Data

It ain't what you don't know that gets you into trouble.
It's what you know for sure that just ain't so.

—Mark Twain

O
ur investment process has three elements: data, analysis, and strategy. This is probably not unusual; in fact, it may be somewhat similar to the process used by other managers and researchers. In actuality the type and depth of the data we gather is, as far as we know, unique. This is especially true of our anecdotal data.

When I began my investment career, I tried to accelerate my learning process by reading all manner of books and articles. We took trial subscriptions to a variety of newsletters, which we diligently reviewed, collated, and saved. At some point, we noticed some curious inconsistencies: newsletters that were bearish congratulated themselves after a rally. Others suggested buying high quality, visible names that they identified as Coke and Sears Roebuck, only after those stocks hit new highs.

In part, to keep track of the actual recommendations and comments, we copied and codified significant news from a wide variety of articles, magazines, and other media, which we term *anecdotal data*. Every quarter we bind the collection of this data, and it usually totals approximately 100 pages. Nothing provides a better understanding of the mood, sentiment, and attitude of a particular time.

Knowing the position of the story, its length, the individuals cited, and so forth, is considerably more instructive than the usual polls. Having a bearish attitude is one thing, but telling the *Wall Street Journal* you are bearish is considerably more significant. A recent David Brooks column in the *New York Times* illustrated our attitude:

What Data Can't Do

Data struggles with the social . . . excels at measuring the quantity but not the quality.

Data struggles with context.

Data creates bigger haystacks . . . we find many more statistically significant correlations. Most of these correlations are spurious and deceive us.

This information has a variety of applications that, again, are not likely to be determined by more conventional approaches. Of these, sentiment might be the most important.

Sentiment can be directly measured in any number of ways. I have already suggested that the popular *Investors Intelligence* numbers are not as accurate as most analysts would suggest. The American Association of Individual Investors produces results, but their poll is based on *voluntary* participation.

Our experience is that critical market bottoms and turning points are regularly marked by extremely lengthy and negative reports. We have already discussed that at the absolute bottom in August 1982, the technical community was adamant that this was not it; lower lows were expected.

The previous significant market bottom, fourth quarter of 1974, exhibited the same characteristic:

The Case for Gloom about Stocks: *Fortune*, October 1974

All of which suggests that the calculation . . . yielding a value of around 550 for the Dow is far from airtight—it isn't exactly irrelevant either.

At the same time, *Forbes* (October 15, 1974) expressed a similar, bearish outlook

A Dow Below 400?

And there were any number of negative newspaper reports:

11/5/74—GM Is Cutting Its Dividend by 64%

11/20/74—Consumer Confidence Reported at a Low (48.9%)

All were clustered at or near the bear market's bottom (see Figure 6.1).

We have previously detailed the technicians' views in the fall of 1990. Also negative were economists ("The 'Dwarf Recession' Might Be a Giant"—*BusinessWeek*, October 15, 1974) and strategists.

FIGURE 6.1 DJIA 1974 through 1976

Source: Birinyi Associates, Inc., Bloomberg.

A *Wall Street Journal* story, "This Bear Could Collapse Without Warning, Some Say" (December 10, 1990), presented our view:

The market is at odds with conventional wisdom and strategists' thinking.

It also presented the views of the chairman of Goldman Asset Management who would want to see price earnings ratios fall to 10 or 11 times from the then current 14 as well as a rise in the dividend yield (4.5 to 5 percent from 3.5 percent). He concluded that stocks were 10 to 15 percent overvalued relative to bonds (see Figure 6.2).

FIGURE 6.2 DJIA: 1H 1991

Source: Birinyi Associates, Inc., Bloomberg.

FIGURE 6.3   S&P 500

Source: Birinyi Associates, Inc., Bloomberg.

Several weeks later, a prominent strategist appeared on *Wall Street Week:*

> *I am still quite sour . . . I think there is still more downside risk in the equity markets. If the consensus outlook is right and we have a short recession . . . the market to me would be fairly valued at 10% lower. If my profit estimates are right, the market does not reach fair value until 2,200 on the Dow and here's something to think about, in a normal bear market, the fair value is not the bottom.*[1]

Both views reflected the general consensus that the fourth quarter rally was only a respite in a bear market. Investors were advised that when the 1991 Gulf War actually commenced, the market would drop sharply and that would be an opportune time to buy. In fact, the market opened sharply *higher* continuing the October rally (see Figure 6.3).

Interestingly, and highlighting the value of the anecdotal approach, the *Investors Intelligence* reading was negative at the bottom and positive as the market spiked in 1991, thus failing as a contrary indicator (see Figure 6.4).

The bear market that ended in October 2002 might have been the exception. There was no overwhelming bearish or head-for-the-hills story. The closest might have been a full-page *BusinessWeek* article (September 23, 2002):

> *Are We Looking at DOW 5,000? Bill Gross Says Maybe*

The S&P 500 bottomed on October 9, 2002, at 776.76 but meandered to 800 in early March. Once again, as was the case six months earlier,

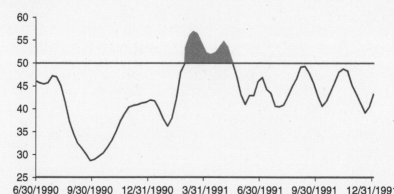

FIGURE 6.4   Investors Intelligence Bullish Sentiment (Four-Week Moving Average)
Source: Investors Intelligence, Birinyi Associates, Inc.

investors were concerned. But there weren't any especially pessimistic or bearish calls.

> *Investment Pros Want No Part of Current Risk*
> *Investors Crave Safety*
> *Investors Are Flocking to Super Safe Treasuries*

What is interesting, as one reads the accounts of those days, is the concern and discussion of the war's impact. No one seemed to remember that when that conflict began [in January 1991], the market went straight up. Indeed that was to be the case in 2003 as well, and even more so as the DJIA added 2.8 percent in one day (see Figure 6.5).

FIGURE 6.5   DJIA: March 21, 2003
Source: Birinyi Associates, Inc., Bloomberg.

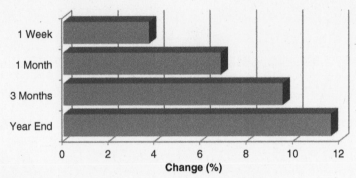

FIGURE 6.6   S&P 500 Performance Post "Special Report"
Source: Birinyi Associates, Inc.

Anecdotal data extends beyond print, although it is more difficult to capture and maintain. On June 3, 2012, with markets down almost 10 percent from their April peak, CNBC ran a "Sunday Night Special Report" (see Figure 6.6). Our notes from the program:

- The May employment report on Friday set off a firestorm of selling—an awful May has been replaced by the start of a frightening June—it's the worst beginning ever for the Nasdaq and S&P—the political landscape heading into the election changes dramatically.
- We don't know what exactly is causing our newfound weakness.
- Futures are already down, just terrible, nasty—these are very thinly traded numbers, but keep in mind the tone is just terrible.
- The contagion [from Europe] is already here, something is very wrong—the Dow wiped out its gains on Friday.
- We are about to head into a European-led recession.
- We have nothing to hang a bullish hat on at the moment.

MAGAZINES AND NEWSPAPERS ARE DATABASES IN DISGUISE

However, the historical approach does not seem to be as useful at market tops. The 2002 bull market went negative on October 9, 2007, but the stories and accounts at the time generally offset one another:

Fed acts to ease credit fears . . . cuts lending rates . . . market up over 1%
Dow rises 1.9% as Fed Letter Stirs Rally
Economists Divided on Recession

The R-word surfaces
Dow Rallies 133 . . . Oil Breaks $80

As the financial crisis played out in late 2008 and early 2009, once again a number of articles suggested that there was more to come and news was consistently negative, perhaps climaxing (if that is the appropriate phrase) on March 9 with a *Wall Street Journal* story:

Dow 5,000? A Bearish Possibility
Strategists Still See Rally, but Earnings Point to 1995 Levels for Stocks

To fully appreciate the anecdotal process, one must incorporate a variety of inputs and do so with some diligence. We read several newspapers daily and a wide number of magazines. We focus on significant stories, days with large moves, lengthy bullish/bearish reports, political/financial and even social stories. One of the best stories on technical analysis actually appeared in the *New York Times'* Arts and Ideas section: "The Patterns Hidden In Market Swings" (June 3, 2000).

Wired magazine may not be on many reading lists but a recent issue (June 2013) had an interesting graphic illustrating high-frequency trading. Meanwhile *Vanity Fair's* editorial on the financial crisis was one of the best we have seen:

The government's attitude toward different professions is strik-
ing. With sports scandals it zeros in on individuals. But when
it comes to banks, federal authorities go after the institutions.
The people at the center of a financial scandal are almost never
touched, and most walk away with compensation packages. . . .
(September 2012)

Our approach includes gathering historical publications as well. As just one example, years ago when the web became viable, we went to the available magazine sellers and bought every available copy of the famous *BusinessWeek* "The Death of Equities" (August 13, 1979).

In addition to overall sentiment, tracking individuals, as well as theories and ideas, can be useful. Therefore, we track the more prominent and vocal commentators, as well as important arguments or approaches.

Robert Bernstein once remarked that "only intuition can save you from the most dangerous individual of all, the articulate incompetent." While that might have been a poor choice of words, we have found it useful to interpret a strategy or advice in light of an individual's attitude. One global strategist told investors (mid-January 2013) to have a "maximum under-weight in stocks" in preparation for another "bear market leg lower."

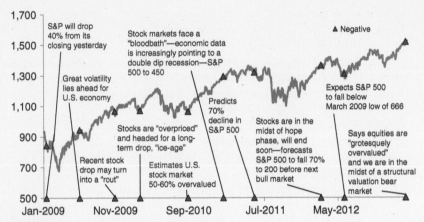

FIGURE 6.7   One Strategist's Commentary

Source: Birinyi Associates, Inc., Bloomberg.

His views were a continuation of a long-held posture and we might give him credit for consistency but not accuracy (see Figure 6.7).

We have previously outlined what we might term *philosophical objections* to technical analysis. A more pragmatic example might be April 26, 2010.

Almost from the bottom in 2009, the technical community disputed the gain: Volume was lacking, breadth was not supportive, and a correction was imminent. On April 23, the market hit a new bull market high, up 80 percent (see Figure 6.8). We were, therefore, surprised to read the *Wall Street Journal*'s lead Money and Finance story on April 26, 2010. In a lengthy 23-paragraph piece, technicians sounded an all clear:

Technical Analysts See Room to Roll

. . . *say all indicators point to more gains ahead.*

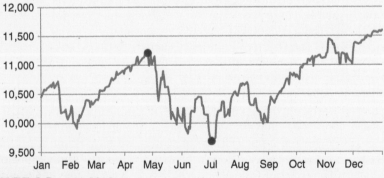

FIGURE 6.8   DJIA 2010

Source: Birinyi Associates, Inc., Bloomberg.

Unfortunately, they were absolutely *wrong* and the market was to go into a 15 percent correction. Then the anecdotal was again of value. At the absolute bottom, with uncanny precision, we were told to *sell!*

Dark Omen Threatens Stock Market Bulls
. . . the current sell off is more likely the start of a longer period of weakness.

***Wall Street Journal*, July 1, 2010**

Technicians Await the Bear
. . . an enduring downtrend emerging.

***Barron's*, July 5, 2010**

Having tracked and catalogued technicians' views, we were not especially fazed by their concerns. We viewed the correction as just that. We were further assured that the market's positive trend was still intact when at the same time and again at the precise bottom, the *New York Times* (June 30, 2010) wrote its longest market story of the year:

Wall St. Tallies New Losses with a Bear Market in Mind
But it was really just another bad day in a bad month, a bad quarter, a bad year.
   If history is any guide it doesn't look all that great.

Our anecdotal approach also provides a historical perspective, which we contend is not otherwise easily available. Following the turn in the market in March 2009, there was concern that the economy was too weak to support the market and economists warned of a double dip. We have no special insights in the area but we regularly noted that a lengthy *New York Times* story (October 3, 1982) questioned the stock market's rally given the weak economy:

The Economic Recovery That Won't Start
. . . the prospect that the recovery may amount to nothing more than a few quarters of a paltry growth . . . is gaining credence . . . among economists. . . .

The *New York Times* concluded:

And to a growing number of analysts, this grim prospect appears all too likely [2% GDP growth].

Obviously the economy recovered, and remarkably so, despite the economists' views. It blew away that 2 percent estimate (see Figure 6.9).

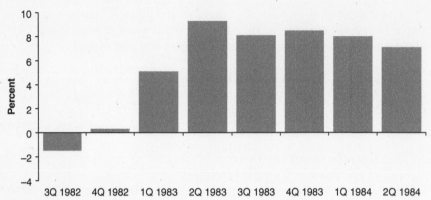

FIGURE 6.9   GDP Quarterly (Annual Rate)
Source: Bloomberg.

DOW THEORY IN REAL TIME

While this was not to be the case in 2010, the previous article provided a counter balance and perspective to the overwhelmingly negative views and to the chorus of commentators arguing against both the economy and the market at the time.

Our information is also useful in researching issues. An example might be that of Dow Theory. Perhaps the oldest of all market indicators, the Dow Theory says that a move in the Industrial Average must be confirmed by a similar move in the Transportation Average. One could undertake an analysis and create a variety of tables and graphs.

Since there are several analysts who allegedly specialize in Dow Theory, we thought it more useful to track their commentary to see if indeed this was a compelling and valuable approach.

We have tracked their commentary back to 1980 and found that the calls are basically random. One call that was especially prominent appeared on the cover of *Barron's* (October 12, 1992):

> *Bear market? Dick Russell says it is. Dick is famous . . . the tireless keeper, defender and explicator of the Dow Theory.*
>
> *And under that venerable but still viable doctrine, according to Dick, on last Monday October 5, we entered a bear market (407.57).*

From October 12th, the market went up eight days in a row and never threatened 407 (see Figure 6.10).

FIGURE 6.10 S&P 500: 4Q 1992
Source: Birinyi Associates, Inc., Bloomberg.

Plotting Dow Theory calls over the past several years is not very supportive of the idea (see Figure 6.11).

Creating and maintaining an anecdotal database might seem difficult. But we suggest keeping the significant stories, of which there are relatively few in any given week. Especially important are the end-of-year stories and publications. Here we would suggest merely saving them until March or early summer, at which point even a perfunctory perusal would highlight that one has really not missed much.

Years ago we compiled a history of the first 25 years of *Barron's* annual roundtable. A mutual fund manager was profuse in his gratitude. We suggested it really wasn't all that useful. But, as he said, it made him realize that he didn't have to engage in the exercise and was therefore able to save five or six hours of reading every year.

FIGURE 6.11 Dow Theory Commentary: 2006 through 2011
Source: Birinyi Associates, Inc., Bloomberg.

FIGURE 6.12   *New Yorker* Cover

Source: New Yorker.

MAGAZINE COVERS—OVERRATED

It might be suggested that this is but an extension of the magazine cover approach, which says that if something makes it to the cover, the story is out and the game is over. We disagree.

One of the more interesting covers we dug up shows trading at the NYSE (see Figure 6.12). Since there was no market story or reference in the magazine, we assume that it was just a random cover, even though the Crash of 1929 was only eight weeks away.

Another example was the *Forbes* cover of June 5, 1995, "Where have all the BEARS gone? The public is nervous, but it's hard to find a real pessimist on Wall Street" -highlighting their concern that everyone was bullish. Rightly so, the market gained another 14 percent that year.

NOTE

1. *Wall Street Week with Louis Rukeyser*, PBS, January 2, 2000.

CHAPTER 7

Always Cut the Cards

I knew few people who made money acting on economic forecasts but a good many that had made it from selling on them.

—Attributed to Friedrich Hayek

In the world of financial reporting, the normal journalistic mandate to undertake critical investigations and objectively report findings to the reader appears not to apply.

—Stieg Larsson, *The Girl with the Dragon Tattoo*

In 1967, Adam Smith's *The Money Game* became a best seller on and off Wall Street (and one that we still regularly read). Games, by definition, have winners. They also have losers, and we hope to help you differentiate between the two.

Over the course of several decades, hundreds of meetings, dozens of seminars, and countless conversations, we have concluded that one of the characteristics of most investors is that they are not very good consumers. Individuals who would not buy a used car without checking the *Kelley Blue Book* or a new television before ascertaining the price at Amazon will seriously consider a stock or sector highlighted in the morning news or the weekend business section.

We regularly stress economic accountability. While one might listen to and consider an idea, no monies should be involved unless the source of that idea can be held somewhat financially responsible if the idea fails. Our monthly newsletter provides a list of conservative stocks, another of growth names, and a few trading ideas. While we make a strenuous effort to do well, if customers, for whatever reason, are not satisfied, we suggest that they cancel and ask for a refund.

If, however, you act on an idea from CNBC or the *Wall Street Journal*, your options are somewhat limited. Disconnecting your cable will probably hurt you more than your cable company, and one less subscriber to the newspaper is not likely to be noticed. A broker, however, will probably feel the loss of a customer (and more than one will be noted by his or her boss as well). A series of bad trades and account withdrawals will, at some point, cause management to raise some questions.

Accountability also suggests an ongoing business relationship. We always advise investors to understand the source, the agenda, and the rationale for an idea. Audience members dutifully listen, nod, smile, and nudge their neighbor. Ten minutes later when we provide a few recent ideas, pencils and pens are unsheathed, notes are made on the backs of envelopes, and hearing aids are turned up.

No one ever asks if these are long-term investments or merely trades, whether they are made for taxable or tax-exempt accounts, what the price targets or other objectives are, and so forth. At restaurants, we question if a dish is gluten-free or made with nuts and the amount of sugar in various dishes and so forth. But in the market, where we should be even more skeptical since it directly involves money, most investors are less wary.

Individuals should also recognize that barriers to entry, in terms of stock market advisors and commentators, are purely economic. Thus literally anyone who can persuade you to pay for a newsletter or charge for some service can do so. To provide research and commentary on financial matters, in most states, one need merely register as a business. As for actually managing money, not until one has $20 million in assets under management need one advise the Securities and Exchange Commission (SEC). But even then, no tests or certifications are required.

There are no educational requirements, either. Media, in whatever form, is therefore available to anyone who can persuade a producer to provide a microphone or camera.

As a result, one should be aware that *expert* is more of a title than a description. While the TV program or magazine reporter may confer it, it is totally discretionary and therefore totally meaningless.

In 1989 when the Berlin Wall fell, I was asked for my views. Reporters were surprised that I had none. True, I was from Eastern Europe and had some language familiarity and had taken a number of college courses on the region. But I had no insights as to the political and economic ramifications. As I told one disappointed reporter: I eat steak but that does not make me a rancher.

STRATEGISTS: MORE MARKETING THAN MARKETS

Strategists are usually the most visible and vocal of the Street's commentators. Charged with the responsibility of taking their firms' investment ingredients and presenting a coherent outlook and strategy, as well as specific recommendations, they usually serve as the firms' spokesperson and write or contribute to the newsletter that most firms provide on a regular basis.

Perhaps their most notable and difficult function is presenting a target for the market. While we appreciate the business pressure to do so, it is an increasingly difficult endeavor, as highlighted by Figure 7.1. Historically, the market was a function of Federal Reserve Board (FRB) policy, corporate earnings, and economic events; today the strategist must be aware of geopolitical events, new market structures, international markets, currencies, and—increasingly—domestic politics.

Furthermore, our experience with money flows suggests that the market discounts three to six months in advance. Thus, producing an end-of-year target on January 1 is, in effect, looking over the horizon and around the corner. We suggest that investors, if possible, keep track of strategists' forecasts if only to appreciate the difficulty of that endeavor. Investors should recognize the marketing element of the exercise. One strategist on December 21, 2012, raised his year-end forecast to 1,450 from 1,440. Are there really indicators or approaches that forecast a 0.7 percent move over a 10-day period?

It is also disconcerting that the rationale and logic for forecasts are often lacking. We once noted that one analyst, whose year-end target called for an 8 or 10 percent gain, reiterated that call after a midyear drop of 5 percent. In effect he was now expecting a 15 percent rally in roughly six

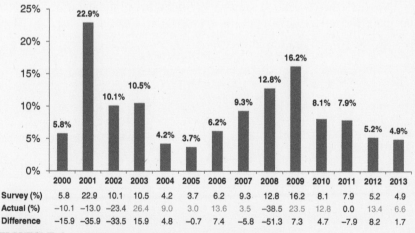

	2000	2001	2002	2003	2004	2005	2006	2007	2008	2009	2010	2011	2012	2013
Survey (%)	5.8	22.9	10.1	10.5	4.2	3.7	6.2	9.3	12.8	16.2	8.1	7.9	5.2	4.9
Actual (%)	−10.1	−13.0	−23.4	26.4	9.0	3.0	13.6	3.5	−38.5	23.5	12.8	0.0	13.4	6.6
Difference	−15.9	−35.9	−33.5	15.9	4.8	−0.7	7.4	−5.8	−51.3	7.3	4.7	−7.9	8.2	1.7

FIGURE 7.1 S&P Forward Forecast versus Actual Return

Source: Birinyi Associates, Inc.

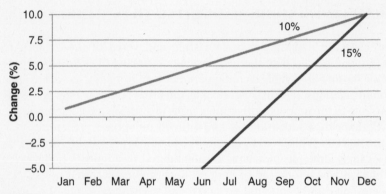

FIGURE 7.2 Analyst Forecast
Source: Birinyi Associates, Inc.

months, or 30 percent annualized. The forecast was now three times *more* bullish than at the beginning of the year (see Figure 7.2). But why?

A second concern is an abundance of commentary and opinion. "I think" should not be a critical ingredient in providing input to fiduciaries. Nor are suggestions that the market or interest rates "could" rise, or speculation on what might or might not transpire. But the ultimate failing of most strategists is that they are not helpful in improving investment returns.

This was most visibly manifested in a series of exercises in 2000 when at least three brokerage firms established mutual funds based on their own research and managed or at least directed by the firm's own strategist.

While they were successful in a business sense, raising many millions of dollars, their investment results were not. One grossly underperformed the S&P (see Figure 7.3).

We track the prominent strategists (and other commentators), including their secondary calls such as sectors (see Figures 7.4 to 7.6). It is

FIGURE 7.3 Strategy Fund versus S&P 500
Source: Birinyi Associates, Inc.

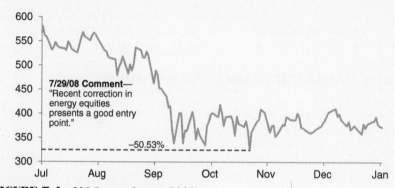

FIGURE 7.4   S&P Energy Sector: 2008

Source: Birinyi Associates, Inc., Bloomberg.

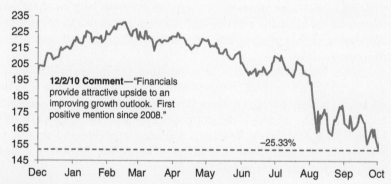

FIGURE 7.5   S&P Financial Sector: 2010 through 2011

Source: Birinyi Associates, Inc., Bloomberg.

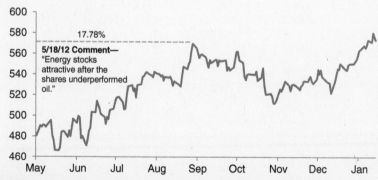

FIGURE 7.6   S&P Energy Sector: 5/18/2012 through 1/31/2013

Source: Birinyi Associates, Inc., Bloomberg.

regularly discouraging to do so and, as shown by one individual's forecast, just as regularly unprofitable.

STOCK *MARKET* RESEARCH: AN OXYMORON

Our issue with strategists is not only with their conclusions, but also with a lack of process and analysis:

- The fourth quarter of 2011 was a difficult one for managers and analysts allegedly because of the high degree of correlation, which made stock selection difficult. But we showed that 95 of the Standard & Poor's 500 stocks had doubled the return of the S&P while another 162 beat the S&P by more than 50 percent, which was not unique, and was in line with similar double-digit quarters (see Table 7.1).
- The oft-forecast or wished-for correction, especially in 2009, was not based on available metrics or historical parallels. As we noted in November of that year, at 224 days and up 62 percent, it was neither *due* nor *overdue*.
- An issue, especially in 2013, was whether public participation was beneficial or detrimental. We presented a graph (see Figure 7.7) that showed it was inconclusive; sometimes the public was early, and sometimes the public lagged. It did not require detailed prose or analysis to come to that realization. The data is readily available and simple, yet we saw no other efforts to actually analyze it. This did not, of course, prevent articulate interpretations and commentary.

TABLE 7.1 S&P 500 Stock Performance

	Beat by 50%	Beat by 100%	Return (%)
2013			
1Q	167	89	10.03
2012			
1Q	145	83	12.00
2011			
4Q	162	95	11.15
2010			
4Q	165	98	10.20
3Q	160	88	10.72
2009			
3Q	184	123	14.98
2Q	194	140	15.22

Source: Birinyi Associates, Inc.

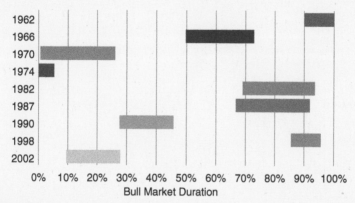

FIGURE 7.7 Period of Strongest Equity Mutual Fund Inflows During Bull Markets
Source: Birinyi Associates, Inc.

THE ISSUE OF CAPE: CYCLICALLY ADJUSTED PRICE-EARNINGS RATIO

Our positive stance since 2009 has, in part, been reinforced by less than compelling negative arguments: bears argued that volume was lacking, economists forecast a double-dip recession, and strategists noted that the cyclically adjusted price-earnings (CAPE) ratio was not cheap.

Benjamin Graham and David Dodd in their *Security Analysis* suggested using the market's 5-, 7-, or 10-year trailing price-earnings (P/E) ratio adjusted for inflation as an indicator. More recently it has been associated with Yale's Robert Shiller, who has often been credited with forecasting the dot-com bubble. In fairness to Dr. Shiller, we are not aware of his trumpeting of that call; rather it was others who did. Our view, hopefully objective, is less enthusiastic. While his 2000 book, *Irrational Exuberance*, did appear coincident with the market top, it articulated his long-held view (see Figure 7.8).

On December 3, 1996, he and John Campbell of Harvard made a presentation to the FRB and Alan Greenspan, which concluded that the market was "widely overvalued." (This allegedly prompted Mr. Greenspan's "irrational exuberance" speech.) The two academics were to write two articles expressing their concerns, including one in the winter 1998 edition of the *Journal of Portfolio Management*.

It presented an outlook that was "extraordinarily bearish for the U.S. stock market" with their "price-smooth earnings ratio . . . predicting that the real value of the market will be 40 percent lower in 10 years," or approximately S&P 629.[1]

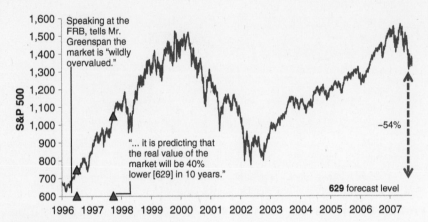

FIGURE 7.8   Dr. Shiller's Forecasts
Source: Birinyi Associates, Inc., Bloomberg.

Given that, we were not worried when the March 30, 2009, issue of *Forbes* presented the 10-year trailing, inflation-adjusted measure (which was then at 12 times earnings) and wrote: "stocks are cheap but could get a lot more so" (see Figure 7.9). The article was entitled "The Case for Bonds."

Three months later the magazine reiterated its view using the same argument: " . . . easy winnings are already off the table."[2]

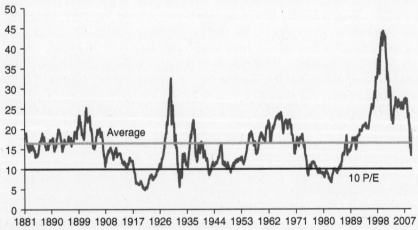

FIGURE 7.9   Shiller P/E as of March 2009
Source: Robert Shiller, Birinyi Associates, Inc.

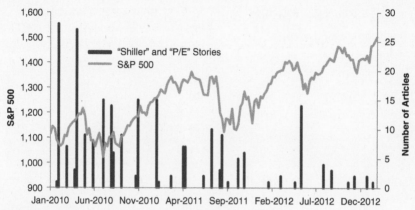

FIGURE 7.10 S&P 500 vs. Number of Shiller P/E Stories

Source: Birinyi Associates, Inc., Bloomberg.

As the rally progressed, bearish strategists made CAPE a staple of their arguments almost to the point of redundancy (see Figure 7.10).

We have never embraced the idea of a 10-year trailing P/E for several reasons. First, it is contrived or artificial. Why 10 years? We prefer natural parameters such as a business cycle or an average bull/bear market. Why 10 years and not 5 or 15? It reminds us of the baseball announcer who tells us that Joe Baseball has hit .375, with eight home runs and 15 RBIs since June 16. That usually also suggests that on June 15, he was 0 for 5, hit into a double play, and struck out three times.

Nevertheless, as the market advanced the argument went from CAPE being "not cheap" to being "expensive." To us that is like an analyst who changes his opinion on a stock from "sell" to "hold." Hold what? Should we not first go buy and then hold?

In 2013, as the market continued to surprise most investors, the measure went to 23 times earnings, which, statistically, was dangerous territory. Perhaps, but as we noted, the last instance of 23× *and rising* was July 1995, from whence the market rose another 170 percent through March 2000 (see Figure 7.11).

STRATEGISTS: ONE MORE THING . . .

Every year end, strategists and brokerage firms produce detailed, multipage outlooks with all manner of indicators, analysis, and commentary. Economic indicators are dissected, scenarios are detailed, and lists of stocks to buy are provided.

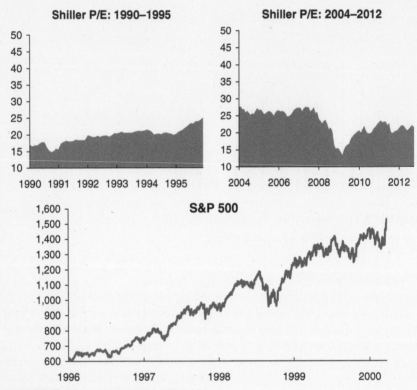

FIGURE 7.11 Shiller P/E and S&P 500

Somewhat surprisingly, there is little discussion of the stock market itself—the current trends, historical perspective, or other market elements. We have always referred to this as the American approach to dinner: plan and then shop. This is in contrast to the French chef approach: present a menu based on what is available at the market itself. Or as one famous chef once said: half of cooking is shopping.

David Dreman in his fine book, *Psychology and the Stock Market*, quotes Robert Plutchik:

> *The observation of naturally occurring events is the starting point of all science.*

He goes on to relate the importance of observation to establish evidence by citing Sir Francis Bacon:

> *In the year of our Lord 1432 there arose a previous quarrel among the brethren over the number of teeth in the mouth of a horse. For 13 days the disputation raged without ceasing. . . .*

At the beginning of the 14th day, a youthful friar . . . beseeched them to look in the open mouth of a horse and find the answer to their questionings. At this, their dignity being grievously hurt . . . they flew upon him and smote him hip and thigh, and cast him out forthwith.

Historically, investors and analysts alike derived their market inputs from the ticker tape. Given the amount and speed of trading that exists today, that is no longer practical. But the process of market-oriented inputs (often termed price discovery) is available but generally not incorporated in today's investing process.

As just one example, we were more positive on housing for much of 2012 because we regularly lost money when shorting the stocks. And we recall a Greek election in 2011 that was much in dispute. Our view was that there would be no surprises because the Greek bank index had gone up eight days in a row leading up to the election.

As discussed earlier, one of our favorite stories from Salomon involved Bill Simon, who would go on to be Secretary of the Treasury. He asked a young man to go buy $10 million of bank acceptances or some other short-term paper at $4.00. The young man came back and said it had traded there, but that he had been unable to buy it at $4.00 and it was now available at $4.10. Mr. Simon told him to buy it at $4.10, but it, too, traded higher so the individual was told to try $4.20.

That didn't work either, nor did $4.30. Finally, Mr. Simon told the young man:

"Son, if you can't buy it at $4.00 or $4.30, then sell!"

So $10 million was sold short at $4.40 and bought back at $4.10, and eventually the original $10 million was bought at $4.00 or thereabouts.

Our approach of questioning and skepticism extends to academics as well. Surely the learned and tenured, without the pressures of day-to-day decisions, can be counted on to provide guidance and value added.

Unfortunately, we have not found this to be the case. Too often we get a sense of arrogance and the attitude of somehow being exempt from the guidelines of scholarship and research.

It is also interesting that financial academics are not necessarily specialists but feel free (if not obligated) to profess opinions on a wide variety of financial and economic topics. One of our associates once called a Nobel Prize winner who had made some comments regarding trading costs. Although he had never written on the subject, he was annoyed that someone questioned his competence.

Our first experience in this regard occurred some years ago when *BusinessWeek* asked, "What to Do about the Dow" (February 22, 1993). Several individuals were asked how "to make the index better reflect the economy." An Ivy League professor suggested adding Capital Cities/ABC, Norfolk Southern, and Pacific Gas and Electric.

Capital Cities was then one of the highest-priced names on the Board (+$500) and would have overwhelmed the price-weighted index. Norfolk Southern is a railroad company, while Pacific Gas is a utility. Had he never heard of the Dow Jones Transportation and Utility indices?

WHAT DO STOCKS REALLY RETURN?

One area we have researched in detail is stock market returns. In 2009, Jason Zweig wrote a *Wall Street Journal* article, "Does Stock-Market Data Really Go Back 200 Years?"[3]

He raised a number of questions regarding Dr. Jeremy Siegel's book, *Stocks for the Long Run*. We undertook an analysis of the subject of historical returns beginning with the book itself. It was a bit disappointing to find that the book, while a good, basic introduction to investing, devoted so little effort to its thesis and contained virtually no detailed data. In fact, the entire issue of long-term returns was basically discussed in one chart and one table.

Our topical study, *What Do Stocks Really Return?*, took issue with some of Dr. Siegel's results.[4]

Dr. Siegel responded to Mr. Zweig and defended his work, citing yet another study by several academics at Yale.[5] We analyzed the Yale study, which only led to more questions and fewer answers. For example, their pricing of America Bank in 1830 seems questionable, while the dividends attributed to another stock are also suspect (see Tables 7.2 and 7.3).

TABLE 7.2   America Bank 1830 through February 1831

	Close (P)
Jan-1830	$93.00
Feb-1830	91.00
Mar-1830	94.00
Apr-1830	93.00
May-1830	93.00
Jun-1830	92.00
Jul-1830	93.00
Aug-1830	93.00
Sep-1830	94.00
Oct-1830	95.00
Nov-1830	96.00
Dec-1830	542.00
Jan-1831	96.00
Feb-1831	96.00

TABLE 7.3 Yale Dividend Database (%)

Name	1841	1842	1843	1844
Neptune Insurance	0	0	72	13.07

Perhaps we are overly cautious or skeptical, but did Neptune Insurance really pay no dividends for two years, then 72 percent and 13.07 percent the year after? Not 13 or even 13.1 percent but 13.07 percent in 1844? Surely, a study from a prestigious institution written by three academics and several graduate students might have undertaken a bit more research.

While stocks have, as Dr. Siegel wrote, fared well over time, other considerations might make that argument less assertive. In 2002, he made the somewhat aggressive statement:

> *I dare any bond enthusiast to look me in the eye and maintain that an investor who buys the 10-year US Treasury bond at the current yield of 4.4% will outperform an investor who buys a diversified portfolio of common stocks over the next decade.*[6]

Overall, stocks did outperform but by the narrowest of margins (see Figure 7.12); most investors would have preferred the consistency of 4.4 percent to the vicissitudes of the stock market.

Dr. Siegel was somewhat ingenuous when he allowed that at one point bonds did outperform because . . . *the returns on Treasury bonds were well above average.*[7]

FIGURE 7.12 S&P 500 versus U.S. Government 10-Year Bond
Source: Birinyi Associates, Inc., Bloomberg.

The Wharton professor, like other academics, has parlayed his reputation and brand beyond academia and has made market forecasts as well. While he has every right to do so, our experience is that observation does not necessarily translate into experience or ability.

Triumph of the Optimists is an oft-cited book (and one of Bill Gross's favorites) that provides data on global markets, and the authors may well be expert and qualified on these issues.[8] But that does not necessarily make them experts on markets *going forward*, as evidenced by the comments of one of the authors at the end of February 2009:

> . . . *estimates that we'll have to wait nine more years before the Dow Average, including dividends, has a 50 percent chance of hitting its 2007 highs.*

A SUCCESSFUL MODEL EXCEPT FOR "IRRATIONAL" INVESTORS

> *The stock market in four years' time is unlikely to be much higher than it is now.*
>
> *That sobering forecast comes from a simple stock-market timing model that has an impressive track record over the past five decades. In fact this model has turned in the best performance of any in forecasting the market's four year return.*[9]

In late 2000, we first read about an approach that incorporated the forecasts of Value Line's analysts. It was developed by a number of academics, and that article, "A Quiet Sign of Better Days Ahead." concluded that *it is truly good news that this indicator is now signaling a buy.*[10]

The market was to lose over 18 percent over the next four years and was down as much as 36 percent after two years (see Figure 7.13).

FIGURE 7.13   S&P 500: November 2000 through November 2002

Source: Birinyi Associates, Inc., Bloomberg.

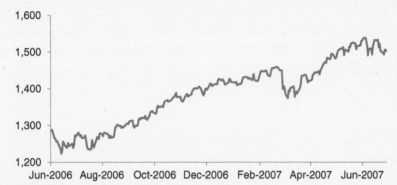

FIGURE 7.14 S&P 500: June 2006 through June 2007
Source: Birinyi Associates, Inc., Bloomberg.

Six years later another article again extolling the virtues of the model was pessimistic:

Expect weakness or worst over the next year.

Even more disappointing than the forecast (see Figure 7.14) was the accompanying text. First we learned that the "impressive track record" was largely a result of back-testing, which, as most investors know, always seems to produce good results. One of the academics did allow that the model was a "failure" in the 1990s not because of the model but because of investor "irrationality."[11]

Mark Hulbert, who wrote the articles and crowned the approach as the "best," also defended the model and its record in the 1990s. He too argued that investors were at fault, not because of "irrationality" but because they were using the wrong benchmark! They should have used the Value Line Geometric Composite (VLGC), which gained only 2.7 percent a year from November 1996 through November 2000, "well below the market's historical return of about 11 percent annually" (see Figure 7.15).

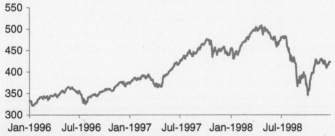

FIGURE 7.15 Value Line Geometric Composite: 1996 through 1998
Source: Birinyi Associates, Inc., Bloomberg.

FIGURE 7.16 S&P 500: 1996 through 1998

Source: Birinyi Associates, Inc., Bloomberg.

That is also questionable, as we have never seen anyone, anywhere, suggest double-digit returns for stocks. Mr. Hulbert wrote that the 2.7 percent return is what investors made who "weren't lucky enough to be holding stocks like Cisco and GE." But most investors *were* holding Cisco and GE, and the S&P 500 almost doubled during those four years (see Figure 7.16), hugely outperforming the VLGC, which, by our calculation, only returned slightly over 15 percent.

Investors should also be aware that academics seemingly ignore the intellectual process and fail to uphold the standards we were expected to adhere to in our educational experiences. An approach to measure transaction costs might serve as a case study of our concern.

The SEC's *Institutional Investor Study,* which we referenced earlier, also determined that the impact of trading was the difference between the prevailing price and the price at which a stock was bought or sold. If a stock was priced at $20 and someone bought 500 shares at $20.10, the trading cost or trading impact (before commissions) was 10 cents times 500 shares or $50 (0.50 percent).

While this was applicable if an institution bought 25,000 shares in one trade, it was not practical if this was a series of trades spread over a day or more. In 1988 a group of researchers, including an academic, introduced the idea of volume-weighted average price (VWAP). Their contention was that if the average price of a stock on a given day, adjusted for volume, was $35.50 and a trader bought it at $35.60, he had cost his portfolio 10 cents per share.

The approach had some merit in evaluating trades and traders, but its advocates wrote that it could also be used to calculate the portfolio impact. We disagreed. If, for example, a stock misses its earnings estimate and trades down $2.00 to $42.00, the portfolio has lost $2 even if the trader is able to sell it at $42.10 or 10 cents above the VWAP.

Of far greater concern were the assertions and allegations made in the accompanying research:

- "Over very long periods, the stock market will rise on roughly two-thirds of the days."

For the 59 years ending 12/31/12, the market has been up 53 percent of the days.

- "Their method suggested a 0.62% market impact cost for what were presumed to be sell transactions, but no market impact for presumed buys."[12] "Their" refers to a publication by Alan Kraus and Hans Stoll, who contributed to the SEC study. They used the data from the SEC to "examine the extent to which block trading contributes to, or detracts from, efficient markets."

The SEC, with its mandate, was able to determine the exact impact of sells (1.13 percent, not 0.62 percent) as well as buys (0.74 percent, not 0). The 0.62 percent comes from the Kraus/Stoll study and is very clearly articulated:

The commission on 10,000 shares of a $40 stock was 0.62%. . . .[13]

There is, we would argue, a significant difference between writing that it cost 0.62 percent for "presumed sell transactions" when it is clearly stated as the commission of a given, singular, detailed trade.

- "This reduction in commission charges was accompanied by an increase in liquidity so that large blocks of stock could be traded with substantially smaller price impacts."

In real life, cheaper does not usually beget better. Given the importance of that comment, we read the article looking for supportive words such as *trading, commissions, discounts*, and the like. Having found none, we read it again—this time backward—and later electronically searched for supporting evidence. Again, we found none.[14]

Over time these are not necessarily unique examples. During the debate on electronic trading and market structure, a number of academics have presented positions despite limited evidence and experience. In 2012 and beyond, professors have defended high-frequency trading while at the same time having business relationships that are not always transparent.

THE PRESS SHOULD BE IN THE REPORTING, NOT FORECASTING, BUSINESS

Experience that has taught us to question, review, and ascertain extends to the media as well. While the press may be the champion of the individual, highlighting the shenanigans and misdeeds of politicians, athletes, and rock stars, when it some to finance the press's allegiance is skewed toward the industry.

This is, to some degree, understandable. Most financial publications or sections are largely underwritten by advertising. A senior editor at the *Wall Street Journal* once admitted that they treated the "names" on Wall Street gingerly because "their firms advertise and we need them [the individuals] as input and sources."

As illustrated by the following, there should be no question as to whose butter is being spread:

> *To the Editor*
> *. . . [Did he forget] to mention that among his favorite stocks . . . Tokos Medical . . . which traded as high as 44 in 1992, closed the year at 16¾ and goes for 8¾ a share?*
>
> *Editor: . . . we were specifically asking him for new ideas . . . not to re-cover old ground.* [15]

While we have some sympathy for the investor, we again strongly suggest that one have some economic response, aside from not buying the newspaper or magazine.

More critical, in our opinion, is when the media goes beyond reporting and becomes an advisor. Over time we have tracked the results of various recommendations with uninspiring results. At the beginning of 2000, both *SmartMoney* and *Fortune* provided "10 Stocks for the Next Decade" shown in Tables 7.4 and 7.5.

Another illustration of the media crossing the line between reporting and forecasting was the *SmartMoney* cover of June 1994: "What's Next for the Market?" A lengthy report provided a stock market model where one could input several data points that would result in superior returns. We duplicated the report's efforts but with different results.

As the market progressed and especially in 1995, this model became increasingly bearish while the market became increasingly bullish. Every month we eagerly awaited the publication, but at some point that spring or early summer, there was no model.

We were told that the editor responsible was on vacation. Finally, in September 1995, in the bowels of the magazine, a small box informed readers that the model was "in the shop for retooling."

TABLE 7.4 *Fortune*'s 10 Stocks for the Next Decade

Name	Ticker	Price[1]		% Change
		7/19/2000	12/31/2009	
Broadcom	BRCM	$154.98	$30.85	−80.09%
Charles Schwab	SCHW	34.68	18.82	−45.73
Enron[2]	ENRNQ	72.56	0.00	−100.00
Genentech[3]	DNA	37.53	94.97	153.04
Morgan Stanley	MS	73.26	29.60	−59.59
Nokia	NOK	53.13	12.85	−75.81
Nortel Networks[4]	NRTLQ	765.00	0.02	−100.00
Oracle	ORCL	36.88	24.53	−33.48
Univision[5]	UVN	56.63	36.23	−36.02
Viacom[6]	CBS	50.21	14.05	−72.02
			Average	**−44.97%**
			S&P 500	−24.76%

TABLE 7.5 *Smart Money*'s 10 Stocks for the Next Decade

Name	Ticker	Price[1]		% Change
		10/22/1999	12/31/2009	
America Online[7]	TWX	$124.24	$29.14	−76.55%
Broadcom	BRCM	37.01	30.85	−16.64
Citigroup	C	336.15	33.10	−90.15
Inktomi[8]	INKT	51.53	1.65	−96.80
Monsanto[9]	748957Q	37.13	45.06	21.37
Nokia	NOK	26.28	12.85	−51.11
Nortel Networks[4]	NRTLQ	276.25	0.02	−99.99
Red Hat	RHT	37.59	30.90	−17.81
Scientific-Atlanta[10]	3026360Q	27.47	42.98	56.47
MCI WorldCom[11]	WCOEQ	47.17	0.00	−100.00
			Average	**−47.12%**
			S&P 500	−14.33%

[1]Adjusted for splits, spinoffs, etc.
[2]Filed for bankruptcy in 2001, completed proceedings 11/17/2004
[3]Acquired by Roche Holding on 3/27/2009
[4]Filed for bankruptcy in 2009, proceedings still ongoing
[5]Acquired by multiple private equity firms 3/29/2007
[6]Split into two companies in 2005, "new Viacom" spun out of CBS
[7]Merged with Time Warner in 2000
[8]Acquired by Yahoo! on 3/20/2003
[9]Acquired by Pharmacia in 2000, Pharmacia acquired by Pfizer on 4/16/2003
[10]Acquired by Cisco on 2/27/2006
[11]Filed for bankruptcy in 2002, completed 4/20/2004

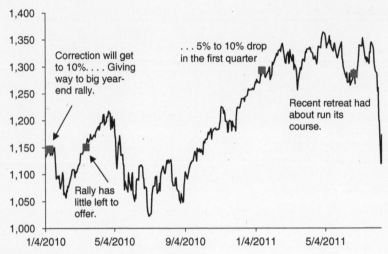

FIGURE 7.17   *Barron's* "Mystery Broker"

Source: Birinyi Associates, Inc.

The media might also be taken to task for congratulating and prais-
ing investors or commentators for their prowess and acumen without even
perfunctory documentation. The former editor of *Barron's* often cited a
"mystery broker" for his prescience. We tracked those calls and they appear
to be—in our view—somewhat overrated (see Figure 7.17).

Alan Abelson, the former editor and columnist for the same paper,
regularly sourced a small group of individuals for their insights and good
calls while overlooking their blemishes. We tracked the positive and negative comments of one (see Figure 7.18), an exercise that was especially
interesting in that his fund's record is considerably better than it should be
based on his public comments.

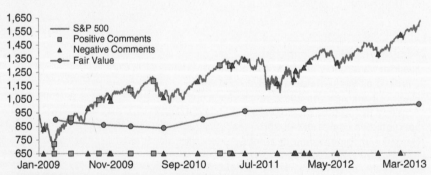

FIGURE 7.18   Fund Manager's Market Commentary

Source: Fund manager's commentary.

Investors should also be aware that the investment results that the media presents are usually not attainable. For example, they are often unwieldy. *Barron's* 2012 picks, for example, did very well. But *Barron's* had 121 positive names, which is a bit unrealistic for most individuals. This is not to suggest that they should be ignored, and they may serve as a starting point. Given those results, it is curious that *Barron's* year-end performance review is sometimes incomplete.

For some reason, we noted in 2008 that General Motors was not one of *Barron's* picks despite being on the cover ("Buy GM," June 2, 2008). In 2012, Sears (SHLD) was panned on the January 2 cover ("Why Sears' stock could plunge 80%"). SHLD doubled that quarter and was up 44 percent for the year but was not included in the end-of-year compilation, which would still have done very well even with SHLD included (see Figure 7.19).

We might also note that even positive, publicity-oriented stories can be harmful. Apple's sharp decline in 2012 was one that we never considered, not only because of how much the stock had enriched us and our portfolios, but also because we had been seduced by the news.

In November 2011, a glowing report on the company's manufacturing advantage and its large profit margins (40 percent versus 10 to 20 percent for competitors) gave us the impression that the firm was invulnerable and would continue to be so. In truth, we probably would have held the stock anyway, but the story made us even more confident.[16]

Another positive story led us to Volkswagen: "Audi Defies Demand Drop as Companies Give Workers Wheels." Deutsche Telekom and other German corporations were taking advantage of tax breaks to support the local automobile industry. Having long owned BMW, to add VW to our portfolio without doing more analysis did not seem especially risky. While the final chapter has yet to be written, the stock has not done especially well (see Figure 7.20).[17]

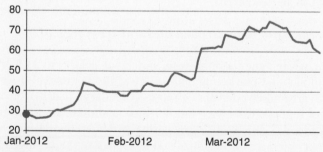

FIGURE 7.19 Sears Holdings

Source: Birinyi Associates, Inc., Bloomberg.

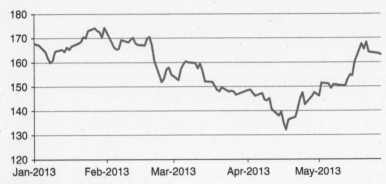

FIGURE 7.20   Volkswagen

Source: Birinyi Associates, Inc., Bloomberg.

Our concern that investors are unlikely to duplicate recommendations is also exhibited with regard to *Investor's Business Daily*, which weekly lists 50 stocks that meet its criteria. *IBD* regularly provides results, but 50 stocks are far too many for most individuals. Complicating matters are the number of changes. In the first week of March 2013, eight stocks were added and eight removed (which was also the case the week following) (see Table 7.6). The performance calculations are based on the close Friday, whereas investors are unable to transact until Monday morning.

This is, of course, even before trading costs and commissions.

Unfortunately, the Wall Street jungle is not limited to Wall Street and the traditional financial sources. With the introduction of the Internet and less regulation, there are opportunities for malfeasance, especially since many advisories and sources are unregulated or have limited regulations.

On July 19, 2012, Intuitive Surgical traded from $544 to $498 on 1.5 million shares, over six times its average activity. The stock was downgraded by Citron Research:

"Has the Halo Been Broken on Intuitive Surgical?"

Citron wrote that there were a variety of issues, including "excessive and unjustified marketing claims." Over the next several weeks, the stock recovered and traded above $500. On January 17, 2013, Citron issued yet another report with a $300 target. Once again the stock swooned and traded as low as $485, before recovering to $515. Several days later the company reported strong earnings and a positive outlook. After closing at $518.49, it traded up $47 in after-hours and added another $1.50 the next day (see Figure 7.21).

TABLE 7.6 *IBD* Changes March 4, 2013

Added

GMCR	Green Mountain Coffee Roasters	8.54
GWRE	Guidewire Software Inc.	2.95
MYL	Mylan Inc/PA	2.22
PRLB	Proto Labs Inc.	2.46
SWI	SolarWinds Inc.	5.53
UTHR	United Therapeutics Corp.	1.31
VRSN	VeriSign Inc.	1.45
WDC	Western Digital Corp.	−1.07
	Average	**2.92**

Removed

AIRM	Air Methods Corp.	6.85
AMCX	AMC Networks Inc.	4.49
EGOV	NIC Inc.	0.11
LOPE	Grand Canyon Education Inc.	0.71
NTSP	Netspend Holdings Inc.	−0.06
SODA	SodaStream International Ltd.	3.41
STRZA	Starz-Liberty Capital	7.1
TSM	Taiwan Semiconductor Manufacturing Co., Ltd.	0.11
	Average	**2.84**

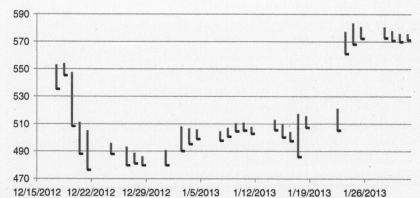

FIGURE 7.21   ISRG: December 2012 through January 2013

Source: Birinyi Associates, Inc., Bloomberg.

The critical question is: Who is Citron Research? As we later discovered, its executive editor, Andrew Left, has a past:

- *The National Futures Association sanctioned Left for "fraudulent communications and attempt to cheat, defraud or deceive customers."*
- *He was ordered to pay separate fines of $26,445 and $2.5 million.*
- *He has been sued four times as a result of his postings.*

Source: www.citronresearch.com/who-is-citron-2.
Superior Court of California, County of Los Angeles

We have often been told that our approach is daunting and difficult. Checking, reviewing, and ascertaining, as we do, are not easily accomplished. We recognize that we have some advantages in doing so. Today, however, with the Internet, individuals can probe deeper, analyze to a greater degree, and engage in more analysis.

Investing is, in the final analysis, no easier than accounting or dentistry. There are no shortcuts, magic pills, or secret sauces. Given that it takes most individuals many years to accumulate a significant portfolio, we think it reasonable that they devote significant time and effort to maintaining it.

NOTES

1. John Y. Campbell and Robert Shiller, "Valuation Ratios and the Long-Run Stock Market Outlook," *Journal of Portfolio Management* (Winter 1998).
2. "The Case for Bonds," *Forbes*, June 24, 2009.
3. Jason Zweig, "Does Stock-Market Data Really Go Back 200 Years?" *Wall Street Journal*, July 11, 2009.
4. *What Do Stocks Really Return?* Birinyi Associates, Inc., October 2009.
5. William N. Goetzmann, Roger G. Ibbotson, and Liang Peng, *A New Historical Database for the NYSE 1815 to 1925: Performance and Predictability*, Yale International Center for Finance, July 14, 2000.
6. Jeremy Siegel, "Stocks Are Still an Oasis," *Wall Street Journal*, July 25, 2002.
7. Jeremy Siegel, "'Stocks for the Long Run' Still Holds in Spite of the Painful Sell-Off," *Financial Times*, October 6, 2009.
8. Elroy Dimson, Paul Marsh, and Mike Staunton, *Triumph of the Optimists: 101 Years of Global Investment Returns* (Princeton, NJ: Princeton University Press, 2002).
9. Mark Hulbert, "One Way to Time the Market," *Wall Street Journal*, April 19, 2013.

10. Mark Hulbert, "STRATEGIES: A Quiet Sign of Better Days Ahead," *New York Times*, November 5, 2000.

11. Mark Hulbert, "An Old Formula That Points to New Worry," *New York Times*, June 18, 2006.

12. Stephen A. Berkowitz, Dennis E. Logue, and Eugene A. Noser, Jr., "Study on Investment Performance of ERISA Plans: Chapter 1-6," and "The Total Cost of Transactions on the NYSE," *Journal of Finance* 42, no. 1, March 1988.

13. Alan Kraus and Hans R. Stoll, "Price Impacts of Block Trading on the New York Stock Exchange," *Journal of Finance* 27, no. 3 (June 1972): 569–588.

14. Alicia H. Munnell, "Who Should Manage the Assets of Collectively Bargained Pension Plans?" *New England Economic Review* (July 1983).

15. Mark Brody, "*Barron's* Mailbag," *Barron's*, March 15, 1993.

16. Adam Satariano and Peter Burrows, "Apple's Supply-Chain Secret? Hoard Lasers," *Bloomberg*, November 3, 2011.

17. Dorothee Tschampa, "Audi Defies Demand Drop as Companies Give Workers Wheels," *Bloomberg*, January 3, 2013.

CHAPTER 8

DOW: 19,792?

Computers were built in the late 1940s because mathematicians like John von Neumann thought that if you had a computer—a machine to handle a lot of variables simultaneously—you would be able to predict the weather. Weather would finally fall to human understanding. And men believed that dream for the next forty years. They believed that prediction was just a function of keeping track of things. If you knew enough, you could predict anything.

—Jurassic Park

In the days before personal computers, perhaps the most common acronym of the day was GIGO (garbage in, garbage out). This served as a warning to programmers and users alike that bad data led to bad decisions. Given today's proliferation of databases and sources, this is not considered an issue. But it should be.

We first became aware of this issue in the financial markets when we tracked the Federal Reserve Board's quarterly flow of fund data. These numbers detail what public and private pension plans are buying or selling as well as that of individuals, mutual funds, and other investors. They are released toward the end of the subsequent three months, so in June we learn what was bought and sold in the quarter ending in March.

When released, we dutifully recorded that corporate pension plans had bought, for example, $850 million in U.S. stocks while insurance companies were net sellers of $250 million. But in each succeeding quarter, preceding quarters were regularly revised. As a result, the $850 million that corporate plans might have bought became net selling of $250 million. And they might again be revised in the next quarter's release.

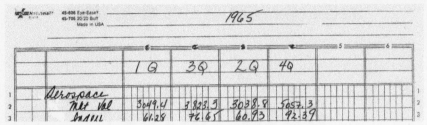

FIGURE 8.1   Handwritten S&P Results

Mutual fund numbers are collected by their trade associations but investors should appreciate that many of the other results of this, and other, data are often estimates or samples. For the most part, they are unlikely to result in investor harm, but one should recognize that even official data is often, as they say in London, "ropey."

Readily accepting data as accurate and facts as truthful is a common failing among individuals and institutions alike.

A second experience was gathering historical Standard & Poor's (S&P) group results. S&P provided those numbers on a weekly basis, which we obtained. We were first surprised that they were handwritten (see Figure 8.1).

More importantly, the weekly data, upon examination, was not Friday to Friday but rather Wednesday to Wednesday, as it took two days to calculate. (Our group at Salomon was probably the first firm to provide Friday to Friday results.) At the time, however, S&P treated the index as almost a public service and not as a potential business enterprise (that changed when the index was licensed to index funds and ETF providers).

As a result, S&P results were sometimes in error. January 1987 was a great month for stocks, up almost 15 percent. Several of the 500 stocks apparently did not participate and actually lost half their value:

Worst-Performing Companies

1.	Whirpool Corp	−49.1%
2.	Johnson Controls	−45.6
3.	Datapoint	−21.8
4.	Yellow Freight Systems	−12.9
5.	Westmoreland Coal	−7.3
6.	Bank America Corp.	−5.9
7.	Handleman Co.	−5.6
8.	Mellon Bank	−5.4
9.	Southland Corp.	−4.0
10.	Wendy's International	−3.7

As of January 20, 1987.
Source: Birinyi Associates, Inc.

We say *apparently* because Whirlpool Corporation and Johnson Controls split mid-month. They did not split on the last day of trading, which might have been acceptable if not excusable. While this probably had no effect on the index results, it was unsettling.

In 1985, corporations began buying back stock in significant and visible amounts. Our traders and bankers asked for a list of companies engaged in doing so. Unable to find a source, we created our own database, which we contend (as do some institutions and brokers who subscribe to the service), is the best available today. Our confidence is only increased when we see lists such as the following:[1]

Financial Times List of Buybacks

Date	Ticker	Value ($, billions)
1/24	INTC	$10.00
1/25	GILD	5.00
2/1	PFE	5.00
2/2	TWX	5.00
2/2	MHS	3.00
1/25	COH	1.50
1/26	BLL	1.40
1/27	APH	1.10
1/27	SYMC	1.00
2/2	UNM	1.00
2/2	WU	1.00

Unfortunately, the "top 10" omits six significant programs in a period of just less than two months (in bold in Table 8.1).[2]

Something as simple as buybacks should be easy to compile but they are not for a variety of reasons:

- Not all buybacks are announced, although most are.
- Historically only 77 percent of announcements are completed. We maintain a list of both announced and completed buybacks.
- Buyback details are sometimes buried in quarterly earnings or other releases. Thus, searching on the key word is often inadequate.

The critical investment takeaway is that *every buyback study or analysis we have seen is incomplete* (as is the case presented earlier), or it does not discriminate between announcements and executions.

TABLE 8.1   Birinyi Data: Largest Share Buyback Programs 2011 YTD (as of 2/8/11)

Date	Ticker	Name	Value ($, billions)	% of S/O
1/24	INTC	Intel Corp.	$10.00	8.61%
1/25	GILD	Gilead Sciences	5.00	16.14
2/1	PFE	Pfizer Inc.	5.00	3.43
1/25	**TRV**	**Travelers Cos. Inc.**	**5.00**	**20.68**
2/2	TWX	Time Warner Inc.	5.00	12.84
2/3	**UNP**	**Union Pac Corp.**	**3.74**	**8.11**
1/25	**KMB**	**Kimberly-Clark**	**3.20**	**12.26**
2/2	MHS	Medco Health	3.00	11.37
2/3	**VZ**	**Verizon**	**1.65**	**3.54**
1/25	COH	Coach Inc.	1.50	9.48
1/25	BLL	Ball Corp.	1.40	22.64
1/26	APH	Amphenol Corp.	1.11	11.45
2/8	**CMI**	**Cummins Inc.**	**1.00**	**4.52**
1/27	**MO**	**Altria Group Inc.**	**1.00**	**1.97**
1/26	SYMC	Symantec Corp.	1.00	7.24
2/2	UNM	Unum Group	1.00	12.54
2/1	WU	Western Union	1.00	7.51

CITIBANK (THE COMPANY) VERSUS CITI (THE STOCK)

The data issue is not easily resolved but its importance might be high-lighted in a *New York Times* story: "Cutting to the Quick" (February 10, 2008). The article discussed FRB policy and its effect on banks and specifically Citibank and detailed its reaction when the Central Bank cut rates:

> *The banks shares responded quickly in early 1991. By March, the stock was at $2.50; it ended 1991 at a split-adjusted $3.04. By 1995, the stock was at $10. The Fed's rate cut had effectively bailed out the bank.*

It would appear that this was indeed the case as "C" did indeed track those prices as shown in Figure 8.2. Except it was not a bank domiciled in New York City.

In October 1998, the bank merged with Travelers Corp. Legally, Travelers took over Citi but adopted the Citi name. Hence, the chart in Figure 8.2 is actually Travelers for the period in question.

While Citi also benefitted from the Fed's action and ultimately recovered, its course was not as smooth and consistent as that of the insurer (see Figure 8.3).

FIGURE 8.2 "Citi" (Traveler's Corp.)

Source: Birinyi Associates, Inc., Bloomberg.

FIGURE 8.3 Citi Actual

Source: Birinyi Associates, Inc., Bloomberg.

An even more intriguing situation arises with regard to the DJIA. In the mid-1980s, when we were awash with interns and trainees, we created a list of the 100 best and worst days. Additionally, we downloaded the original news reports to determine rationale for the move on any given day. Somewhat to our surprise, we found a number of errors, including the one seen in Figure 8.4.

The Real Thing . . .
It was a specialty market yesterday and some individual stocks advanced from 1 to more than 8 points. Meanwhile, the

Date	High	Low	Close	Change	Industrials

	Industrials				
Date	**High**	**Low**	**Close**	**Change**	
6..............	190.77	189.39	190.28	-0.11%	Actual
7..............	191.93	190.30	(181.46)	-4.63%	Close
8..............	194.40	192.08	193.70	1.17%	191.46

FIGURE 8.4   Dow Jones' Own Book . . . March 1946

Source: The Dow Jones Average: 1995–1985.

> *leaders were quiet and higher with the three averages ending with good gains.*
>
> **Wall Street Journal, March 8, 1946**

WORLD WAR I: THE MARKET SWOONS, OOPS, RALLIES

More intriguing was the trading halt that accompanied World War I. On July 31, 1914, there was a run on the Bank of England, which raised its Bank rate from 4 percent to 8 percent. The previous day the U.S. market was down 6.9 percent so the NYSE never opened and remained closed until Saturday, December 14. A chart of the year reflects not only the stoppage but also the impact of the war (see Figure 8.5).

We suspect that most analysts have missed this because it is not readily apparent on most charts. If, for example, we look at the *Bloomberg* graph in Figure 8.6 for that period it shows a sharp drop, which one might associate with World War I.

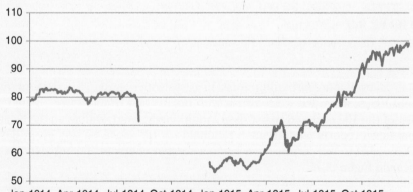

FIGURE 8.5   DJIA: 1914 through 1915

Source: Birinyi Associates, Inc., Bloomberg.

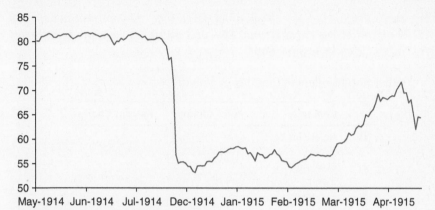

FIGURE 8.6 DJIA: 1914 through 1915

Source: Birinyi Associates, Inc., Bloomberg.

Upon closer inspection, you might note that the period July 30, 1914 to December 31, 1914 is compressed and takes up less space than most months.

This is also reflected in a popular chart that shows "secular" bear markets over the last century as the DJIA went from 71.42 on 7/30 to 56.76 on December 14 (see Figure 8.7). This has always been used by bearish forecasters as it shows that every 15 or so years we have a lengthy, difficult period.[3]

The newspaper reports of December 16 are somewhat in contrast to the apparent decline in Figure 8.5:

Stock Market Resumes and Prices Advance Sharply

With the heaviest attendance on the floor for many years and with both galleries crowded to capacity stock trading was resumed

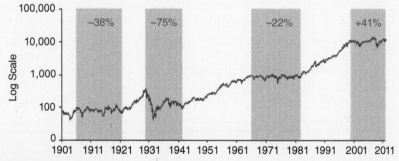

FIGURE 8.7 DJIA: 1901 through 2011

Saturday on the New York Stock Exchange. The market acted very well and prices ruled strong. Sharpest advances were made in Reading, Lehigh Valley, St. Paul. . . .

Other notable gainers that day included:

	Company	Point Change	Percent Change
1.	American Beet Sugar	+11 3/8	59.9%
2.	Bethlehem Steel	+12	40.0
3.	General Motors	+27 1/4	46.4
4.	Lehigh Valley	+12	9.8
5.	Peoples Gas	+11	10.4
6.	Texas Co	+19 1/8	16.9

The five most active were:

	Company	Shares	Point Change	Percent Change
1.	Amal Copper	7,990	+2 5/8	5.3%
2.	Erie	6,150	+2	9.8
3.	International Metals	4,500	+1 3/8	12.0
4.	Nevada Consol	4,700	+1 3/8	12.9
5.	Rock Island	4,150	+ 1/2	57.1

The reports of the day and the Dow results are, of course, incompatible. The market clearly did not lose 20.52 percent if "prices advanced sharply." We eventually determined that on October 4, 1916, Dow Jones & Company reconstituted the index. They dropped four stocks (including GM) and added 12, for a stock-only index of 20 names.

Rather than make allowances for the change, the new index was recalculated back to December 12, 1914 and the actual Dow from then to 1916 was replaced. That might have been "kosher" except that no allowance was made for the fact that this was not a case of apples to apples and the two were simply stapled together to create the chart shown in Figure 8.8.

Interestingly, had a divisor been created (which is the case today for revisions, splits, and spinoffs) and the DJIA been correctly computed, it would have ended 2012 at 19,792 (see Figure 8.9).

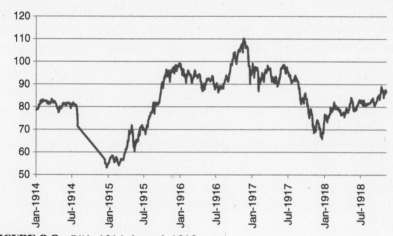

FIGURE 8.8 DJIA: 1914 through 1918

Source: Birinyi Associates, Inc., Bloomberg.

FIGURE 8.9 DJIA Logarithmic: 1901 through 2011

Source: Birinyi Associates, Inc., Bloomberg.

THE DOW TRADES ABOVE 1,000

The fact that even simple market averages can be misleading is also illustrated by the question of Dow 1,000. A common artifact among institutional investors is a photo of their Quotron screen on October 19,

1987 showing the 500-point loss and the key stocks. For years, we sought to find something similar for Dow 1,000. Surely someone somewhere had a Polaroid of that historic event, which occurred on January 18, 1966.[4]

March 12, 1956—Closes above 500 for the first time at 500.24.
January 18, 1966—Reaches 1,000 for the first time in mid-session, but drops back to close at 994.20.
November 14, 1972—Reaches 1,000 for the first time, at 1,003.16.

News accounts that day are somewhat murky. While some reports tell us that the market traded above 1,000, others did not. The *Wall Street Journal*'s high for the day was 1,000.50, which would seem to be the last word. However:

It was reached intraday, on a theoretical basis for the first time on January 18, 1966. . . . intraday highs and lows were calculated by taking the high and the low of all Dow stocks at any time during a trading session and assuming they had occurred simultaneously.[5]

Finally, on November 11, 1972, the *New York Times* business page confirmed that we had breached the 1,000 mark for the first time intraday and three days later (November 14, 1972) finally closed above 1,000:

Stock Market Soars to Record High; Average Tops 1,000 Before Dropping

There is, we submit, a significant investment ingredient in what might be a trivia question: the psychology of significant numbers. Economists and strategists attach relatively little importance to whole numbers but we still remember when Washington Post traded to $999 in 2004 and couldn't quite make it. The DJIA stalled at 996 in 1966, and subsequently took six years to get over that barrier.

S&P results might also carry a warning label. For one, it was not introduced until 1928 (although we regularly see S&P numbers back to 1900). From 1928 to 1957, the S&P 90 was the market standard. That gave way to the 500 stocks on March 4, 1957.

And not until July 1976 were financial stocks included. Thus, the popular graphs that showed the 1929 market with the financial crisis of 2007 were somewhat misleading, as the former index had no banks (see Figure 8.10).

This was important as those names fared badly and would have resulted in an even more dramatic decline:

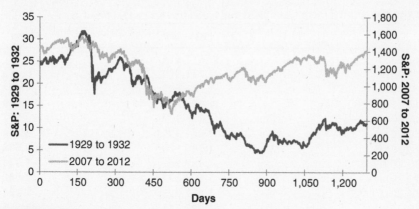

FIGURE 8.10 "S&P" During Financial Crisis 1932 versus 2008
Source: Birinyi Associates, Inc., Bloomberg.

Selected Manhattan/Bronx Banks 1929 through 1932

Bank	8/30/1929	6/30/1932	Change (%)
Chase	220	20.25	−90.80
First National	7,840	900	−88.52
Manhattan Co.	935	17.50	−98.13
Sterling National	121	8.50	−92.98
City	416	26	−93.75

As with the Dow, we have had issues with S&P. One in particular was their decision not to include a $30 billion dividend by Microsoft in 2004.[6] They argued, somewhat after the fact, that since it was a special it should be treated as such.

Had they included it, the S&P's total return would have been 35 bps higher or 11.23 percent vs. 10.88 percent. This raised an interesting question: What did index funds do with this income? It should have given them a significant advantage and led to outperformance, but Vanguard 500 Index Fund that year reported 10.74 percent vs. the S&P's total return of 10.88 percent.

Our focus on data also incorporates understanding the sources and reliability. Earlier we discussed our concern with the weekly bull bear survey. Another weekly report is that of the American Association of Individual Investors, which is a voluntary and therefore statistically questionable result.

Ordinarily the number of respondents approximates 300, but we are aware of instances where it is just over 100, making it even more dubious (week ending April 11, 2013).

TABLE 8.2 State and Local Plans Implied Performance ($, MM)

	Assets	Flows
4Q 2009	$1,617,814	
1Q 2010	1,713,915	$16,460
2Q 2010	1,522,645	24,992
3Q 2010	1,639,758	−199,880
4Q 2010	1,778,227	−177,592
1Q 2011	1,839,395	−176,224
2Q 2011	1,780,120	−202,688
3Q 2011	1,499,092	−9,524
4Q 2011	1,662,221	−37,080
1Q 2012	1,867,593	224
2Q 2012	1,793,145	−28,536
3Q 2012	1,885,007	−36,660
4Q 2012	1,861,606	−63,344
Change	$243,792	−$889,852
Adjusted Change	$1,133,644	
Implied Return	70.07%	
S&P 500	35.85%	
Europe 500	10.48%	

Source: Birinyi Associates, Inc.

Earlier in this chapter, we shared our historic concerns regarding the FRB's flow of fund numbers. While some analysts cite pension levels in their analysis we still have our doubts. Table 8.2 lists the equity holdings of state and local pension plans from the years 2010 through 2012.

We might consider the assets as a stock price and the flows as a purchase or sale. As shown over the three years ending 2012, the value of the "stock price" increased by $243 billion despite "sales" of just under $900 billion. The implied return is +70 percent at a time when the S&P 500 was up 35.8 percent.

Our approach was to assume beginning of quarter purchases or sales (flows) while end of quarter would have had a slightly different result. Other math games could also be applied, but the end result is the same— the numbers are not real.

NOTES

1. "Pace of U.S. Equity Buy-Backs Picks Up," *Financial Times*, February 8, 2011.

2. "Buyback Data ????" Birinyi Associates, Inc., February 11, 2011.

3. "Is This Bull Cyclical or Secular?" *Wall Street Journal*, June 15, 2009.

4. "Historical Dow Dates—Listed," Associated Press, July 13, 1990.

5. Peter Eliader, "Nasty Numbers," *Barron's*, March 22, 1999.

6. Jonathan Fuerbringer, "Redoing the Math of an Index," *New York Times*, June 12, 2005.

CHAPTER 9

That's Easy for You to Say!

. . . quite simply the best security analyst operating in the 1990s . . . the reigning champion of stock pickers.
—Louis Rukeyser inducting Laszlo Birinyi into the
Wall Street Week Hall of Fame (April 23, 1999)

It ain't bragging if you do it.

—Dizzy Dean

A t some point, a reader might rightly ask, given my attitude toward most commentators and providers of financial guidance, what qualifies me to make these judgments. In response, I might begin with the technical community. Interestingly, when I have presented my views, the response has usually been personal. A two-page *Forbes* column, "Diagnosticians Who Can't Prescribe,"[1] drew a strong response suggesting the editors should terminate my contract and objecting to me personally while failing to address my specific concerns.

Few will remember that in 1989, *Wall Street Week* instituted a new version of its "elves." Previously, the Elves Index was a series of technical indicators that had a passable record until they didn't, and the provider of the results left the show.

The new feature asked 10 market timers, including me, to present one-, three-, and six-month forecasts. In another one of those incidents that undermines these analysts, one of the original ten withdrew when he learned that his name would be associated with each call and he would therefore be held accountable.

At the end of one year, Mr. Rukeyser provided the results:

In the thirty-six weeks that we've been able to match the Elves' forecast with actual Dow performance three months later, the most accurate forecaster has been Laszlo Birinyi.

Birinyi [also] gets the blue ribbon if we count either four or five months from the original calls. . . .

Merging all the results, here are our current top five elves. Birinyi holds onto first place. . . .[2]

I might also highlight some of our market calls:

- On October 30, 1987, we published our views on the post-Crash stock market:[3]

  . . . a period of consolidation and generally shows little gain for the next several months. We believe that the US stock market will follow a similar period. . . .

  Our expectation was that it would parallel the sharp decline of 1978, which had a 5 percent gain in its post-six months (see Figure 9.1).

  Although the picture was not perfect, the 2 percent gain over the next six months qualifies, we think, as "little gain."
- We had previously presented our stance after the 1990 invasion of Kuwait. The prevailing view then, and in the fourth quarter, was either out and out negative or, at best, a bear market rally. Money flows showed buying not only *before* the market bottom but consistently through the balance of the year, as well as through the sharp decline in January (see Figure 9.2).

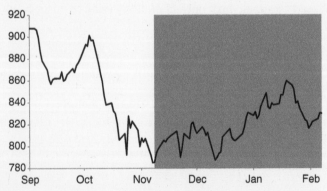

FIGURE 9.1   DJIA: September 8, 1978 through February 14, 1979
Source: Birinyi Associates, Inc., Bloomberg.

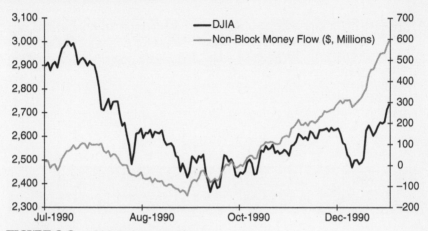

FIGURE 9.2 1990 DJIA Money Flows

Source: Birinyi Associates, Inc., Bloomberg.

- In 1995, for the only time in *Wall Street Week* history, my high/low/close forecast was the most correct of any of the 25 panelists, although my close was woefully short of the actual:

  Birinyi was closest of the panelists on all three Dow forecasts: the high, the low, and the final reading, and was, in fact, just 32 points off in predicting the 1995 low.[4]

BUSINESSWEEK: 1998, 1999, AND AMERICA ONLINE

- Of the 50 respondents in *BusinessWeek's* then-annual poll, our 1998 and 1999 forecasts were not only bullish but within 2 percent of the actual year-end result.

  In both years, our single best idea was America Online (AOL), which gained 585 percent in 1998 and 95 percent the next year (see Figure 9.3).
- At the beginning of 1999, we also forecast an audacious 50 percent rise in the NASDAQ.[5]

Wall St. Experts Were Caught with Their Predictions Down
Laszlo Birinyi of Deutsche Bank Securities wins kudos . . . by predicting year-end NASDAQ of 2,800 [up 50%].
New York Post, November 4, 1999

As some later noted, we were in error by a magnitude of 50 percent as the index went up 75 percent!

| 1998 | | DOW JONES INDUSTRIAL | | STANDARD & POOR'S 500 | FAVORITE |
NAME	FIRM	MID YEAR	YEAR END	YEAR END	STOCK
LASZLO BIRINYI, JR.	Birinyi Associates	9,500	10,250	1,200	America Online
ROBERT J. FROEHLICH	Zurich Kemper Investments	9,300	10,000	1,200	--------
EUGENE E. PERONI, JR.	Janney Montgomery Scott	8,800	9,850	-----	Wm. Wrigley Jr. Co.

| 1999 | | DOW JONES INDUSTRIAL | | STANDARD & POOR'S 500 | FAVORITE |
NAME	FIRM	MID YEAR	YEAR END	YEAR END	STOCK
LASZLO BIRINYI, JR.	Deutsche Bank Securities	10,050	12,010	1,500	America Online
ELAINE GARZARELLI	Garzarelli Capital	------	12,000	1,550	Merrill Lynch
TOM GALVIN	Donaldson Lufkin & Jenrette	10,100	11,000	1,300	Merrill Lynch

FIGURE 9.3   1998 and 1999 *BusinessWeek* Forecast Tables

- In December 2008, our publication, *S&P 750: The Bottom*,[6] was too
  optimistic by 8 percent. But given that the market rallied 20 percent
  in just two weeks when it bottomed, we contend that being early was
  considerably more profitable than being late.

We will acknowledge that we were too optimistic in 2000, stayed positive too long, and failed to appreciate the depth of the financial crisis of
2008. We did, however, publish a piece, *The Next CRASH*, just before the
crisis in August 2007. We were concerned regarding systemic risk, new
instruments, and trading practices that at some point would coalesce and
have a negative impact. We did not suggest it would be soon or what shape
it would take.

We also manifested our concerns by removing Citibank from our recommendations on October 30, 2007 at $42.11, but *we did neither antici-
pate nor forecast the severity of the financial crisis* (see Figure 9.4).

INSIDE THIS ISSUE
- The Financial Press
- Housing - Yes Again
- Strategy

Reminiscences

PUBLISHED BY BIRINYI ASSOCIATES, INC.   VOLUME 15, NUMBER 11   NUMBER 2007

> **Changes to the Portfolios**
>
> To the Conservative portfolio we have made the following change:
>
> | Removed | Added |
> | --- | --- |
> | Citigroup | Enerplus Resources (ERF) |

Source: Birinyi Associates, Inc.

Even more critical, in our view, is the issue of actual performance and recommendations, specifically recommendations. Hopefully, our record there warrants your attention beginning with *Wall Street Week*.

I reported our results as a *Wall Street Week* panelist in Chapter 5 where our results were more than double the second best result, and over four times that of the average forecaster. We did not do well in the post dot-com period, but in 2003 when the S&P added 28 percent, our 84 percent gain was double that of the median return of 39 percent for the 22 panelists.

It has been suggested that I had the good fortune of being positive during a positive period (isn't that what one is supposed to do?). One of those years, 1994, was not a great year with the S&P down 1.3 percent and our gains were a result of shorts. In fact, they might have been even better had it not been for our Hong Kong trade.

One of the instruments in that "portfolio" was a put option on the Hang Seng Index, which went down 31 percent. Financial theory and Investments 101 teach us that if a stock or index goes down, the put should go *up*. Despite that and the decline in the index, this put actually went down

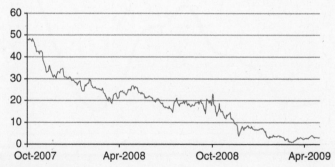

FIGURE 9.4 Citigroup

Source: Birinyi Associates, Inc., Bloomberg.

a similar 30 percent! Hence, we have always been leery of derivatives as a result.

BEST: REAL TIME, REAL MONEY, REAL RESULTS

It could be argued that these results are only on paper. In 2000, we introduced a real-world portfolio in the form of a unit investment trust. Like the *Wall Street Week* experience it would be a limited number of stocks held for 13 months to minimize taxes.

The Birinyi Equity Select Trust (BEST) had a March (Even) series and another in September (Odd). Over the next 12 years, the record of both was well ahead of the market (see Figure 9.5 and 9.6).

Unfortunately, the underwriter of the trusts sold the franchise to an organization whose greater interest was its own branded vehicles.

In 2001, we constructed our unit odd trust. The 10 stocks were outperforming the market by over 1,000 basis points after the first three months. Unfortunately, the instrument was a strict buy and hold. By its maturity, an earnings shortfall, downgrade or some other event had impacted every issue in the portfolio (see Figure 9.7 and 9.8).

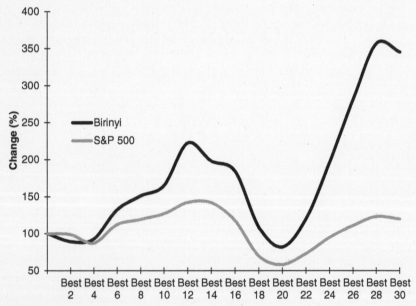

FIGURE 9.5 Master Performance for Even Trusts

Source: Birinyi Associates, Inc.

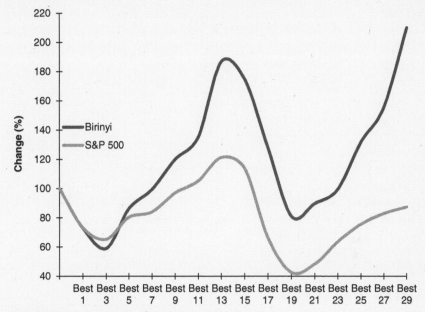

FIGURE 9.6 Master Performance for Odd Trusts

Source: Birinyi Associates, Inc.

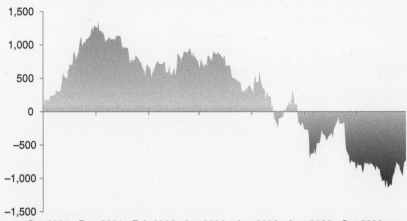

FIGURE 9.7 Best Three versus S&P 500

Source: Birinyi Associates, Inc.

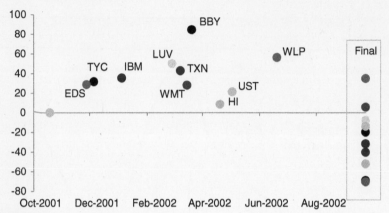

FIGURE 9.8   Best Three Individual Results: Peak Performance versus Maturity
Source: Birinyi Associates, Inc.

NOTES

1. Laszlo Birinyi, "Diagnosticians Who Can't Prescribe," *Forbes*, December 1, 1997.

2. "The *Continued* Failure of Technical Analysis," Birinyi Associates, Inc., May 2006.

3. "The U.S. Stock Market—October 19, 1987, and Beyond," Salomon Brothers, October 30, 1987.

4. "Year-End Review," *Wall Street Week with Louis Rukeyser*, PBS (Maryland Public Television), December 29, 1995.

5. "Wall St. Experts Were Caught With Their Predictions Down," *New York Post*, November 4, 1999.

6. "S&P 750: The Bottom," Birinyi Associates, Inc., December 2008.

CHAPTER 10

Playing the Game

The game of professional investment is intolerably boring and over exacting to anyone who is entirely exempt from the gambling instinct. . . .

—John Keynes

Like all of life's rich emotional experiences, the full flavor of losing important money cannot be conveyed by literature.

—Fred Schwed

At some point, it becomes time to put away the textbook, fold the paper, turn off the computer, and actually enter the arena. This is true for the MBA going into the training program at Merrill or American Capital, the individual who is retiring or scaling back, and the lucky bloke whose rich uncle left him an inheritance.

To begin, one must accept certain realities and limitations. First, recall, if not frame, our introductory headline:

Wall Street Always Wins.

Translating that into a more pragmatic response, it suggests: You can't beat the market and, more importantly, don't berate yourself for not doing so. Here we make the comparison to golf. There may be 5 or 25 truly gifted individuals who could play on the professional tour. But for whatever reason, they never did; however, there are still millions of golfers who enjoy the experience even if their handicap is in the high double digits.

And surely they will regale you with their detailed, 45-minute account of the day they broke 80 or had back-to-back birdies. You might, therefore, begin by having some reasonable expectations based on your own experience, requirements, and lifestyle. Among the questions we attempt to ascertain for our managed accounts are the following:

- Are you likely to need a significant sum in the next twelve months, such as for school tuition? (Tuition, as you may already know, is only the first step on an expensive ladder.)
- Will you be able to make regular contributions to grow this portfolio? If so, we tend to be a bit more aggressive.
- Where are you in your life cycle? Given long-term historical returns (7 percent for stocks, 5 percent for treasuries, and 2 percent for cash) what do you think you will need to retire at 65 or 70 *before* Social Security? Is it enough?

In the graph in Figure 10.1, we plot our assumptions for two 30-year-olds. One begins with $10,000 and the other with $25,000. Both contribute $5,000 a year to an IRA. As shown, the importance of regular contributions over a long period is evident.

This is further highlighted by another chart in Figure 10.2 that shows the importance of timing. If you miss the best five days of every year, you lose your entire savings:

(Details on the above are available in Appendix B.)

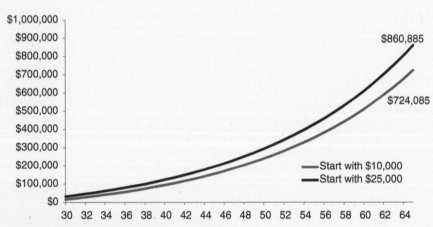

FIGURE 10.1   Investing for the Long Run
Source: Birinyi Associates, Inc.

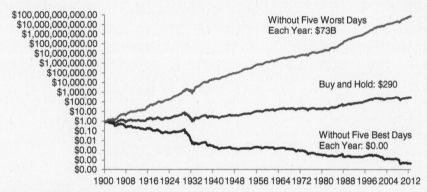

FIGURE 10.2 Cost of Timing the Market: DJIA 1900 through 2012

Source: Birinyi Associates, Inc.

MR. BUFFETT BUYS AND SELLS SILVER

Another consideration is taxes (losses in a tax-deferred account such as an IRA or 401(k) are not usually deductible and cannot be replenished). Most important of all, and hardest to determine, is the issue of risk.

Our preferred measure thereof is the first sleepless night. If it occurs when your overall portfolio is down 5 percent, that is your risk parameter. It suggests that when you are down 4 percent, you should reassess and recognize that more cash might be in order going forward.

And don't even think about bringing Mr. Buffett into the conversation. In our best days, we didn't approach his results and you won't either, for several reasons, most importantly:

- His time parameter is forever.

An example of this might be his purchase of silver in January 1998 at an average price of $5.88. Not until 2004 did it trade above there and in the interim traded as low as $4.01 so he had a drawdown of 31.8 percent (also known as a loss) (see Figure 10.3). In addition, he bought *physical* silver on the order of 130 million ounces, which meant he had to store it and insure it so even when it traded to $6, he was still probably losing money.

In 2006, someone wanted to introduce a silver ETF where shares traded based on the price of the metal. But to do so they had to have physical silver and a lot of it. Guess who was able to accommodate them, allegedly at $12.5 an ounce? His total return was 113 percent (less expenses) for an annualized gain of 13.6 percent.

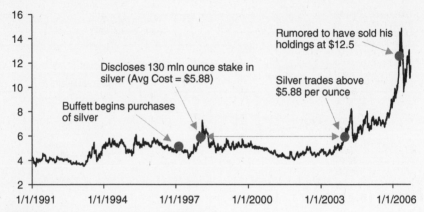

FIGURE 10.3   Silver and Warren Buffett
Source: Birinyi Associates, Inc., Bloomberg.

If anyone else was down 30 percent or so after five years, they or their customers would surely have bailed.

- Mr. Buffett has no customers.

The institutional business of money management and especially for pensions and endowments is difficult in part because managers are required to report quarterly results and often in great detail. The rationale for decisions is reviewed, the manager's style or philosophy is questioned, and the results are scrutinized.

To accommodate these requirements, larger pension plans and other large pools of money employ outside consultants to monitor managers and make sure that the value manager does not buy growth stocks or that the growth manager avoids utilities. Outside consultants are, we have been told, if nothing else, time consuming. Mr. Buffett's only "explanation" of his efforts is at his annual "lovefest."

Lastly, of course, even if his roof leaks or cellar floods, he won't need to take out a loan or sell any of his stock.

The individual who has decided to invest is only beginning the process. The next step, for most individuals, is limited by their assets as very little useful guidance is available for portfolios of less than $100,000. The fees for most instruments and stocks make it difficult to accumulate wealth at these levels.

For these accounts we suggest a portfolio of 60 to 70 percent stocks via a low cost index fund, 20 to 30 percent in U.S. Treasuries, and 5 to 10 percent cash.

In truth, not until $250,000 or more is one likely to be of interest to a knowledgeable broker or advisor and even then interest is likely to be lukewarm.

The traditional path of asset enrichment has come from stockbrokers. Unfortunately, the traditional stockbroker is an anachronism. Today, brokerage offices are populated by financial advisors or account executives or even portfolio managers. In part, this reflects the reality of the times. Individually, customized approaches are both difficult and, frankly, not profitable.

Over time (and it has diminished), we regularly received portfolios reflecting a brokerage firm's recommended list. Even million-dollar portfolios had 65 names that ranged from positions with 26 shares to others with perhaps 500 shares. These portfolios were, in effect, guaranteed mediocrity.

Brokers themselves had no great interest in this approach, as once established there was likely to be little or limited activity and, therefore, irregular (at best) commissions.

Even a more aggressive or directed portfolio had limited profit potential for brokers.

Consider, for example, a million-dollar portfolio that was to focus on dividend paying low-growth (and therefore low-volatility) stocks. If we assume the average stock is $40, the portfolio will own 25,000 shares. Even at a generous 20 cents a share the total commissions total $5,000 of which the individual broker will retain $1,000 to maybe $1,500.

In all likelihood that will be it for some time, and that "some time" might be a year or three. If it is a year, the broker will have made 0.10 percent on the transaction. An annuity or a fund or some instrument, by comparison, is likely to have a 1 percent associated charge per year and every year. Obviously the correct answer, for a broker, is B.

Too often, too, those other products are homegrown and are—for the broker or wealth manager—more profitable. Our BEST instrument, which we detailed earlier, was eventually scrapped in spite of its historical record.

Furthermore, brokers are often limited by compliance and internal regulations. Every Monday our firm produces a "stock of the week" (see Figure 10.4). Over time, it has done well, but in 2009 we had an especially good run and picked a number of short-term winners. Many of our broker clients were discouraged from implementing the ideas as it suggested "churning" or aggressive trading which, they were told, is not a characteristic of a fiduciary.

Then there are financial advisors and/or financial planners. For the most part they, unlike traditional brokers, are unregulated. They can provide investment advice, financial and estate planning, and other services.

In addition to their flying below the radar (advisors need not register with the SEC until their assets total $20 million), we question the need to pay a fee to someone who recommends buying a fund that will charge you yet another fee.

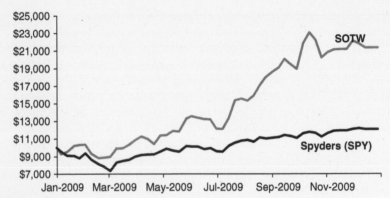

FIGURE 10.4 Stock of the Week (SOTW) Performance 2009

Source: Birinyi Associates, Inc.

Should you consider an advisor (or any professional for that matter) we would recommend:

- Ascertain the individual's academic credentials. Every doctor's office is decorated with diplomas and certificates. Pictures of whaling ships or nineteenth-century schooners may be impressive but they are not enlightening.
- Be very clear on how the advisor gets paid. Is it a flat fee or might she or he have some interest or agenda in a given fund or money manager? We might suggest you do so in writing but doubt that most firms would, for obvious reasons, comply. But you can always ask.
- Ask regarding investment objectives. Interestingly for many individuals, beating the market may not be suitable. To do so often entails undo risk, significant turnover or a lack of diversification. In 1999, some managers had spectacular results because they owned an abundance of dot-com stocks and in 2009 financial stocks had great returns. In both cases, a year later the tables turned. Our objective is, for the greater majority of our accounts, disciplined reasonable returns and never being 100 percent invested, which allows us to take advantage of short-term opportunities.
- Discuss communication. Will you have any input or dialogue? Our preference is for complete control, but we do share our thoughts with our clients. One argument we have against indexing, and other passive approaches, is that financial decisions should not be "one and done." You should have some sort of an on-going relationship, even if it is only tangential.

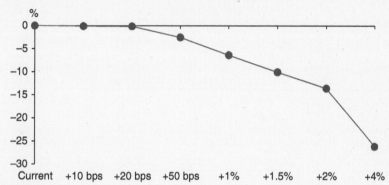

FIGURE 10.5 Percent Change in Bond Price versus Yield Change

Source: Birinyi Associates, Inc.

BONDS CAN GO DOWN

While this is not a constant, we provide some parameters next. In this case, if rates were to go from the current 2 to 3 percent, the value of the bond decreases by 6 percent; if they rise to 4 percent, the loss would be 13 percent (see Figure 10.5).

So, we are basically left with mutual funds and do-it-yourself investing.

Bluntly, we are bearish on professional managers and especially mutual funds. Especially to be avoided are any funds that charge in excess of 1 percent. We recently did a quick scan and found that over 15 percent of all funds have charges of 5 percent on entry, and another 10 percent have exit fees. (In truth, some of these lower or waive the charges depending on the amount of the investment, but even so. . . .) As we noted previously, market returns over time approximate 5 percent and to pay one year's charge for the privilege of managing your money is an example of what Bob Dylan wrote: "Some people rob you with a fountain pen."

When considering a fund, read the ads. Yes, you will get a prospectus, which is 30+ pages written by lawyers and accountants for other lawyers and accountants. The marketing information and ads are often clearer and more useful.

Consider an ad we have often criticized. This fund had a great 2009, which made its three-year results outstanding. But looking at the more recent results in Table 10.1, the *one-year* was 15.72 percent, a bit under the Russell 1000 Growth Index of 18.26 percent, which ranked them at 56 percent (44 percent of the funds did worse). Note that *after* the sales charge, the 15.72 percent is reduced by 42 percent to 9.07 percent, or less than half

TABLE 10.1   Annualized Total Return as of 3/3/11

Class A Shares Inception 4/1/69	Before Sales Charge	After Sales Charge	Russell 1000 Growth Index	Lipper Large-Cap Growth Funds average	Upper Rankings Large-Cap Growth Funds category
1 year	15.72%	9.07%	18.26%	16.06%	56% (459/823)
3 years	13.87	11.64	5.19	3.17	1% (2/728)
5 years	6.69	5.70	4.34	2.91	1% (3/631)
10 years	3.33	2.27	2.99	2.47	26% (99/386)
Life of Fund	11.01	10.85	—	9.29	29% (4/13)

Total expense ratio: 1.30 %
After-sales-charge returns reflect a maximum 5.75% load. For a portion of the periods, the fund had expense limitations, without which returns would have been lower.

Source: Birinyi Associates, Inc.

of the benchmark. Not noted is that if you want to leave, there is another 1 percent exit fee.

We have not included another portion of the ad that tells us that the fund invests "some or all of its assets in small and midsize companies." But it is benchmarked against large-cap growth funds. Small caps have historically outperformed large growth by the order of 5 percent, or more. This would suggest the fund had a bit of an advantage, as the comparison is not strictly apples to apples.

Our attitude on funds notwithstanding, here too we think there is more confusion than illumination. Critics (and especially academics) continually note that funds, on balance, underperform, and this is especially the case with hedge funds.

The first issue, we contend, is inclusion. In any given year, x or y percent of the funds don't match the S&P 500. But many of those funds are not trying to do so. A small-cap value fund has a different set of metrics than a large-cap growth fund.

Then there is the issue of averaging. A $5 billion fund that does better than the market may more than make up for four $50 million funds that don't. To be sure, there are measures that adjust and compensate for the difference but too often those are buried by the headline number of "Sixty-two percent of funds failed. . . . "

There is another issue that critics fail to consider, which is the matter of styles. Some funds are oriented toward growth stocks or aggressive growth while others have a value orientation. Thus it is highly unlikely at any one point that they all are outperforming at the same time. In the 1990s, when the Internet and technology were the flavor of the day, traditional Graham

FIGURE 10.6   Berkshire Hathaway Relative Strength
Source: Birinyi Associates, Inc., Bloomberg.

and Dodd portfolios, which might have owned utilities or individual names, trailed as they should have, given their mandate.

A well-known portfolio hugely underperformed for much of 1998 and all of 1999, but we saw no editorials criticizing the Berkshire Hathaway "fund" for lagging results (see Figure 10.6).

As for hedge funds, one might remember the critical term: Hedge. Some funds are truly hedged funds as they go both long and short in an attempt to limit market risk and may not measure themselves against the market. Furthermore, their clients do not expect or even request market returns.[1]

We once considered such a circumstance where a client wanted the portfolio to be 50 percent long and 50 percent short, which neutralized market risk. The goal was not to beat or replicate the S&P 500 but to provide greater returns than a risk-free short term U.S. Treasury. Unfortunately, it meant selling stocks that did too well (as the portfolio would therefore be 52 percent or 55 percent long and covering stocks that performed poorly). It also meant constant rebalancing, almost daily, and constant monitoring and review from the client.

The client, having significant assets, was not especially concerned about gains but rather protection of existing assets. Thus, if it were a hedge fund, it would have performed badly by most measures.

This does not, however, alter our longstanding bearish attitude toward mutual funds. After a lifetime on Wall Street, we are bearish on managers, not only because of marketing such as illustrated previously, nor necessarily because of the overall record of managers. Our ultimate concern can be synthesized very simply: *Professionals do not practice investing.*

MR. ELLIS: THE LOSER'S GAME

In 1974, Charlie Ellis, a longtime observer and practitioner wrote, what might be termed a classic essay: "The Loser's Game." There he outlined the difficulties that even professionals face. One sentence especially struck us then and has stayed with us:

Investing should be a profession but it is not.

In our five decades and more meetings than we can recount, no one, ever, not even once ever suggested that they were *practicing* investing. The concept of continually learning, seeking new approaches, updating a skill set, and whatever else, as is entailed with practicing law or medicine, is sadly lacking on Wall Street. Skimming the latest research reports, attending a seminar in Palm Beach, lunching with the management of GE, or other activities, which are often considered as work by members of the financial community, also fail the test of "practicing."

This is not to suggest that it is totally absent. We have been told that Fidelity's Peter Lynch worked most Saturdays, at his office. And we know of one manager who literally takes (or took) a two-suit Samsonite case full of research home, more weekends than not. But those are the proverbial exceptions.

Years ago, when we were more involved in sales, we regularly sent market articles from *Time* magazine and *Fortune* to managers and analysts who thanked us for doing so. (A money manager who doesn't read *Fortune* or much else?) On another occasion we sent our clients a copy of a particularly interesting article from the *Financial Analysts Journal* and again were stunned to learn that, almost without exception, it had not previously crossed their desk.

Sadly for their customers' sake, professionals have an attitude that suggests that they need not seek out ideas, develop information, and extend themselves. They act as if surely anything of significance will be delivered by one of the many brokerage firms seeking their business and good graces.

Long ago, we termed this the *Liberty Square Syndrome* after the area of Boston that is surrounded by a large number of institutions, most of which share this complacency. Having mentioned this at several professional forums, more than one sell-side salesperson or trader congratulated me on the term and detailed their own experience with this characteristic.

Historically, institutions allocated commissions and payments to brokerages by compiling votes. A large fund might determine that they will generate $5 million in commissions for the forthcoming year. The managers of the various funds might be given 200 votes with another 150 given to analysts, while another 50 might be allocated for marketing. In this case, each vote should be worth $12,500.

The manager of the technology fund might have 25 votes that are used to reward a brokerage firm for its ideas, reports, and other services. The analyst responsible for banks and other financial institutions might have ten votes to reward the analysts at AW Jones or Deutsche Bank who recommended stocks that did very well.

In the second half of 1983, although not even a member of the research department, I received the second largest number of votes at the firm, but only one of them came from a Boston institution:

Salomon Brothers Inc. Analyst Voting Results 7/31/1983		
	7/1983 Votes	12/1982 Votes
Analyst 1	106	83
Birinyi	102	78
Analyst 3	101	82
Analyst 4	98	64
Analyst 5	97	79

Source: Salomon Brothers, Inc.

One nameless fund was occasionally receptive to a visit but our work in the 1980s was especially negative on Hewlett-Packard, one of their largest holdings (see Figure 10.7). Even though we had been right on the stock

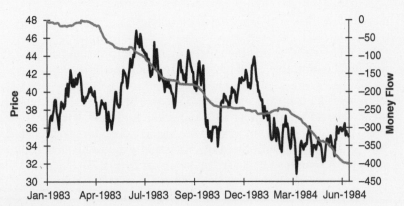

FIGURE 10.7 Hewlett-Packard Money Flow

Source: Birinyi Associates, Inc., Salomon Brothers.

for years, the fund would not entertain the idea that maybe they might, just for a moment, listen.

(At the same time, the electronics analyst at Salomon was a big bull on HWP, Hewlett's ticker at the time, and received business from them as a result. He once wrote a report: "Hewlett—Last Chance to Buy in the 30s." I totally agreed with him, although we differed on the direction!)

In a word, fund managers are arrogant, closed minded, or both. In part, this is understandable given the brokerage communities' attempts to ingratiate themselves and increase their (the brokers') business. Ten or more suitors a day would distort our perspective as well.

WALL STREET WEEK: WE WERE LUCKY (FOR EIGHT YEARS)

We might also again review my *Wall Street Week* experience. From 1992 through 1999, our annual compounded stock selections returned 42.5 percent vs. the market's 19.7 percent. And I appeared on the year-end show six of those eight years placing first in 1993, 1996, and 1997.

The other panelists were all professional, full-time investors with a variety of backgrounds including portfolio managers, proprietors of management firms, analysts, and the like. During that eight-year run, not a single one ever suggested that I visit their next strategy session or inquired as to the availability of our research or in any way acknowledged that maybe, just maybe, I had some useful insights.

In 1999, while on our way to the mid-year show where the top four panelists updated their views, one manager noting our first-half gains said:

Once again, this year you have been lucky!

Since then, our view that the money management business is basically fat, rich, and comfortable continues to be regularly reinforced:

- We received a call from an operation with $100 billion under management who had heard that we had done some study and would we please share it. No, we could not as we were trying to be a for-profit business. We were told that, unfortunately, they had exhausted their commissions for research so could we make an exception. We suggested that they could pay for it themselves and not necessarily use their customers' commissions. That ended the conversation.
- After a *CNBC* appearance where I highlighted our recent study on dividends, a large fund asked for a copy suggesting they were doing us a

favor. Given their prominence, their attitude was that we should be proud that they inquired!

- Some years ago, the trader at a $10 billion fund asked for a personal favor which, given our friendship, was easy to accommodate. He wanted to pay us, but said traders were not allowed to allocate business; the commissions were limited to the managers and analysts.
- In 2001, *Financial Analysts Journal* published "Can Money Flows Predict Stock Returns?"[2] This article analyzed our methodology and "documented strong positive correlation between money flow and return." (See discussion in Chapter 5.) Here was the business' primary professional journal in effect professionally endorsing our approach. We received one phone call. One.

Sadly, we have had numerous other examples of this failing. In years past, we have discussed issues relating to market cycles and showed volume one of our study that is over 1,000 pages in length.

Despite seminars being populated by professional investors, including some sell-side strategists and economists (the study includes details of economic cycles), not one has ever inquired about the study. Despite that, we regularly see commentary and advice on strategy and tactics relating to group and market movements. They are, almost without exception, wrong, incomplete, or theoretical.

While there may have been others, the one unilateral phone call we readily recall was from George Soros himself. He had heard about our efforts and asked that I stop by, but without the salesperson.

In the course of our experience, we are chagrined in not only the lack of intellectual curiosity but also the apparent indifference to what we would term "required reading." To us *Time*, the *New York Times*, *Bloomberg BusinessWeek*, the *Financial Times*, and even the weekend *Wall Street Journal* are the oxygen of our system, but are only incidental to too many so-called professionals.

(Lest we be misunderstood, our concern is with the business, not *our* business. While institutions ignored our *Wall Street Week* picks, individuals did not and our newsletter and asset management efforts flourished. And they did so with relatively little marketing expenses or overhead.)

MONEY MANAGERS DON'T GET IT?

Also disappointing and detrimental to their customers' performance is the truly astonishing fact that *too many portfolio managers today don't appreciate, understand, or incorporate the stock market.*

As we discussed earlier, this was especially true when we introduced the idea of money flows. It was also in evidence when we introduced the idea of "money made" in the mid-1980s.

Then as now, there were all manner of programs that detailed the performance of stocks and groups, sectors, and other slices of the market. However the critical issue is not which stocks went up or down the most, but which stocks had the greatest change in market capitalization. While everyone agrees that the S&P is capitalization weighted, their analysis is invariably based only on price change. GE may only gain $1 this quarter, but the value of the company (given that it has 10 billion shares outstanding) will rise by $10,000,000,000 as a result.

Avon (432 million shares outstanding) may have a good quarter and gain $2, but its value will only increase by $864,000,000. Avon is not chopped liver, but less than 9 percent of GE's increase.

We began reporting these new results which were not well accepted. How could we write that Walmart, with its measly 5.5 percent gain, was more important than the 42 percent move in Delta? Or the $1.75 decline in IBM had a bigger impact on the S&P than the $8 loss in Control Data (CDA). Surely, managers told us, their performance would have been better except for that damned CDA.

In 2012 for example, the 10 best performing stocks added $120 billion in value to the S&P 500 and accounted for 7.8 percent of the gain. The 10 that gained the most in market value did not perform as well but were responsible for 28.8 percent of the gain (see Tables 10.2 and 10.3).

TABLE 10.2　Ten Best Performing Stocks: 2012

	Market Cap Change ($, millions)	Cumulative Market Change ($, millions)	Cumulative Percent Impact	Percent Change (%)
PHM	2,543	2,543	0.2	187.80
S	9,561	12,105	0.8	142.31
WHR	4,009	16,113	1.0	114.44
EXPE	3,914	20,028	1.3	111.75
BAC	48,848	68,875	4.4	108.63
LEN	2,685	71,561	4.6	96.79
MPC	10,591	82,152	5.3	89.25
TSO	2,863	85,014	5.5	88.57
STX	5,987	91,001	5.9	85.85
GILD	29,476	120,477	7.8	79.45

Source: Birinyi Associates, Inc.

TABLE 10.3 Ten Greatest Market Value Changes: 2012

	Market Cap Change ($, millions)	Cumulative Market Cap Change ($, millions)	Cumulative Percent Impact	Percent Change (%)
AAPL	114,217	114,217	7.4	31.61
BAC	48,848	163,065	10.5	108.63
JPM	41,820	204,885	13.2	32.24
CMCSA	39,416	244,301	15.8	57.65
ORCL	38,436	282,737	18.3	29.90
C	36,838	319,575	20.6	50.36
HD	33,603	353,179	22.8	47.12
GE	32,616	385,795	24.9	17.20
WFC	30,823	416,617	26.9	24.02
GILD	29,476	446,093	28.8	79.45

Source: Birinyi Associates, Inc.

There are obvious exceptions, but given the relative lack of educational and licensing requirements for a Wall Street career, coupled with a focus on salesmanship, marketing and presentability, generally unwarranted compensation, and limited accountability, very few in the community can truly say that they are professionals in the same vein as those who practice medicine or the law.

For most individuals, there are limited alternatives, especially if you don't have a favorite uncle who used to be an accountant or a savvy grandfather who has been investing for 50 years. And you are really out of luck if you have trouble balancing your checkbook and think the tax form is written in Swahili. Despite what we wrote a page or two ago, you might consider a mutual fund with these caveats:

- Never buy a fund whose fees exceed 1 percent (maybe on occasion 1.5). Almost 15 percent of the funds charge a 5 percent fee (in many cases less depending on how much you invest). Given that stocks return 5 to 7 percent on average over time, why give up one year's return as an entry fee?
- Management fees should likewise be limited to 1 percent.
- Ascertain that there are no other fees. Over 10 percent of all funds charge an exit fee. If they do a poor job, you have to pay to leave?
- If possible, determine if the fund's record was achieved by the current manager.
- Be leery of funds that advertise heavily; who do you think is paying for those ads?

Don't get hung up on performance. Outperforming, almost by definition, requires risk, often excessive risk. Here again, take your own profile
into account. If your goal is to retire with X or Y, will you get there by being
up 18 percent one year and down 10 percent the next?

Consistency matters, which may have been Bernie Madoff's secret. In
great years, he was good, in average years, he was good, and in bad years,
he was good.

You might want to shortcut and accelerate the process by subscrib-
ing or getting access to Morningstar, a Chicago firm that monitors and
rates mutual funds and provides other financial services. Their April/May
Advisor listed 178 of "Our Favorite Mutual Funds." Of the four large-value
funds, two had three stars and two had four stars. For each asset's return,
yield and expense ratios were detailed.

Not provided is the sales charge and you should walk that extra mile.
The two four-star funds were both having a good year: 6.3 and 7.1 percent
(vs. 6.2 percent for the market), and had good 12-month results as well:
13.4 and 15.8 percent. Expense ratios were similar: 0.63 and 0.68 percent. If
you drill down, as you absolutely must, you will find that one fund charges
a front load of 5.75 percent so your $10,000 takes an immediate haircut
to $9,425. There is also a 12B-1 fee, which the manager uses to advertise,
which is another 0.23 percent and is assessed every year while another fee
of 1 percent is charged should you desire to "exit." The other fund charges
no front- or back-end load, an annual management fee of 0.53 percent, and
has no 12B-1 fee. Two funds with similar results, but their charges are quite
different.

The issue of fees and charges is illustrated by a table in that same issue
of the *Advisor* (see Table 10.4).

Morningstar terms this the "behavior gap," which they attribute to
investors' buying high and selling low. Perhaps, but recommending funds
with 5 percent loads might be a factor as well.

Our last concern regarding mutual funds in general (although there are
notable exceptions) is indifference toward the greater financial community.
In the debate regarding high-frequency trading and other broad issues,
mutual funds have been, for the most part, notably absent. Their general
attitude toward commissions has to be a contributing factor in the performance equation.

TABLE 10.4 Five-Year Annualized Returns

	Total Return	Investor Return
U.S. Stock Funds	1.55%	0.75%

In our experience, the most memorable example of this mentality was a large Boston fund that was featured in a *Wall Street Journal* article on October 12, 2004, for its "penny pinching." The firm waxed pride in its efforts to cut costs, lower commissions, and foster change.

Recently *Barron's* interviewed the manager of the Villere Balanced Fund (VILLX), a New Orleans-based fund which, the paper reports, has gained 8.8 percent annually (since 1999) vs. the S&P's 3.4 percent. There are no sales charges and the annual expense is 0.99 percent. We have never heard of this fund, have no relationship and no interest whatsoever. But the fund fits the template of what we would be looking for if we were looking for a mutual fund for ourselves.

Investors should be especially leery of blogs and irregular research, as they are unregulated and generally worthless.

On May 3, 2010, we were offered an opportunity to buy Big Bear Mining (BGBR) stock and our $5,000 investment could be "sold for $27,000 in 60 days." Had we bought the stock at $1.22 that day we would have lost 81 percent in 60 days. In May 2013, the stock was trading at $0.009 per share (see Figure 10.8).

The next May we were given another opportunity in Lithium Exploration:

. . . estimates as much as 1,000% gains for investors who lead up . . .

This stock was $5 then-but not now (see Figure 10.9).

The producer of the flier was paid $3,296,800, while the distributor received a payment of $50,000.

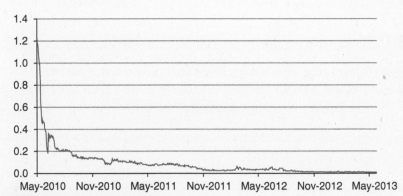

FIGURE 10.8 Big Bear Mining

Source: Birinyi Associates, Inc., Bloomberg.

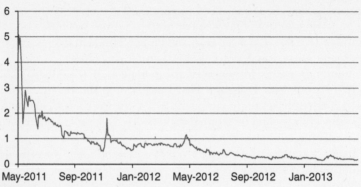

FIGURE 10.9 Lithium Exploration

Or consider the ads that promise to "Double Your Money 20 Times in the Next 20 Days." Thus, your $1,000 investment would become $1,048,576,000 — well over a billion dollars — in just one month.

We Googled one individual to see if we could get some insight into his remarkable gains and the first three results were:

1. (Individual)
2. (Individual) scam
3. (Individual) complaints

If you disagree and think it is still worth considering these "opportunities," you might also be interested in someone we know in Nigeria. . . .

NOTES

1. Carol Loomis, "The Jones Nobody Keeps Up With," *Fortune*, April 1966.
2. James Bennett, and Richard Sias, "Can Money Flows Predict Stock Returns?" *Financial Analysts Journal* (November/December 2001).

CHAPTER 11

Have It Your Way

If you want to see a rainbow, you have to stand a little rain.

—Jimmy Durante

O ur comments regarding mutual funds and advisors might or might not surprise you, depending on your own experience. Perhaps you wondered why the market was hitting new highs while your portfolio seemed to move in only two directions: neutral and reverse. Despite a lack of real progress, somehow your fund holdings still created taxable income.

You told your advisor that you wanted growth and were not adverse to risk and you ended up with GE? He also did you a big "favor" and got you into the latest IPO at, as he reminded you, no commission, although you read that his firm made $2 million on the deal.

The financial advisor you visited was impressive, but somewhat less than forthcoming on compensation (his) and potential results (yours). He wasn't too clear on the questions you asked regarding specific tax situations and, seemed to be more of a sales type than an accountant or lawyer.

Now that you are about to retire, even after a daily walk and three visits to the gym each week, you will have time to go it alone. Those "experts" or pros on TV disagree almost as much as the guys in Washington, and it seems to you that one was a buyer last week, but this week is a seller. Maybe it was the other way around. Or perhaps you just want to take more control of this facet of your life so that one day you can retire. Given that the average IRA at the end of 2011 was $87,668, according to the Employee Benefit Research Institute (EBRI), it suggests that life after 65 for far too many people will not play out as planned.

You recall that you did pretty well in the economics courses you took 20 years ago (okay, it was more like 35) and how hard could it be to buy

Exxon or Intel? With discount brokers advertising their bare bones commissions and costs, it is not a free lunch but they claim to provide services and assistance.

On the other hand, the experts and newspaper supplements all suggest financial planning where you can put your retirement and other funds on cruise control and travel, garden, and play with the grandchildren. Our simple response is: Don't.

Yes, indexing is seductive and a favored tactic of many "pros" and other commentators. But individuals too often put their financial awareness on the back burner. No one is watching or concerned about those funds, no one is monitoring developments, or considering changes. Too often that approach, in our experience, leads to what we might term *financial negligence*. Having made a decision, investors do not revisit, review, or reconsider even as market and personal circumstances change. Furthermore, too often no one is monitoring developments or suggesting a change or reallocation. Like all financial decisions, even this should be tracked and revisited on a regular basis. Be aware, however, that given the paucity of fees, most brokers and advisors aren't likely to spend too much of their time on your portfolio.

It is, therefore, somewhat curious that one of the most important elements of one's life (especially for those who are retired) is then put on autopilot. And there are target-dated funds, which become more conservative—allocating more to bonds—as you grow older. In the markets following the financial crisis when interest rates were at unprecedented lows, this led to a large portion of retired individuals' assets being allocated to low-yielding, fixed-income investments (more money, earning less and less). It might not be a "perfect storm", but it certainly was not astute. Yet some portion of the $550 billion in those funds was doing just that.

Our concern with these investments and many other ideas is that they are historically sound, but history changes. Markets change, they evolve, sometimes they dissolve because, as you may recall, backtesting and historical precedents *always* work.

You might have invested in one of them five years ago. Since then, one component of target funds, bonds, have done well (see Figure 11.1).

Over that period, two of the largest funds were up just over 4 percent and 5 percent, respectively, while the S&P returned 6 percent. So for all your huffing and puffing, even given some portion of the dismal returns of late 2008/early 2009, you have not fared well.

You might also be a new hire at a brokerage or financial firm who, having taken a slow ride through academia, is interested in a faster track so you won't have to share a bathroom with three other guys.

FIGURE 11.1 iShares IBOXX Investment Grade Corporate Bond

Source: Birinyi Associates, Inc., Bloomberg.

So for the investor who wants to take more control or do better either in their portfolio or their career, with what and where might we begin? First of two caveats:

1. Making money is hard work.

We are continually surprised by the public's attitude that Wall Streeters lead charmed lives, abbreviated hours, and four-day weeks from Memorial Day through Labor Day. True, we are unlikely to strain our lower backs by lifting heavy objects and bankers and traders seldom suffer from exposure. But every banker or trader has taken the red eye from LA, a 22-seater to Charleston, not to mention a charming Holiday Inn or its equivalent in Wheeling.

For one thing, the market is open every day and every day, there is news to digest. There are reports to read or, in some cases, to write. Decisions have to be made and at least one stock or five will put you on the spot. Dow Chemical is reporting earnings tomorrow; should we buy more or sell, and if not, why not? Credit Suisse just downgraded United Airlines, should we take advantage of the lower price to add or should we agree with them and sell our shares? Macy's is up on a rumor that it might be taken over.

The almost instant feedback of the market is a unique characteristic of the business. Real estate developers will not likely get their results for several years, the buyer for a department store will have to wait months to see if blue really is this year's color. On Wall Street, many a lunch has been soured by a decision made at 11 A.M., which also negates whatever positive trade one made the day before.

2. Have a realistic performance goal.

If you are going to go it alone, have a realistic objective, which should not be the market itself. As discussed earlier, outperforming the market is neither rational nor easily achievable. Okay, there will be a year where you might get lucky or a bad market where you have a good stock. Yes, we know that every year someone passes away and is found to have left a shoebox with $800,000 in gains, but the two million individuals who leave $80 are never heard from.

Our professional target is usually about 10 percent below the S&P, which reflects that we will usually have between 5 and 10 percent cash for "sprained-wrists trading" (see Chapter 16). For tax-advantaged accounts (IRA, ROTH IRA, 401k, pension, etc.) where we will regularly hold more cash and be more likely to take short-term profits, our return objective is 5 to 10 percent a year. There will be years, such as 2009, where the market was +23 percent, we would hope to do somewhat better than our goal but given the nature of tax-advantaged accounts, the issue is preservation so our goals are more conservative.

We will again make the point that in tax-preferenced accounts you cannot deduct losses and you are limited in your ability to replenish the account. The implication, therefore, is that the strategies and tactics should differ. Our firm has clients who have their IRAs and their taxable accounts with very little overlap. The IRA may contain utilities and stocks, which have limited growth prospects but are slow, steady, and consistent, such as foods. The other account knows the Amazons and technology names.

(Although to illustrate the perversity of the market, things sometime go awry. In early 2013, we bought Walgreens for tortoise-like characteristics only to watch it perform like a rabbit and gain almost 40 percent in the first five months of the year. As a result, for the first time in our experience, some tax-preferenced accounts are outperforming the taxable accounts in a rising market!)

Having decided to be your own money manager, the first step must be one of education and we have provided a reading list for that purpose. Your education should continue by developing a disciplined, rigorous process. On a daily or weekly basis you should read the same periodicals whether it be the *New York Times, Wall Street Journal, Barron's,* or *Time;* investing, like exercise, cannot be incidental to your other activities.

Furthermore, you must read as an investor or student. At Salomon, one of my more interesting responsibilities was to take the new employees to dinner in small groups. These were off-the-record opportunities for them to ask some pointed questions and for me to share some stories and experiences.

It was also a chance for me to try new restaurants and update old ones. As a result, I read restaurant reviews with a totally different perspective than previously. No longer was I reading just a review, but instead I was now looking for a place to eat. Was there a dish that I might try, how crowded and noisy was it likely to be (given six to eight people, an important factor if one wanted to converse), were reservations required, and so forth.

After a season or two, I became the firm's walking Zagat, especially on the better establishments. Salomon, after all, was paying for those dinners.

Reading the various publications and digesting news should be different than reading the sports page or op-ed section. In our case, we not only ask "what is wrong with this picture" but also what is missing, if there is something obvious that is not included. More specifically, since we keep track of individuals' and firms' outlooks, we know where they stand and look for changes in their views and arguments.

Our approach to discipline and a different perspective was once illustrated by an individual who regularly watched *Wall Street Week*. Over the years hundreds of people have told us how much they missed, enjoyed, and "wouldn't miss a week" of that program. While that was fine, what was really heartening were the comments, letters, and gifts (a case of champagne, for example) from individuals who not only watched but *listened* and bought our recommendations.

Or the individual who watched Friday night, but did so again Saturday morning with pen in hand so he could write whatever ideas or names he might have missed the previous evening.

This approach should lead you to develop your own anecdotal database where you save the significant stories (in a normal week there might be only two or three) and maybe even an investing diary of what you did or did not do. One of the most helpful elements in my investing approach is the physical. First, I process, not just read, the various reports and journals. Then I copy them for future reference.

Years ago, we realized the failings and shortcomings of data because we physically copied them into ledger books (known today as *spreadsheets*). Even today, I weekly transcribe my personal accounts from my brokerage statements to a personal spreadsheet. This copying can be done electronically and automatically, but doing it by hand makes it more meaningful.

This is also why I read newspapers. Online journalism does not reflect the size of the headline or the position of the story.

It reminds me too of the gentleman who read some of my critical comments on technical analysis. He had been successful in his own technical efforts and described them. Every day he noted the prices of his key stocks and used blue for up days, red for down, circled the stock if it had outperformed, and so on.

I would argue that the very act and discipline, more than technical analysis itself, is what made him successful. If you use blue for the market three days in a row and red for a stock, it should be pretty clear that your stock is underperforming.

The discipline, the attention, the process, all may seem a bit too much. But we are, in the last analysis, talking about money, which is the common denominator for most of your other activities. While you can't keep up with the Joneses of Wall Street, be aware that they are putting in 60 hours a week playing in the same sandpit. Most people work very hard for their money; why not let your money work for you?

So, as Steve Jobs used to say, "There's one more thing."

At the risk of insulting our new friends, we might simplify and condense our view into one word: Think. We are regularly surprised and disappointed that educated, professional individuals seem mesmerized by the world of finance. Individuals who would require a second opinion on a medical procedure subscribe to an investment idea because the speaker is logical, educated, and well-known.

WEASEL WORDS: NOT OUR CHOICE, BUT KNOW AND RECOGNIZE

We have already suggested that comments such as "we expect a rally to mid-year and then a correction before the next leg up" should be dismissed, not only because they regularly fail but also because there is no supporting evidence. And we too often read technical conclusions such as:

The market is likely to have a positive bias into early or mid-July. Thereafter probabilities favor either a test or more correction.

Perhaps it is oversimplification but we translate this as "the market will probably go up until July and then try to go higher or go lower." But if we are going to go up, where does the "more correction" fit in?

Another chartist once wrote:

*. . . it will be important to look for the standard-type **negative** internal divergences that can occur on rally efforts, the flip side is to be looking for any **positive** divergences on the downside probes.*

Unfortunately, we weren't told what to do if we encountered any negative divergences if the market rallied nor were we told what they might be.

One last example:

It will be crucial for the major benchmarks to break through their respective long-term trend measures on a closing basis. If they fail to do so, it will confirm US equities have entered another cyclical downtrend.

For those not familiar with Wall Street speak, this could be translated as, "if the markets don't go up, they will go down."

In 1989, there was a conference on technical analysis in Chicago and one speaker talked about the importance of sentiment. He suggested that investors should determine the prevailing conventional wisdom. Then one should decide if the conventional wisdom was right. If it was indeed right, then one should go with the crowd. But if the crowd was wrong, one should take a contrary view. We are among the minority who did not scribble these pearls on our napkin or notepad.

Markets, at the end of the day, go up or they go down. As someone once said, it is better to be approximately right than precisely wrong and, as traders have often said, "It ain't brain surgery."

When reviewing market letters, strategy, and commentary, we have also found it most helpful to avoid what someone else termed "weasel words." These are regularly heard comments with little or no meaning including the often heard *could* as in the market *could make a new high*. This phrase also suggests, with almost as much conviction, that it could not.

Other indifferent or meaningless words (we dislike the previous term) include *average, typical, usual, normal, should, might*, and so forth. There is, as we have hopefully shown, no *average* or *typical* market, and while the market *might* rally, it also might not. By thinking, being a somewhat demanding consumer, and requiring facts, investors will avoid many of the pitfalls and blind alleys that they encounter on a regular basis. In addition, they will find an unexpected reward: time.

In the post-2008 financial crisis environment, concerns continue regarding black swans or totally unexpected and unpredictable events. Articles, editorials, and predications regarding potential black swans were regular features especially on blogs. Given that they are what they are, we find little reward in determining the impact of a totally unexpected event.

CHAPTER 12

The Market: Yesterday, Today, and Tomorrow?

*Somehow if you are called Retail, it means there's some-
one else in the game called Wholesale, and he's . . . gotcha.*
Thomas Tom Wolfe, *Eunuchs of the Universe*

S ome time ago, when cars had fins and *Life* was a magazine, buying
stocks was similar to buying a shirt or groceries. You decided what
you wanted, placed an order, and wrote a check, or more typically,
paid cash. There were a few differences, however: one being that your
choice was usually limited to NYSE issues and the other being that you
usually paid in advance, with money already at your broker. There were
other, more subtle, differences; one being that at Brooks Brothers, the second shirt cost as much as the first one, and so did the fifth.

On Wall Street, prices changed and your second or third hundred
shares might be priced higher (never lower) depending on how aggressive
you and other buyers might be. At your local liquor store, a case of wine
probably entitles you to a discount; on Wall Street a large amount might
actually be priced at a premium.

Unlike your local deli or gas station, the individual who was actually
filling your order had a vested interest in the transaction. Your grandfather's
market was considerably slower paced and we did not trade 100 million
shares until 1982. In those days, orders were handwritten by a clerk on
the floor of the Exchange. The firm's representative, or floor broker, would
then walk over to the "post" where the stock was located, just as we know
that cereals are in aisle four at the local supermarket.

Then another broker (the "specialist" in the stock) would advise as to the
present interest from both buyers and sellers. Assume, for example, an order
to buy 200 shares of GE. Your broker would ask the specialist for a market
that in an active stock like GE might be 22½ to 22¾, 500 up. In effect, you

163

could buy up to 500 shares immediately at $22.75 or sell 500 shares immediately and receive $22.50. If indeed it was a market order to buy (which meant buy at the prevailing price) you were "done" or "filled" at $22.75.

If, however, you wanted to pay only $22.50, your floor broker could hang around and wait for a seller and try to negotiate. It was more likely that he gave the order to the specialist. This order might be added to the previous interest at $22.50 so now the market became $22.50 to $22.75 but 1,000 shares was sought with 500 being for sale.

The specialist now has a vested interest in the order because acting as the broker's agent, he will collect a commission known as *brokerage*. In addition, and differing from your grocery clerk, he also had the responsibility for making an orderly market. That is to say that if there are no sellers, he had to become one. He offered stock either out of his inventory or created stock (by shorting). In an active stock like GE that was seldom an issue, but in times of market turmoil, as we witnessed during the Crash in 1987 or bad news in GE, it could be expensive if the specialist was the buyer of last resort.

If it was not a monopoly, it was a near-monopoly, and critics argued that the specialist had an unfair advantage (which he did). But because of the ticker tape all transactions were transparent and subject to scrutiny. Furthermore, with regard to sizeable transactions, trading desks at both brokerage firms and institutions limited any shenanigans or misdeeds that might have occurred. Nevertheless, specialists prospered and none of their children—to our knowledge—ever required financial aid.[1]

For the individual, this was of little interest. In the overwhelming majority of instances, he was able to buy or sell his stock at a reasonable price.

COMMISSIONS GO DOWN; ERISA CHANGES THE RULES

The early 1960s were to see a series of changes, which continued to take place over the next several decades revolutionizing the industry. As Adam Smith wrote in the *The Money Game:*[2]

> There were two legal changes that were to change the theater or stadium in which the game was played. When the brokers first met a kind of club was formed with the members agreeing on the fees or commissions to be charged. That fee was the same for each share whether you were buying one share or a million.
>
> But by the early seventies, the fixed-fee system had been broken. The institutions bargained for—and got—reduced rates. Diminished

commissions meant that the river of income for research and for all those brokers calling customers with tips dried up.

The other legal action [ERISA] was more complex. It involved pensions . . . and the pension money grew until it was the biggest factor in the marketplace. Then came a law which allowed investors to sue their managers for improper investments. Stocks go down; you ask the court for the manager's car and his house.

The latter reformed and revolutionized the investment business. Banks that had formerly managed the pension plan as part of their commercial banking relationships initially prospered. JP Morgan became the 900-pound gorilla and the NYC banks dominated the business. But banks were still banks, as reflected in the fact that the senior trader at one NYC bank had a title reflecting both his paycheck and lack of stature in the organization: assistant cashier.

As a result, the more aggressive portfolio managers left the bank trust departments with their trust department trappings and set up businesses specializing in managing pension plans. The new firms or boutiques including Alliance Capital, Jennison Associates, Batterymarch, and others flourished.

They pointed to the well publicized remarks of McGeorge Bundy, the head of the Ford Foundation, as justification for more performance and growth-oriented portfolios:

It is far from clear that trustees have reason to be proud of their performance in making money for their colleges. We recognize the risks of unconventional investing, but the true test of performance in the handling of money is the record of achievement, not the opinion of the respectable. We have the preliminary impression that over the long run caution has cost our colleges and universities much more than imprudence or excessive risk taking.

While Mr. Bundy was specifically commenting on college endowments, his remarks were interpreted as critical of institutions in general. Gerald Tsai did not pioneer performance, but the industry noted that his fund, which had hoped to raise $25 million, underestimated that by a factor of ten on day one and was to reach $400 million in its first year. Fiduciaries saw that the trustees of the University of Rochester heeded Bundy's comments and bought out local companies such as Xerox and Bausch and Lomb, becoming the fifth richest school in the country.

Ironically, years later two college endowments, those run by Yale's David Swensen and Harvard's Jack Meyer, became the new model for large funds by encompassing a broader range of assets far beyond the traditional debt/equity model.

Measured growth became the order of the day. Unlike the go-go 60s, the goal was not to maximize returns but to meet, and beat, actuarial assumptions on a regular basis. Risk was not to be avoided but, if possible, contained. After all, the new law made the managers personally responsible.

Adam Smith's book, *The Money Game*, shed light on an industry that was generally unknown to the world at large and illuminated the changes in that industry, and showed that in addition to greed and avarice, making money was fun.

On the sell-side (the brokers) a new firm called Donaldson, Lufkin, and Jenrette (DLJ) introduced the idea of detailed, almost scholarly, research for this new market. No longer was a one-page tear sheet from S&P adequate to understand the business of Dow Chemical or Texaco. Wall Street generally welcomed the transition to a more sophisticated and professional market. As DLJ had done, research departments were upgraded, and institutional departments were established and staffed by salesmen and specialized traders.

Unlike their retail brethren, the institutional brokers were not forced to solicit business and persuade Aunt Mae to buy stocks. After all, their customers were investing professionals whose business it was to buy and sell. And they wanted to buy what was being sold. As a result, the salesman at DLJ might have from 10 to 20 accounts with whom he spoke daily. Most of his calls were to the portfolio manager, or managers, as well as the director of research and, if needed, the individual analysts.

While he was termed a "salesman," his role was more like an account executive for an advertising agency. He was DLJ's or Goldman's point man, not only for passing along research from his research department but he was also responsible for client relations. This may have also included Broadway tickets for the Chicago account that was visiting New York City and helping someone's son get into Columbia or Georgetown.

The institutional trader, too, had a limited number of accounts depending on the amount of business and the size of the institution. Usually connected via a direct line to the institution's trading desk, he would make his clients aware of what the firm was buying and selling in the hopes of finding other buyers and sellers.

No longer were orders sent to the floor of the Exchange willy-nilly. An order to buy 5,000 shares of Polaroid or Kresge could not, after all, be treated with the same approach as 100 shares. A strategy had to be undertaken, as a market accustomed to buying or selling several hundred shares at a time could not easily dispose of thousands of shares in an orderly fashion.

It often meant that trades were partially executed "upstairs" on the trading desk itself. A significant order might be received from Dreyfus

or Harris Bank. Rather than disturb the Exchange floor and make the
world aware that Merrill was a "size" buyer, traders would call institutions to solicit interest in both amount and price. A sale of 50,000 shares
of Atlantic Richfield at $120, for example, was not likely to be easily
accomplished. A bank in St. Louis might take 5,000 shares. A mutual
fund in Minneapolis might have an interest, but not at $120, which was
important to note for the next time. At the same time, someone in Boston could use 10,000 shares, but only if the entire 50,000 shares are
traded. Otherwise, some overhang in the market might depress prices
later that day.

In many cases, the broker could not place all the shares, in which
case he might use his own capital to buy the balance, a term known as
positioning. After the trade, he would be left with a *long* position that he
could hopefully sell with a minimum loss over the next day or two.

The increased institutionalization of the market was initially a boon for
Wall Street. Trading larger amounts of stock was more efficient and more
profitable even as commissions were negotiated.

Even then, there was a lot of slippage or overflow. A significant institution, such as Bankers Trust in New York or a Boston fund, might generate
$10 million in commissions in any given year. The commission or, as they
were often called, "soft dollars," would be credited to pay for research,
trading prowess, and services. Services could include the tracking system
provided by AG Becker, where institutions could review (anonymously)
their results against their peers.

In most cases, commissions more than covered those costs. The traders at the banks and funds might reward their friends at First Boston or
Prudential by giving them business above and beyond what was generally
agreed upon. While it was never clearly articulated and written, a fund
might allocate $100,000 to a firm for its research and services. But they
might actually give the firm $150,000, if the recommendations were espe-
cially valuable in a given year or because the traders at the respective firms
were especially compatible and were both Red Sox fans.

The institution might also use its commission for execution services.
Firms such as Shields, Goldman, and Salomon were known not only for
their distribution capabilities when underwriting securities, but also for
their capital and appetite for risk. Thus a fund that had a particularly sour
position might ask one of them to sell the stock, which entailed positioning the stock. Both sides accepted that the broker would probably lose
money, which would be somewhat offset by subsequent less treacherous,
trades.

As time went on, the public became more conscious of financial markets both by their direct involvement via mutual funds, IRAs, 401(k)s,
NOW accounts, and by increased media exposure. Although *Wall Street*

Week went on the air in 1970, not until 1982 did the market become an integral element in the public's consciousness. We were introduced to *FNN* and eventually *CNBC*, *Fox Business*, and *Bloomberg TV*. The *Wall Street Journal* also began writing about the stock market on a regular basis. Previously, with only rare exceptions, their coverage had been limited to two daily columns: "Abreast of the Market" and "Heard on the Street."

At the same time, financial markets were expanding with new instruments such as put and call options in 1976 and later index funds, stock index futures, and an assortment of approaches to quickly separate investors from their savings.

For an investor today, the more critical changes were structural. Institutions railed at the specialist system as it exposed their orders. They lobbied for electronic trading, the ability to trade before and after the usual trading session. The buy-side lobbied for lower commissions and tighter spreads. Commercial banks wondered why they too could not underwrite securities and share in the expanding financial pie. In only a few years, Wall Street was no longer a location on lower Manhattan but, like Hollywood, a state of mind (or mindlessness).

The overhaul of the financial markets in the decade was, in the final analysis, detrimental to the individual investor but beneficial to the professional. The introduction of trading in decimals, after-hours trading, fragmenting the markets, new unvetted vehicles, and the general deregulation of the markets, despite the comments of officials, was not a boon to the man on the street. It actually placed him at a greater and greater disadvantage.

Regulators and legislators applauded their own efforts saying that the individual now had access to more and better information, was in a better position to make investment decisions, and that the market had become more transparent.

We took a different view. Marshall McLuhan, for one, had written extensively regarding the impact of structural change and its unintended consequences.[3] As we have often suggested, if one squeezes one end of the sausage, something happens at the other.

Today's investors should recognize that indeed they have more tools, more resources, and more opportunity. Unfortunately, the field is even more skewed *against* the individual.

We detailed our concerns with the structural changes of the 1990s in a variety of publications.[4] Our first concern was that many of the arguments in favor of reform were tepid. The chairman of the SEC argued that our practice of pricing eighths was in contrast to the global convention of decimals.[5] This, he reasoned, put our markets at a competitive disadvantage. We question how many investors were buying BMW, rather than GM, because they understood $0.10 and not $0.125.

LONDON'S BIG BANG: A FAILURE THERE, A GOOD IDEA HERE?

A more important issue was that regulators apparently ignored, or were unaware of, experiences in other markets such as London. In 1986, the London Stock Exchange (LSE) underwent a total overhaul of its trading process in a series of reforms, known as Big Bang:

> *Fixed minimum commission rates were abolished. Mandated separation of brokering and dealing functions also. . . . British banks were allowed, for the first time, to become full-service financial institutions, restrictions on foreign ownership ended . . . market-makers spent millions on computer systems.*

Disaster might be too strong a term, but it surely did not go as intended. For one, the Exchange trading floor was remodeled and updated at considerable cost. On day one of Big Bang, Merrill Lynch closed their floor operations and within six months the floor, where there had been trading since 1801, closed.

In early 1989, it was reported that British brokerage firms had lost $2 billion since Big Bang as well as thousands of jobs. In addition there were any number of incidents of irregularities and failings, of which the most extraordinary might have been the unilateral early closing of the market on December 31, 1997.

> *Trading in shares was cut short yesterday as the LSE took unprecedented action to prevent manipulation of the market by rogue dealers.*
>
> *The exchange halted trading 20 minutes ahead of schedule fearing that thin share volumes would leave the market open to manipulation by City traders hoping to take advantage of weakness already inherent in the new order driven trading system. . . .*
>
> *For the first time a panel of academics was called in to review the closing prices of all FTSE 100 shares in the light of the unusual trading conditions. The panel found it necessary to alter the prices of 11 constituents of the index, making some significant changes.*[6]

In 1990, an internal policy group, the Elwes Committee, suggested ". . . reverting to the old rules, restoring the obligations of market-makers for firm bids and offers, dealing with all customers at displayed quotes and reporting large trades' prices immediately." Or as someone dryly commented, "they wanted to undue everything Big Bang has done."

Despite the obvious and available issues of trading in London, we saw no mention of their experience in the various and abundant documents proposing similar changes in the United States.

We argued that the decision to implement changes, such as decimal trading, in New York was based on spurious or even nonexistent research. Since most stocks were quoted with an eighth of a point spread, it was charged that market makers were making excess profits at the expense of individuals. Thus if GM was quoted 32 ½ to 32 ⅝, market makers bought low and sold high, in this case making an eighth of a point. Repeating this 20 or 100 times a day on several hundred shares was taking advantage of the public.

In reality, that was not the case and the specialist could do so only if there were no public orders at that price. One "study" concluded that investors might save as much as $10 billion in trading costs.[7] Upon further review, the estimate was lowered to $1 billion. Other estimates were equally artificial. *Investors Business Daily* wrote that market makers made money on *every* trade by buying at the bid and selling at the ask. We knew that these and other comments were wrong.

Our computer programs that produced money flows analyzed every single trade in every single stock for a variety of reports, all of which were proprietary except money flows. We *knew* exactly what costs, spreads, volatility, and other characteristics were, for every stock.

Our daily 15-page report for October 3, 1984 (DJIA –8.50, –0.71 percent) showed that there were 1,785,200 trades of 100 shares, which equaled 0.7 percent of the day's volume. As shown, 57.6 percent were transacted with no change in price. Even the trades of 5,000 to 9,999 had well over 50 percent of the trades done at the last sale:

Shares	Volume (%)		
	Up	Down	Unchanged
< or = 100	22.1	29.1	57.6
200–400	22.4	21.5	56.0
500–900	23.8	21.7	54.4
1,000–4,900	24.7	19.9	55.2
5,000–9,900	27.6	17.9	54.3

Our greater concern was, and remains, the residual effect. Nowhere could we find any discussion of the impact of trading in decimals instead of fractions or of after-hours activity or fragmented markets.

The overwhelming consensus was that trading costs would decline, market makers would be squeezed, and customers would benefit. Like the Edsel, it looked good on paper until reality interfered.

First, one NYSE specialist firm was also a listed stock. LaBranche and Company went from $11 to over $50 from January 2000 to February 2001 at a time when the S&P fell 15 percent and the market was transitioning to decimals (see Figure 12.1).

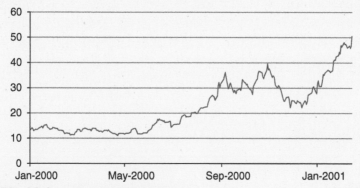

FIGURE 12.1 LaBranche and Company

Source: Birinyi Associates, Inc., Bloomberg.

Interestingly, specialists were actually making more money largely because they were increasing their shorting activities (see Figure 12.2 and 12.3).

Second, trading costs for some stocks actually went up, including Wal-Mart, which has always been considered a liquid stock. With the spread in Wal-Mart narrowing from ⅛ to ¹⁄₁₆, it suggests that some brokers who would not have paid up +⅛ to buy stock were willing to pay +¹⁄₁₆ and thus avoid paying brokerage to the specialist and at the same time get an immediate fill.

Another development, which had been under way for some time, was the deterioration of the broker/client relationship.

Electronic trading, narrower spreads, limits on research, and increasing demands from institutions greatly reduced the commission pool that was so critical to the Street. At the same time, brokers realized that trading for its own account (proprietary or prop trading) was considerably more profitable than working for commissions. They were now as low as two

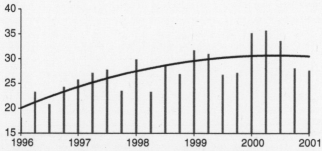

FIGURE 12.2 Specialist Quarterly Operating Margin (%)

Source: Birinyi Associates, Inc., NYSE.

FIGURE 12.3   Specialist Short Sales as a Percent of NYSE Volume
Source: Birinyi Associates, Inc., NYSE.

or three cents per share (and even lower). While firms might still give lip service to the concept of fiduciary responsibility and customer service, informed clients knew better, as illustrated by Inktomi.

On April 14, 2000, we entered an order to sell 1,000 shares of Inktomi at 10:27:49. Two hundred shares were done immediately at $105 at, or close to, the last sale.

We suspect that the other 800 shares were also executed at or around the same price. It is likely that the trader either sold 800 shares out of his inventory or shorted the same amount. We received a report that we sold our remaining 800 shares: $103.875 at 10:30:22 or two minutes later.

As shown in Figure 12.4, there was significant activity during those intervening minutes and in all probability the trader may have made almost $900 ($105 – $103.875 = $1.125 × 800). Actually, we were told he waited because he thought he could get a better price.

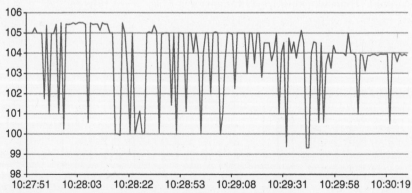

FIGURE 12.4   Inktomi 1,000 Share Sale: April 14, 2000
Source: Birinyi Associates, Inc., Bloomberg.

THE PUBLIC VERSUS "ALL OTHERS"

In one notable case, the head trader of Knight Securities actually detailed his activities on page one of the *Wall Street Journal*:

> *When Egghead.com Inc. released good news early one morning in December, before the Nasdaq Stock market opened, many online investors thought its stock would open higher. Kenneth Pasternak knew it would.*
>
> *Mr. Pasternak sat before a screen at Knight/Trimark Group Inc., a market maker whose job it is to execute trades. His screen showed that orders to buy Egghead exceeded orders to sell by 100,000 shares. Because it would be Knight's job to fill those orders, Mr. Pasternak quickly went to work buying up 50,000 shares in informal trading before the market opened. When it did open—with Egghead sharply higher—he sold them to online buyers, nailing a quick $15,000 profit.*[8]

It is surprising that the trader was so candid regarding his activities, and especially with the detail that he made $15,000 so quickly. To do so, he either collected 15 cents commission from both the buyer and the seller, or bought it for his own account and sold it to customers at a higher price, a practice usually termed "front running."

Later in the same article, Knight revealed more of their business practices:

> *Knight takes steps to limit its risk. For example it chooses whom to trade with. Mr. Pasternak welcomes the "uninformed" orders of thousands of individual investors because he is confident that, on average, Knight will be smarter than them . . . for investors who consistently make money, Knight may restrict or suspend the promise to automatically execute all trades at the best price.*[8]

Two years later there was another *Journal* article regarding Knight:

> *Regulators Are Investigating a Big Nasdaq Trader—Knight Trading Faces Allegations That It Violated Rules and Cost Investors Millions of Dollars*[9]

In 2004, it was announced that the firm ". . . agrees to pay $79 million to settle regulators' allegations firm put itself ahead of clients," while in December of the same year, two further articles provided even more "color" on their business model:

> *Client Comes First? On Wall Street, It Isn't Always So (Knight and other brokers' practices are detailed)*[10]

How Knight Clients Failed to Recognize Questionable Trades[11]

Equally disturbing was the fact that the investigation was a result of an executive filing an arbitration claim in 2002. Two years prior, on page one of the *WSJ*, it should have been abundantly clear to any regulator that Knight's activity was outside the lines.

In fact, Knight's failing was probably its blatancy as the Street increasingly (and understandably) focused on its own P&L. Unfortunately, the intrusion of electronics and the inability of regulators to keep pace have resulted in a marketplace increasingly more difficult for individuals and unsuspecting institutions to navigate. They have created new opportunities for, if not breaking the rules, certainly bending them, as in the case of mutual funds and after-hours trading.

In 2003, a number of mutual funds were charged with "late trading," where significant clients could place orders after the usual 4 p.m. close as if they had been placed at or before the close and take advantage of what could be market-moving news. A number of funds paid multimillion-dollar fines to settle without, as usual, admitting to any wrongdoing.

Individuals, for the most part, were only indirectly affected by these and other questionable practices, but increasingly, electronic trading, fragmented markets, decimalization, and other developments inexorably altered the investment process, as we learned in the case of Google.

On July 20, 2006, Google reported earnings (see Figure 12.5). As had been their practice, they reported just after the closing bell. The stock had closed at $387 but the results were disappointing and the stock traded lower. We entered an order to buy at $360 and watched as the stock traded below that price before recovering.

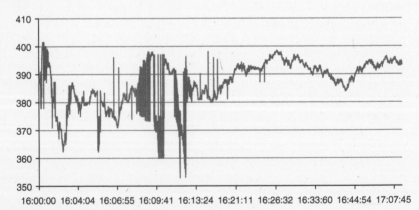

FIGURE 12.5   Google After Hours: July 20, 2006

Source: Birinyi Associates, Inc., Bloomberg.

Confident that we had a "winner," we were somewhat anxious as the execution was not forthcoming. We finally received the following, which showed a purchase price of $38! By that time, the stock had traded considerably back above $360 and the broker claimed electronic failure or glitch. The only recourse we had was the local tavern.

Date	7/20/2006
Ticker	GOOG
Security Name	GOOGLE INC-CL A
Order Side	BUY
Order Limit Price	360.1
Average Fill Price	38
Bang Style	NORMAL
Order Type	LIMIT
Pegging	Not Pegged
Order State	ACTIVE
Order Entry Time	16:03:13:028
TIF	DAY
Last Update Time	16:03:13:028
Tradebook Order ID#	13132702

Source: Birinyi Associates, Inc.

Given our trading background, skeptical nature, and experience, we monitor our activity more closely than most managers and regularly note traditional irregularities, never to our benefit.

Among the more significant developments was the new role of the exchanges. Where the NYSE and Nasdaq had been quasi-public institutions, they now became legitimate businesses and could no longer be assured of continuous order flow. As a result, brokerage firms monetized their business by selling their order flow to hedge funds and other traders. Citadel Capital, for one, invested in E-trade and obtained the right to "peek" at 20 percent of their orders.

If possible, brokers first matched buyers and sellers in their internal systems in order to reduce costs and we found that our personal orders on Exchange stocks were never traded at 11 Wall Street. Clearly, individuals were unaware of the nuts and bolts of their orders. The *CFA Institute Magazine* discussed the issue in the article ["An Ugly High Frequency Mess" (January/February 2013)]:

A retail brokerage charges its customers $7 per trade. If a customer placed a market order to buy 3,000 shares and the brokerage routed this order to the NYSE/ARCA, the take fee would *be $0.003 per share for a total cost of $9. The brokerage would lose money on this trade.*

Instead the brokerage routes the trade to an OTC market maker that actually pays for the order (usually $0.001 and $0.003).

In 2009, a number of articles detailed yet another change in the process, the high-frequency trader (HFT).[12] Using sophisticated algorithms and massive computer capabilities, they exploited minute inefficiencies and opportunities. By buying space from the exchanges and sharing the same facilities, they traded literally millions of shares daily for allegedly minute increments, invariably less than one cent. Incredibly efficient, they usually ended the trading day flat and therefore enjoyed minimal risk.

Interestingly, high-frequency trading was not as unique or new as some have suggested. Years earlier several articles were written regarding "noise traders":

> . . . *noise trading takes so many forms in the theoretical literature that it can be defined most accurately by what it is not: noise trading is not rationally based on the arrival of new information about asset values.*[13]
> . . . *noise trading might cause a permanent divergence between prices and fundamental values.*[14]
> . . . *noise traders can come to dominate the market.*[14]

Proponents of high-frequency trading, often researchers hired by trading firms, contend that their activity has increased liquidity and reduced trading costs.

Unfortunately, the issue of liquidity is difficult to segregate as it is closely related to news and market events. We plotted volume for one month in 2013 and found no effective relationship (see Figure 12.6). When volume dropped in the second week, there was a slight increase in volatility. As volume recovered, volatility rose but then dropped. Further analysis was also inconclusive. Thus, the question remains unanswered: Does increased trading (especially by high-frequency trades) increase or decrease volatility?

The other argument, that trading costs have been reduced, is not sustainable. In 2005, the Government Accountability Office (GAO) published *Securities Markets. Decimal Pricing Has Contributed to Lower Trading Costs and a More Challenging Trading Environment.* The study concluded that, in the 2000 to 2004 period, trading costs for NYSE issues had declined by 16 to 28 basis points (0.16 to 0.28 percent).

In addition to a number of shortcomings (including citing studies without providing any details as to source, author, or title), the analysis failed to

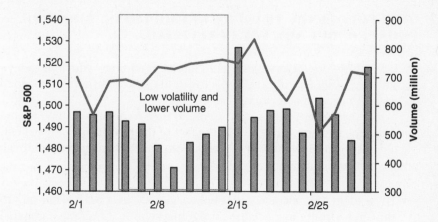

FIGURE 12.6 S&P 500: February 2013
Source: Birinyi Associates, Inc., Bloomberg.

note that while trading impact had indeed been reduced, the market during the same period was 50 percent lower.

Earlier in this book, we have referred to other studies regarding transaction costs. As a result of our analysis and experience, we consider ourselves more than amateur observers and have been critical of what most consider trading measurement systems. As another example, we might note a report that showed that over an 18-month period, Salomon Brothers regularly had excessive trading costs for this particular account:

	Salomon/Client Trading Costs		
	1985 First Half	1985 Second Half	1986 First Half
Benchmark Market Impact	−2.3¢	−7.3¢	−5.3¢
Client Market Impact	29.1	10.6	13.8

Source: Salomon Brothers.

The client's trades were compared to a database that collected transaction costs from an allegedly large number of clients. As shown, the client had reason to complain. The key issue, however, was not the client's trade but everyone else's. For all the other portfolios totaling many millions of shares, Salomon produced *negative* (savings) results. They would have us believe that the firm consistently, over an 18-month period, bought stocks below the last sale and sold them higher than existing prices.

While we prided ourselves on good executions, we were not *that* good.

HIGH-FREQUENCY TRADERS GET BILLIONS, BROKERS PROSPER, BUT ARE YOU BENEFITING?

We have, therefore, reservations as to any methodology, which in today's markets can truly capture the impact of trading. Furthermore, anecdotal analysis argues against customer benefits as well.

While the controversy as to the role of high-frequency trading is contentious, one element is not that is, the fact of their profits as they benefitted not only by trading but by payments from the Exchanges for their business, which is significant:

- HF traders ". . . earned $12.9 billion in 2009 and 2010 according to the Tabb Group, a specialist on the markets. . . ." And an estimated $1.25 billion in 2011.[15]
- Tradeworx, a HFT firm, had a good day (8/8/11) when the market lost 635 points, the next day when it was +430 "even better."[16]
- Tradebot, a HFT firm in Kansas City, Missouri said (in 2008) that it had not had a losing day in four years.[17]

Their greater source of revenue comes from payment for order flow whereby exchanges rebate some portion of their fee. One former SEC official has suggested that "in any other business this would be termed a kick back" and it is banned in Canada and limited in the UK. As shown in Table 12.1, the numbers are not just rounding errors.

TABLE 12.1 Exchanges' Liquidity Payments: 2010 through 2012 ($, B)

Liquidity Payments	2010	2011	2012
NYSE	$1.60	$1.51	$1.12
NASDAQ	$1.31	$1.34	$1.10
BATS	$0.54	$0.57	—
HFT Profits	$1.09–$2.17	$0.99–$1.95	$0.81–$1.21
Days of Trading Gains*	2010	2011	2012
Goldman Sachs	227	198	236
Morgan Stanley	214	188	215
JP Morgan	239	225	245
BofA	226	216	246

*Based on 252 equity trading days.

Source: Rosenblatt Securities, SEC Filings.

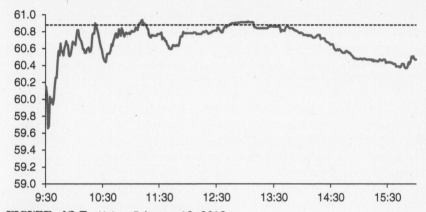

FIGURE 12.7 Heinz: February 13, 2013

Source: Birinyi Associates, Inc., Bloomberg.

It requires, we believe, some creativity to suggest that exchanges rebate billions of dollars and HFT firms make significant profits as do major brokerage firms and yet, after all this, the customer ultimately benefits?

Furthermore, we have too many examples of questionable executions, fiduciary irresponsibility, and other practices that were either a real cost, or an opportunity cost, for our portfolios.

Investors and especially individuals should recognize that their order flow is often subject to abuse:

- *The opening and non-opening execution.* The stock market's regular hours are 9:30 to 4:00. It is probably the norm to enter orders for 9:30 execution. On February 13, 2013, Heinz opened sharply lower but quickly recovered (see Figure 12.7).[18]

Why were these trades sold so aggressively and quickly? Many trading systems are programmed to coincide with the beginning of trading at 9:30 a.m. For a variety of reasons, trading at the preferred location, such as the NYSE, may not begin in a particular stock at that time. In the intervening 25 seconds, or minute, a trading firm may capture the sell and trade it at another exchange. In this case, the most probable scenario was that a HF trader bought the stock at the lower price, sold it when the Exchange opened, and booked a quick and handsome profit with minimal risk.

We cite this with some confidence. On Sept. 30, 2011, our order to buy Chipotle was executed at 9:30:01 at $311.02. Milliseconds later, it opened at $308.20 at the NYSE.

- *The trade-through exemptions.* The intent of the National Market System (NMS) is to provide the best available price to any and all investors. Thus, if one Exchange is offering AT&T at $33, while another is showing an offer of $32.90, buyers should be directed toward the lower price. In theory.

Exceptions to the rule are allowed via the trade-through exemption amendment to regulation NMS. One is volume. If, for example, a buyer in the AT&T case wants 10,000 shares, which are available at $33 at one exchange while the $32.90 offering is only for 100 shares, the trader can bypass the better price.

Unfortunately, the exemptions provide an abundance of opportunities. In the period of February 2012 through August of the same year, we noted that over half the trades in Priceline claimed some sort of exemption from the best available price (see Figure 12.8).

In November 2012, we were bidding $128,100 for one share of Berkshire Hathaway. The stock traded at $128,000.20 and the trader apparently claimed the volume exemption because two shares traded. His buyer paid $99.80 more than he should have and we lost the opportunity to make some immediate profit as the stock traded higher that morning.

- *Broken trades are still costly.* Clearly errant trades are increasingly flagged and noted. But the remedy is seldom satisfying. In the next case, Garmin spiked from $41.00 to $47.50 (see Figure 12.9).

While "NASDAQ Marketwatch is investigating potentially erroneous transactions . . ." in the stock, they canceled all trades above $42.76. Why at that price, why not $42 or even $41? Our view was that the 23,843 shares

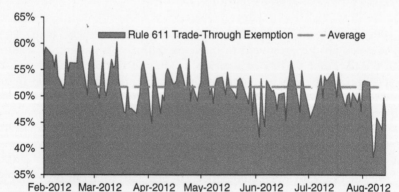

FIGURE 12.8 Priceline Trade-Through Exemptions
Source: Birinyi Associates, Inc., Bloomberg.

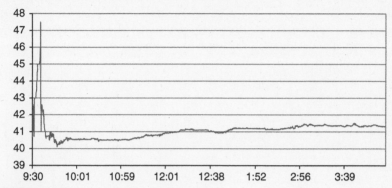

FIGURE 12.9 Garmin: December 27, 2012

Source: Birinyi Associates, Inc., Bloomberg.

between $40.71 and $42.76 should have been cancelled as well. They were not, and investors lost $18,571.

- *Not all trades are "broken"* as in the case of Dollar Tree on August 16, 2012 (see Figure 12.10). The company lowered guidance and, as expected, traded lower. But $10?

At 9:30:03 for one second, 73,000 shares traded with a spread as wide as $4 or 400 basis points (see Figure 12.11). We submit that the abrupt decline and recovery of the stock reflects a trading failure, not fundamental overreaction or corrections.

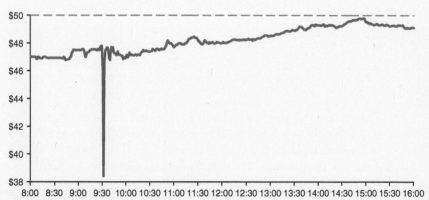

FIGURE 12.10 Dollar Tree: August 16, 2012

Source: Birinyi Associates, Inc., Bloomberg.

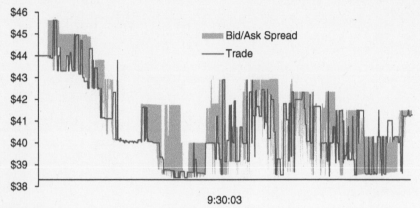

FIGURE 12.11 Dollar Tree: August 16, 2012 at 9:30:03
Source: Birinyi Associates, Inc., Bloomberg.

- *NVR is almost a case study.* This is a home builder/mortgage banker that in times past would have been called a stock that "trades by appointment." Given its high price (over $1,000) and light volume, it is prone to wide swings and even wider spreads.

We occasionally trade the stock, and on March 26, 2013, it closed at $1,068.48 and opened at $1,069 the next morning. The next 100-share trade was $1,035.32 and then 100 shares one minute later at $1,054.01 and so on:

Date	Time	Size*	Price	$ Change
3/26	16:06:58	6.63	1,068.48	2.48
3/27	9:30:26	1.54	1,069.00	0.52
3/27	9:42:18	1	1,035.32	−27.18
3/27	9:43:25	1	1,054.01	$18.69

*Volume Scaled by 100
Source: Bloomberg.

That afternoon the stock was up to $1,079, and we were offering 100 shares at $1,085 only to see 100 shares trade at $1,100 (as shown in Figure 12.12). Five minutes before the close it was back to $1,082, only to trade at $1,057.15 right at the close-except that the official close was 1,077.55!

We, however, bought 100 shares at $1,057.15 as evidenced by our report:

15:59:55 Fill has Occurred 80 shares at 1,057.15
    BOT 80 at 1057.15 from ARCX

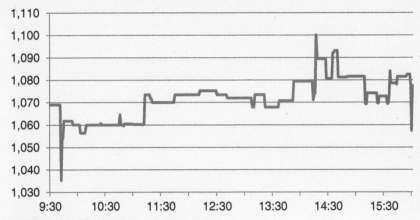

FIGURE 12.12 NVR: March 27, 2013

Source: Birinyi Associates, Inc., Bloomberg.

> 15:59:56 Filled 20 shares at 1,057.15
> BOT 20 at 1057.15 from ARCX

For reasons unknown, our order was filled by two odd-lot sales and since odd lots do not have to be reported, they were not. We first noticed this inconsistency in January when we bought 50 + 50 shares of NVR which, again, were never printed:

NVR Trade Execution: January 18, 2013

13:19:14 Fill has Occurred 50 shares at 982.00
    EDGA TRD: BOT 50 at 982.00
13:19:14 Filled 50 shares at 982.00
    EDGA TRD: 50 at 982.00

Time	Exc	Bid/Trade/Ask	Exc	Size
13:19:25	O	977.40/981.99	O	1×1
13:19:18	O	977.40/982.00	T	1×1
13:19:10	O	977.40/982.00	T	2×1
13:19:10	O	977.40/982.00	T	1×1
13:19:00	B	977.39/982.00	T	1×1

Even more extraordinary, the next day (March 28) we were again trading NVR and at the close bought stock at $1,065.35 while shorting the stock at $1,088.80.

> 15:59:57:578 BOT 41 at 1065.35 from BATS
> 15:59:59:002 SOLD (SS) 1 at 1088.80 to BATS
> 15:59:59:341 SOLD (SS) 2 at 1088.80 to BATS

It will be argued that NVR is a special case and not representative of the greater majority of names. Perhaps, but if we can isolate the extraordinary, why assume that it does not occur with the ordinary as well?

We have experienced too many rogue trades where someone has been abused. MasterCard on April 3, 2013 is one example (see Figure 12.13).

FIGURE 12.13 MasterCard: April 3, 2013
Source: Birinyi Associates, Inc., Bloomberg.

The stock was trading $532–533 and we placed an order to buy 500 shares at $530.50. A few minutes later, we bought the stock as someone for some reason needed to urgently sell 2,000 shares. While thankful for the trade, it illustrates that liquidity can be trumpeted by sloppy or mindless executions in the best of names.

We also benefitted from someone's desire to sell Chipotle on April 29, 2013. As shown in Figure 12.14, the stock dropped like a stone and bounced

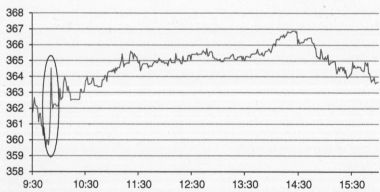

FIGURE 12.14 Chipotle Mexican Grill: April 29, 2013
Source: Birinyi Associates, Inc., Bloomberg.

like a ball. Among the sales during that window were 100 shares that went from $364.62 to $363.70 (–$0.92) while another 100 shares took the stock from $363.91 to $364.52 (+$0.61) (see Table 12.2).

We have long maintained that the execution process does not receive the emphasis and focus of investors. This continues and is becoming even more the case. Unfortunately, it is understood by the hedge fund, electronic crossing networks, and exchanges. Individuals should recognize that they

TABLE 12.2 Chipotle Egregious Trades: April 29, 2013

Time	Trade	Previous Trade	Volume	Tick Change (bps)	Exchange	Code
9:51:53	364.52	363.80	100	17	NASDAQ OMX BX	IS
9:51:29	363.23	362.84	100	16	FINRA ADF	T
9:51:11	362.36	361.80	200	15	FINRA ADF	T
9:50:10	360.72	360.17	100	13	FINRA ADF	T
9:51:34	363.68	363.23	100	12	BATS	R6,IS
9:50:21	361.16	360.80	100	10	EDGA	R6,IS
9:51:48	364.62	363.64	400	9	FINRA ADF	T
9:51:48	364.25	364.62	100	8	NASDAQ InterMarket	R6,IS
9:51:26	362.64	362.54	100	8	NASDAQ InterMarket	R6,IS
9:51:26	362.80	362.35	100	8	EDGA	
9:51:42	363.94	363.68	100	7	NASDAQ InterMarket	R6,IS
9:50:15	361.05	360.72	100	7	BATS	R6,IS
9:51:51	363.80	363.91	100	7	New York	R6,IS
9:51:48	363.94	363.70	100	6	National Stock Exchange	
9:51:10	361.80	361.59	200	6	FINRA ADF	T
9:50:25	361.37	361.16	100	6	FINRA ADF	T
9:51:28	362.65	362.80	100	–4	FINRA ADF	T
9:50:15	360.82	360.80	100	–6	NASDAQ InterMarket	R6,IS
9:51:26	362.40	362.80	100	–7	NASDAQ OMX BX	
9:51:26	362.54	362.52	100	–7	EDGX	R6,IS
9:51:48	363.64	363.58	100	–8	EDGX	
9:51:48	363.70	364.29	100	–25	NASDAQ OMX BX	

Source: Birinyi Associates, Inc., Bloomberg.

are "red meat" to the markets. They may hope that their brokers serve as a buffer, but that is not necessarily the reality.

Our concern goes beyond trading and the potential leakage, which can—in the short term—affect portfolios. In my occasional speeches, I have often suggested that stock trading and the NYC Marathon are two of the most democratic of all institutions. Unfortunately, as noted in the CFA *Institute Magazine* in October 2012, *Dark Pools, Internalization, and Equity Market Quality*:

> *Because retail investors are typically less well-informed than professional or institutional investors, retail order flow is very desirable to wholesale market makers.*

In addition to the philosophical argument, Themis Trading a firm that admittedly has taken a stance against HFT has written that the next systemic failure will be one of technology, a point with which we not only agree but have long suggested. We did so in August 2007 in our publication, *The Next Crash:*

> *There is an increase in systemic risk as regulators fiddle, brokers rush in, and traders prosper while the individual investor is the odd man out. For rent: 11 Wall Street—large rooms, high ceilings, abundant light.*

We did not forecast the financial crisis but did note that at some point, somewhere, the combination of technology, structural reforms, new instruments, and regulatory lag would be disruptive.

THE DEMISE OF THE JAPANESE MARKET WAS STRUCTURAL

New instruments, we contend, were the "smoking gun" in the Japanese stock market. Most observers would point to inflated real estate prices (on every visit to Tokyo I was reminded that the Palace's real estate value equaled all of California), but in addition to weakening fundamentals, fast money, and other factors, we would cite Japanese warrants as the needle that burst the bubble.

Those who experienced the era will remember that the Ministry of Finance (MOF) kept a tight grip on the proceedings. It was considered especially desirable to be granted a seat on the Tokyo Stock Exchange, a privilege that came only with the blessing of the MOF.

In early 1990, for reasons that it surely regrets, the MOF allowed warrants to be traded on the Nikkei. For the first time investors and traders

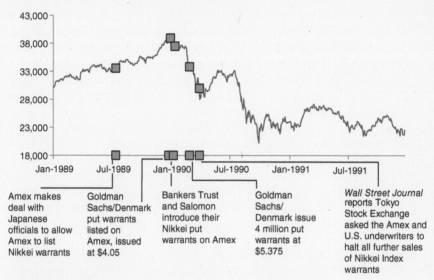

FIGURE 12.15 Nikkei versus Introduction of Put Warrants

Source: Birinyi Associates, Inc., Bloomberg.

could engage in activity without the sanction and knowledge of the Ministry. Put warrants were especially active, as now one could easily short Japan, hedge one's holdings, and even trade actively (see Figure 12.15).

Real estate might have eventually stopped the market or even fundamentals but the introduction of warrants was when the market stopped being bulletproof. Inevitably, the short term affects the long term.

In addition to our friends at Themis Trading, other, credible voices have also been heard on this subject:

- "How the Quest for Efficiency Corroded the Market" (*Harvard Business Review*, July 2013). In a textbook instance of unintended consequences, policy makers' attempts to improve U.S. financial markets critically weakened the institutions that protect investors from abuse.
- "Stock Markets That Flummox Masses . . ." was an article written by Amy Butte, the former CFO of the NYSE: "Want to know a dirty little secret? Our stock markets no longer work. They have grown so complex, fragmented and opaque that they don't serve their stated purpose . . . look more like a video game. The trouble is, it's one where only a few understand the rules. . . ." (*Bloomberg*, December 3, 2012).
- "Time for SEC to Act and Put a Stop to Casino Markets," Leon Cooperman (*Financial Times*, September 25, 2012): "Regulators have done little while recent events have wreaked havoc on what had been the best source of capital formation and creation in the world."

- "A Speed Limit for the Stock Market", Roger Lowenstein (*New York Times*, October 2, 2012). "High-frequency trading does investors far more harm than good."
- "NYSE Says Regulation Hits Retail Investors" (*Financial Times*, December 18, 2012). "Professional traders are benefiting at the expense of retail investors due to a combination of technological change and the rules that govern US equity markets."
- "Exchanges Fault Complexity" (*Wall Street Journal*, December 18, 2012). Joe Mecane, head of U.S. equities at NYSE Euronext: ". . . some of the exchange operator's orders were designed to comply with regulations, while other were written to 'guarantee economic results' for clients."
- "Trading in the Dark" (*New York Times*, op-ed, April 6, 2013). ". . . there is mounting evidence that the shift is obscuring the true prices of stocks, raising the cost of trading and, by extension, damaging investor confidence."
- "Time for a Reboot for Tech on the Street" (*Wall Street Journal*, April 30, 2013). "This score just in: Faulty Technology 2, Capital Markets 0."

Unfortunately, given the reality of economics and the reality that high-frequency and other traders create income for exchanges, we should expect no near-term response.

NOTES

1. The story is told of an alleged mafia member who visited the NYSE floor one day. Being street smart, he quickly understood the process and was heard saying as he left: "I joined the wrong mob."

2. Adam Smith, *The Money Game* (New York: Random House, 1967).

3. After one of Peter Drucker's classes, I suggested to him that he sounded a lot like McLuhan. He looked at me with a twinkle in his eye and said, "Marshall's been stealing my stuff for years."

4. "Decimals, ECNs, and 24/7," December 2000; "Pennies: First Blush," June 2001; "NYSE: Issues," November 2003; "The Next CRASH," August 2007; "The Next CRASH: II," August 2012.

5. "Decimals Pricing in the Securities and Options Markets," U.S. Securities & Exchange Commission, June 13, 2000. http://www.sec.gov/news/testimony/ts092000.htm.

6. "Share Trading Cut Short to Thwart Rogue Dealer," *The Times of London*, January 1, 1998.

7. "SEC Member Says Decimal Stock Quotes Could Save Billions," *Dow Jones Newswire*, September 30, 1996.

8. Greg Ip, "Catbird Seat—Nasdaq Market Maker, Seeing All the Orders, Becomes Canny Trader," *Wall Street Journal*, March 3, 2000.

9. Kate Kelly, "Regulators Are Investigating a Big Nasdaq Trader—Knight Trading Faces Allegations That It Violated Rules and Cost Investors Millions of Dollars," *Wall Street Journal*, June 4, 2002.

10. Ann Davis, "Client Comes First? On Wall Street, It Isn't Always So," *Wall Street Journal*, December 16, 2004.

11. Ann Davis, "How Knight Clients Failed to Recognize Questionable Trades," *Wall Street Journal*, December 17, 2004.

12. "Stealth Trading," *Forbes*, January 12, 2009; Joe Hagan, "Stock-Surfing the Tsunami," *New York Magazine*, February 2, 2009; Jacob Bunge, "NYSE Adjusts Charges in Bid to Draw Traders," February 3, 2009; Charles Duhigg, "Stock Traders Find Speed Pays, in Milliseconds," *New York Times*, July 24, 2009; Scott Patterson, "NYSE's Fast-Trade Hub Rises Up in New Jersey," *Wall Street Journal*, July 31, 2009; Michael Mackenzie, "SEC Runs Eye over High-Speed Trading," *Financial Times*, August 4, 2009.

13. C. L. Osler, "Identifying Noise Traders: The Head-and-Shoulders Pattern in U.S. Equities," Federal Reserve Bank of New York, February 1998.

14. J. Bradford De Long, Andrei Shleifer, Lawrence H. Summers, and Robert J. Waldman, "The Survival of Noise Traders in Financial Markets," *Journal of Business* 64, no. 1 (1991): 1–20.

15. "High Frequency Trading," *New York Times*, October 10, 2011.

16. Sal Arnuk and Joseph Saluzzi, *Broken Markets—How High Frequency Trading and Predatory Practices on Wall Street Are Destroying Investor Confidence* (Upper Saddle River, NJ: FT Press, 2012).

17. "Speedy New Traders Make Waves Far from Wall Street," *New York Times*, April 19, 2010.

18. The next day, Berkshire Hathaway bid $72.50 a share for the company. The trades illustrated here were not related to the merger.

CHAPTER 13

Get Ready, Get Set . . .

Foul-cankering rust the hidden treasure frets, but gold that's put to use more gold begets.
— William Shakespeare, *Venus and Adonis*

A nyone who has ever ridden the New York City subway system has heard "there's another train right behind this one." This is also true of the stock market, and despite today's electronic high-speed access, patience truly is a virtue in investing. The old cliché used to be "invest in haste, repent in leisure," but no one has said that in years.

The focus today on immediate executions and expediting transactions has a major failing, as it assumes that prices will be higher 10 milliseconds from now or that the broker or trader will step ahead of the order because he knows how smart the fund is and wants to get there first.

Your first step is perhaps the easiest: What is the state of the market? Looking at a long-term chart, which is available from any number of websites, find the last multi-year high and low. The conventional definition of *bull* and *bear market* is a 20 percent move from a recent low or high. Thus, a rise of that magnitude from the most recent low defines a bull market; a decline of 20 percent from a top suggests a bear market. We would not, however, cast that number in stone and have also tended to take sentiment into account.

Thus, in 1998, the combination of the Russian default as well as issues with Long-Term Capital, resulted in a 19.31 percent decline, which had all the characteristics of a bear market. While there are other definitions, such as a 15 percent move in six months or that a bull market doesn't begin until the market is higher than its previous peak, the 20 percent rule is what most investors and analysts use.

Be leery of secondary concerns, such as earnings or price earnings ratios, as some strategists have argued against the 2009 market as it took

191

place without strong underlying fundamentals or economic underpinnings. In the case of markets, it is all about price (see Figure 13.1 and Table 13.1).

In the mid-1980s, someone made what to us is almost a classic comment: "This is only a bull market in price." Maybe an academic or a purist might agree but to us our responsibility is to provide financial peace of mind.

Having determined the state of the market, the next step is to determine its status. More specifically, is it rising or having a respite? Table 13.2 lists corrections (a decline of 10 percent).

The 17 corrections listed in Table 13.2 had an average decline of 14.04 percent lasting 118 calendar days and took almost five months to recover. On average, a single day accounted for 30 percent of the drop and *tended* to occur toward the end of the correction. The corresponding median correction was 13.94 percent lasting 70 days and taking 43 days to recover.

We would highlight the last column in Table 13.2, which illustrates the randomness of corrections or the lack thereof. For each bull market, the very last entry is the time not to the next correction, but to the start of the next bear market. Thus, in 1962, there was a 10.5 percent decline two months into the rally, which lasted 62 days. That market then rallied without a 10 percent decline for over three years (1,205 days) before a bear market. The 2002 rally likewise corrected early but went over four and a half years without another drop.

More frequent are 5 percent declines. Since 1962, there have been 93 declines of 5 to 10 percent, 22 percent of which led to an official correction.[1]

In bear markets, rallies are less frequent because bear markets tend to be shorter (see Table 13.3). Their average gain is 14.36 percent lasting 48 days but not every bear market has a rally.

For those whose primary interest is trading ETFs and sectors, the same exercise should be undertaken. While this is not easily achieved, other traders will have access to this information and therefore a substantial advantage.

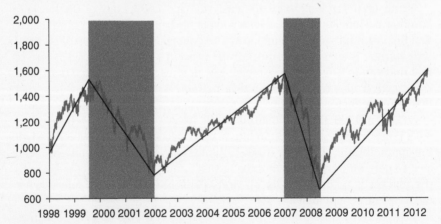

FIGURE 13.1   S&P 500: Bull and Bear Markets
Source: Birinyi Associates, Inc., Bloomberg.

TABLE 13.1 Bull and Bear Markets

Move	Begin	End	Percent Change	Length (Days)
Bull	8/31/98	3/24/00	59.52	571
Bear	3/24/00	10/9/02	−49.15	929
Bull	10/9/02	10/9/07	101.50	1,826
Bear	10/9/07	3/9/09	−56.78	517
Bull	**3/9/09**	**4/29/13**	**136.00**	**1,512**

Source: Birinyi Associates, Inc.

We then look for similar markets. Even casual investors will have heard that the most expensive words are "it's different this time." In truth, it is different *every* time but there are tendencies and characteristics. We took the position early in the 2009 bull market that it would be a protracted, extended rally, and similar markets (1962, 1974, 1982, 1990, and 2002) had four loosely defined periods (see Table 13.4):

1. Reluctance—this can't be a bull market because I'm not invested.
2. Consolidation—finally a chance to catch my breath.

TABLE 13.2 S&P 500 Bull Market Corrections

	Bull Market			10% Corrections		Days to Correction	Days to Next Correction
	% Change	Length	#	% Change	Length	Days to Correction	Days to Next Correction
1962	79.78	1,324	1	−10.52%	62	57	1,205
1966	48.05	784	1	−10.11	162	353	269
1970	73.53	961	1	−13.94	206	337	415
1974	125.63	2,248	6	−13.56	29	35	221
				−14.14	63		371
				−19.41	531		190
				−13.55	63		325
				−10.25	33		98
				−17.07	43		246
1982	228.81	1,839	1	−14.38	288	424	1,127
1987	64.77	955	1	−10.23	113	675	167
1990	301.66	2,836	1	−10.80	20	2,553	263
1998	59.52	571	2	−10.00	15	23	281
				−12.08	91		161
2002	101.50	1,826	1	−14.71	104	49	1,673
2009	119.65	1,411	2	−15.99	70	410	301
				−19.39	157		—

Source: Birinyi Associates, Inc.

TABLE 13.3　S&P 500 Bear Market Rallies

	Bear Market			10% Rally		Days to First Rally	Rally to Next Trough
	% Change	Length	#	% Change	Length		
1966	−22.18	240	—				
1968	−36.06	543	—				
1973	−48.2	630	2	10.85	51	223	39
				10.02	30		
1980	−27.11	622	2	12.04	66	465	84
				11.30	60		
1987	−33.51	101	2	14.92	2	55	44
				12.33	7		
1990	−19.92	87	—				
1998	−19.31	45	—				
2000	−49.15	929	4	12.10	140	21	41
				19.00	47		
				21.40	105		
				20.68	30		
2007	−56.78	517	3	12.04	70	153	44
				11.58	3		
				18.47	8		

Source: Birinyi Associates, Inc.

3. Acceptance—maybe I'll get half invested.
4. Exuberance—everyone in the pool.

These markets could also be characterized as barbell, as they have historically made most of their gains in the first and last stages.

We would then endeavor to gauge the mood of the market and—as we have often done especially at the end of any year—actually make a checklist of issues:

2013 Consensus View as of 1/1/13

Positives	Negatives
In a bull market	Economy sluggish
Corporate profits strong	Corporate revenues slowing
European bank prices up	Europe's financial crisis continues
Housing recovery	Unemployment high
Bearish sentiment	Gold expected to rally 10%
S&P forecasted to gain 6.2%	Oil expectation $100 (14%)
	Bonds to decline: 10 year 2.3% to 1.7%
	10 year P/E above norm

Source: Birinyi Associates, Inc.

TABLE 13.4   S&P 500 Performance by Stage

| | **S&P 500 Performance by Stage** | | | |
	Reluctance	**Consolidation**	**Acceptance**	**Exuberance**
1962	34.0%	14.9%	8.3%	7.8%
1974	61.6	–8.3	6.6	42.8
1982	62.6	9.0	32.2	40.3
1990	43.1	12.2	39.9	78.7
2002	45.7	4.4	7.1	23.7
2009	79.9	5.9	7.5	19.6*
Average	49.4	6.4	18.8	38.7

*Stage four began on July 27, 2012 and this data is as of May 30, 2013.

Source: Birinyi Associates, Inc.

By gauging the market, one establishes a base to track the market going forward. In 2013, the market's first half strength was somewhat a result of the implosion of the negatives: Gold went down and we continued to argue that the 10-year adjusted P/E argument was somewhat neutered by the fact that it had been cited from day one of the 2009 bottom (see Figure 13.2).

TRACKING SENTIMENT, OR, KEEPING SCORE OF THE PLAYERS

If possible, one should also track the attitude of commentators and economists. For example, it was helpful to us that we knew that one

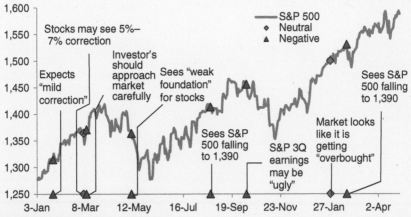

FIGURE 13.2   Market Commentary

Source: Birinyi Associates, Inc., Bloomberg.

strategist had been consistently negative, not helpful, articulate or composed.

Given that it is our job, we drill even deeper and track strategists' detailed views. One of the ironies of the first half of 2013 was that of the nine firms who provided sector outlooks, five were positive on health care, which was up 22 percent going into June 2013; three of the five were bearish on the market.

Having made these suggestions in other forums, we expect the usual retort: That is a lot of work. Yes, it is, but consider a portfolio of $100,000 which hopes to make 10 percent or $10,000. Working as a teacher or administrator or chef, how long would it take to accumulate $10,000? Three months, half a year? Why should you make it on Wall Street in only three days or six weeks?

NOTE

1. "Corrections: 1982–2007," Birinyi Associates, Inc., October 2007.

CHAPTER 14

Market Cycles and Rotation

The sun don't shine on the same dog's ass all the time.
—Jim "Catfish" Hunter

O f all the issues that analysts should dissect, the greatest omission is probably that of *market cycles*. While there are all manner of commentary about group movements, relationships, alleged characteristics, and articulate discussion, in reality almost nothing useful results.

Technicians and strategists alike regularly write "at this stage of the cycle" and recommend buying energy or health care, small or large stocks, or value/dividend paying names. Or they suggest a correction or further advance or increased merger activity. In the bull market of 2009, one of the more common cycle comments was the calling for a correction, which one should expect, is due, would be normal, or is overdue.

Analysis is undertaken on annual cycles, 12-month cycles or, in the case of the Kondratieff wave, 30-year cycles but we have never found them to be especially compelling and/or profitable. Seasonal characteristics (sell in May and go away) are trumpeted and when they coincide, they are hailed as examples of diligent research.

Too often, we submit, cycle theories are merely coincidental and not causal, as in the case of the Super Bowl indicator, which we will willingly ignore. Some years back, one researcher, apparently with a really *big* computer, determined that of all the indicators the one that best fit the stock market's result was butter production in Bangladesh.[1]

While there are some seasonal characteristics that investors should recognize, such as end-of-the-year tax selling, we have never found that they presented significant opportunities. Years ago, we found that most major corporations paid their dividends on the tenth day of the third month of the quarter and created a slightly positive bias on March 10, June 10, etcetera,

197

as investors reinvested the funds. But the difference between those days and the norm were of use only to a statistician. Interestingly, the second highest day of dividend payments was the first day of the second month: February 1, May 1. . . .

Then, however, it appeared to create a slightly negative bias as the distribution of AT&T (which paid on that day) resulted in more people selling than reinvesting.

Analysts have long tried to provide guidance by detailing a typical or normal cycle. Graphs and tables similar to the one in Figure 14.1 suggest the traditional or usual course of a bull market and or the economy.

Other studies have been more detailed. Prudential-Bache, in January 1988 published an 87-page study, *Group Rotation Forecaster*, which was, to be polite, not helpful:

Aerospace/Defense	Buy at top of the investment cycle. Sell at the first sign of a bottom.
Paper	Buy one quarter after the top in the housing cycle. Sell at the top.
Computer	Buy at the top of the investment cycle. Sell at the bottom [of the investment cycle].

Another report regarding the interest rate cycle was more detailed, but also less than prescient (see Table 14.1).

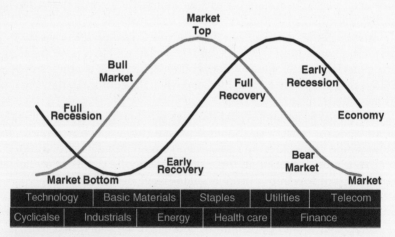

FIGURE 14.1   Idealized Investment Cycle
Source: Birinyi Associates, Inc.

TABLE 14.1 Strategy for Rising Rates: Groups to Buy

Immediate		After	
Group	**Average Change (%)**	**Group**	**Average Change (%)**
Oil and Gas	−1.07	HC Equipment	15.95
Brewers	−2.91	Paper Packaging	8.43
Soft Drinks	−7.07	Chemicals	8.39
		Papers	7.24
		Food Retail	7.20
		Drugs	6.79
		Packaged Foods	4.88
		Tobacco	0.39
		Metals & Mining	−0.70
Groups Not Listed			
Computers	−1.68	Semiconductors	30.48
Metals & Mining	−2.97	Retail	23.89
Energy Equipment	−3.29	Software	23.10
		Brokers	22.27
S&P 500	−5.38	S&P 500	6.43

Source: Birinyi Associates, Inc.

To some degree, we sympathize with these efforts because historically data was limited to 89 S&P groups including:

- Electrical Equipment
- Electronics: Major companies
- Electrical Appliances
- Electronics: Instrumentation
- Electronics: Semiconductors

Lest we forget, one of the groups was called *Miscellaneous*. But in reality, in the early 1980s it was anything but miscellaneous as it was the largest group in the S&P 500 at 8.6 percent.

Juggling and analyzing 89 pieces of information is a formidable task. Fortunately in 2001 (and backdated to 1989), S&P created ten economic sectors, which made analysis more manageable but for a limited period. We extended that period back to 1962 and analyzed market movements on a cycle of price rather than of time.

We began by segregating bull and bear markets using the prevailing convention of 20 percent: a market that gains 20 percent from a trough is a bull market; a bear market is a 20 percent drop from the market's peak.

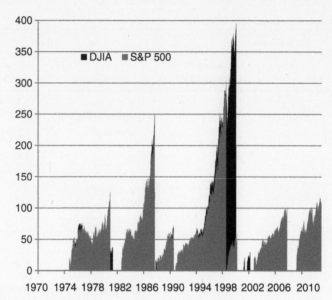

FIGURE 14.2 S&P 500 versus DJIA Bull Market (%)
Source: Birinyi Associates, Inc.

While that might provide definite parameters, we found it was not that simple. As detailed in Appendix A and illustrated in Figure 14.2, the results are different depending on whether one uses the S&P or the DJIA.

There is also the decision regarding rounding or truncation as several of the S&P bull markets had 19+ percent "corrections" which, one could argue, could be rounded up and become bear markets, which has been our practice given the underlying negative sentiment during those periods (see Table 14.2).

TABLE 14.2 Corrections During 1987 Bull Market

	Start	End	Percent Change	Length (Days)
Decline	10/21/87	10/26/87	−11.89%	5
Decline	11/2/87	12/4/87	−12.45	32
Decline	10/9/89	1/30/90	−10.23	113
Decline	7/16/90	10/11/90	−19.92	87
Decline	10/7/97	10/27/97	−10.80	20
Decline	7/17/98	8/31/98	−19.34	45
Decline	9/23/98	10/8/98	−10.00	15
Decline	7/16/99	10/15/99	−12.08	91

Source: Birinyi Associates, Inc.

HOW TO TELL WHETHER WE ARE IN THE EIGHTH OR NINTH INNING

To further complicate matters, there is the issue of intraday prices, which we do not use, but another analyst might and thereby produce yet another set of results.

Having addressed the issue of bull and bear markets, we addressed a critical issue: Which sectors "forecast" or lead bull markets? Conventional wisdom holds that small stocks, which are more sensitive to nuances in the economy, are "bellwethers." Others argue that financial names, especially banks, are leading indicators since bull markets are usually a function of actions by the Federal Reserve.

Going back to 1962 (when reliable data first becomes available), one might first remind investors that there is no single technical indicator that anticipates rallies. As shown in Figure 14.3, the advance/decline line, for one, bottoms coincidentally with every bear market except 2000.

If we look at sectors in the last three months of a bear market and the first three months of a bull market, it would appear that no sector is the "robin" of a bull market while financials and technology are "early bull market cycle" groups (see Tables 14.3 and 14.4).

This assumes, however, that we know when the bull market actually begins. We might therefore introduce what we term "belt" charts, where we

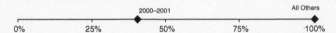

FIGURE 14.3 Trough of NYSE Advance/Decline Line During Bear Markets
Source: Birinyi Associates, Inc.

TABLE 14.3 Last Three Months of a Bear Market

	Minimum	Maximum	Average
Consumer Disc.	−41.1%	−10.7%	−23.7%
Consumer Stap.	−34.8	−4.7	−15.3
Energy	−25.3	−5.1	−15.3
Financial	−51.9	−15.3	−26.7
Health Care	−30.7	4.5	−15.1
Industrials	−34.7	−12.4	−24.6
Materials	−27.9	−2.4	−18.3
Technology	−33.0	−7.5	−23.3
Telecom	−21.7	17.5	−9.3
Utilities	−30.3	−3.6	−12.6
S&P 500	−29.3	−13.2	−20.8

Source: Birinyi Associates, Inc.

TABLE 14.4   First Three Months of a Bull Market

	Minimum	Maximum	Average
Financial	5.3%	96.8%	28.2%
Technology	−6.8	44.5	22.1
Industrials	3.6	55.9	18.5
Materials	−0.8	51.9	17.1
Consumer Disc.	−3.5	50.2	16.8
Energy	−3.4	28.4	13.6
Health Care	−2.0	28.2	13.3
Consumer Stap.	0.3	30.7	12.4
Utilities	1.4	33.0	11.3
Telecom	−18.6	28.7	8.8
S&P 500	5.4	39.0	19.2

Source: Birinyi Associates, Inc.

highlight 20 percent moves (in either direction) as we have done with the
S&P (see Figure 14.4).

We might then compare the S&P bull and bear markets with coinciding
moves (20 percent) in technology. As shown in Figure 14.5, technology did
very well in the 1982 rally and it did so early.

If we expand this to all rallies, tech is a leading/coincident indicator
and bottomed well before the 1982 market, somewhat before the bull
market of 1962 but at or near the beginning of the others (see Figure 14.6).

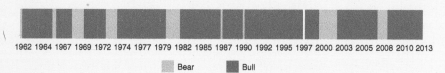

1962 1964 1967 1969 1972 1974 1977 1979 1982 1985 1987 1990 1992 1995 1997 2000 2003 2005 2008 2010 2013

Bear   Bull

FIGURE 14.4   S&P 500 Bull and Bear Markets since 1962
Source: Birinyi Associates, Inc.

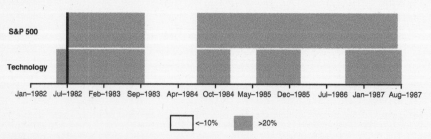

Jan–1982 Jul–1982 Feb–1983 Sep–1983 Apr–1984 Oct–1984 May–1985 Dec–1985 Jul–1986 Jan–1987 Aug–1987

<−10%   >20%

FIGURE 14.5   S&P 500 versus Technology During 1982 Bull Market
Source: Birinyi Associates, Inc.

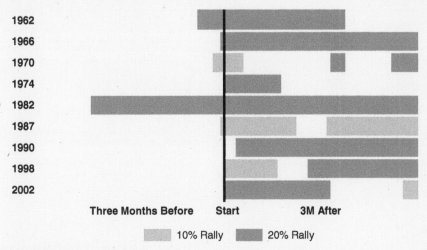

FIGURE 14.6 Technology versus Start of All Bull Markets
Source: Birinyi Associates, Inc.

Now we consider the idea that small stocks are names to buy early. Here, too, we have another old wives' tale. While in several instances such as 1982, they do well early, they do not bottom before the market. In half of the markets they are either average or below average performers (see Figure 14.7).

We can go a bit deeper, and further define bull markets by their ultimate gains and characteristics (see Table 14.5).

TABLE 14.5 Bull Market Characteristics

| | | | Annualized Rate | | Change in |
| | | Length | | Industrial | 10-Year T-Note |
Begin	End	(Days)	S&P 500	Production	Yield (bps)
6/26/1962	2/9/1966	1,324	17.6%	7.9%	77
10/7/1966	11/29/1968	784	20.0	3.2	76
5/26/1970	1/11/1973	961	23.3	5.7	−179
10/3/1974	11/28/1980	2,248	14.1	1.7	468
8/12/1982	8/25/1987	1,839	26.6	3.7	−482
12/4/1987	7/16/1990	955	21.0	1.7	−50
10/11/1990	7/17/1998	2,836	19.6	3.9	−341
8/31/1998	3/24/2000	571	34.8	4.2	115
10/9/2002	10/9/2007	1,826	15.0	2.3	106
3/9/2009	4/11/2013	1,494	23.3	3.3	−107

Source: Birinyi Associates, Inc.

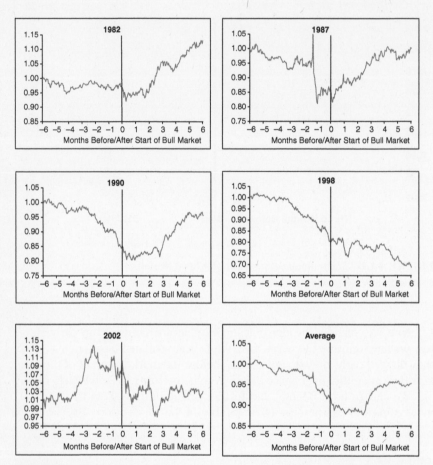

FIGURE 14.7 Relative Strength of Small versus Large Caps at Bull Market Turns
Source: Birinyi Associates, Inc.

GROUP ROTATION EXISTS; IT IS RANDOM BUT WORTH UNDERSTANDING

Having identified and classified the rallies, we then sought to isolate group rotation by detailing when the various sectors produced their strongest gains (relative to the market).

While there are some tendencies, such as technology doing well toward the latter part of a bull market, they are far from concrete. The triangle in the charts shown in Figure 14.8 represents the average, and there seems to be a progression from utilities to telecom to materials and so on but none of the individual markets follow that path.

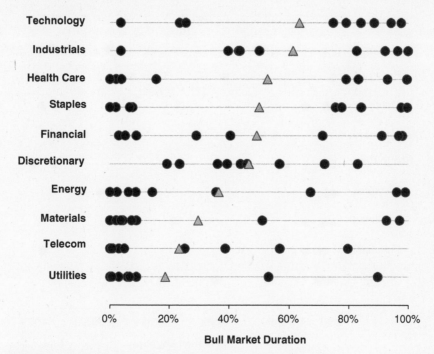

FIGURE 14.8 Relative Strength Peak During All Bull Markets
Source: Birinyi Associates, Inc.

The chart in Figure 14.8 suggests a noteworthy characteristic of bull markets and investment returns. Bull markets are disjointed. Clearly the greatest portion of their gains occurs early and, to a lesser extent, late. Most observers criticize the idea of market timing. Figure 14.8 suggests that an effort to time the beginning of a bull is the most critical. Thereafter, the opportunities for timing are less rewarding.

This is probably a factor in performance. Given the resistance to our *S&P 750: The Bottom* piece in 2009, and to our comments in 1990, professional investors are overly skeptical at market bottoms. While the train may come back to the station, boarding the first one provides a significant advantage.

If we go one step further and segregate markets by strength/length, it becomes more illuminating especially with regard to financials (see Figure 14.9). In the longer bull markets financials do very well early on (1990 excepted); in shorter rallies they tend to exhibit strength late. Thus, financials are an early cycle group in some instances, and late in others.

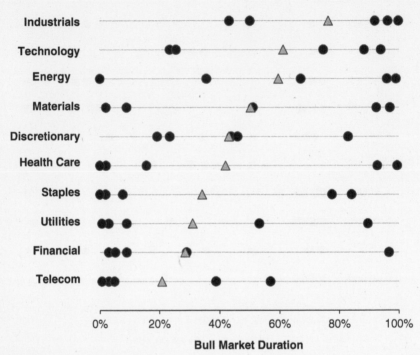

FIGURE 14.9   Relative Strength Peak During Long Bull Markets
Source: Birinyi Associates, Inc.

While this might seem like another example of "on one hand, but on the other hand" it has been, in our experience, very useful. In the 2009 bull market, the financial names doubled in the first eight weeks (see Figure 14.10).

We therefore concluded that this was to be a stronger bull market than many analysts who termed it only a bear market rally. Furthermore, as

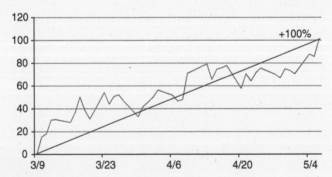

FIGURE 14.10   S&P Financials: March 9, 2009 through May 6, 2009
Source: Birinyi Associates, Inc., Bloomberg.

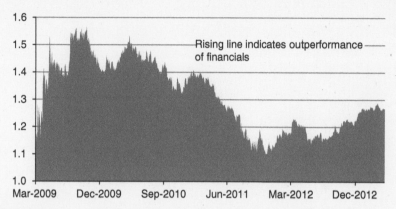

FIGURE 14.11 Relative Strength of Financials versus S&P 500
Source: Birinyi Associates, Inc., Bloomberg.

we noted in a number of publications, historically in these instances, the sector makes over 40 percent of its ultimate bull market gains in just that initial surge and we recommended avoiding these names in 2011. Given that the market was virtually flat that year, not owning the sector added 400 basis points to one's performance.[2]

As shown in Figure 14.11, in the 2009 rally, the financial sector has been a notable underperformer since then. The sector has gained 218 percent, but 50 percent of the gain was in the first two months of the bull market, or 7 percent of the total elapsed time.

Clearly, the concept of some stylized group rotation is not easily discernible. We therefore analyzed those markets characterized by a strengthening economy. Neither they nor markets where interest rates were falling provided any startling conclusions (see Figures 14.12 and 14.13).

In fact, the whole issue of defined group rotation might be characterized as yet another myth as evidenced by another series. If one compares the bear market of 2000 to that of 2007, both were of the same duration but had limited similarities.

More importantly, in March 2001, all the sectors had a coincident rally and again in September of that year. In the second bear market, most of the sectors rallied together in October 2008 after declining together in mid-May of that year (see Figures 14.14 and 14.15).

One final illustration might be to determine the order of sector moves. Specifically, we have taken the financial and technology sectors and asked: After a strong move in these sectors, what should we buy?

The 11 instances where financials rallied more than 50 percent they saw "rotation" into six different sectors. In the 14 instances where

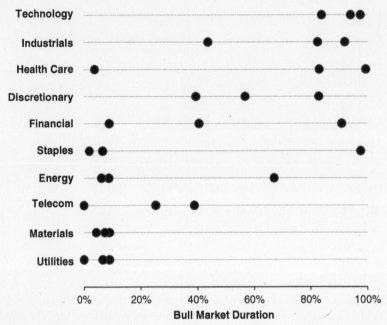

FIGURE 14.12 Relative Strength Peak During Bull Markets with Strong Economic Growth (1962, 1970, 1998)

Source: Birinyi Associates, Inc.

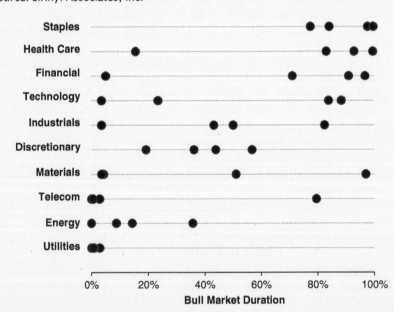

FIGURE 14.13 Relative Strength Peak During Bull Markets with Declining Interest Rates (1970, 1982, 1987, 1990)

Source: Birinyi Associates, Inc.

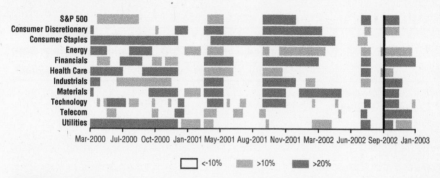

FIGURE 14.14 Market and Sector Filter: 2000 Bear Market and First Three Months of Bull Market

Source: Birinyi Associates, Inc.

technology rallied more than 50 percent, they saw "rotation" into five different sectors (see Tables 14.6 and 14.7).

Thus, the idea that sectors or groups rotate or hop-scotch from one area of interest to another is not readily apparent and the concept of late cycle or stocks that do well early in a bull or bear market is more wishful thinking than reality.

Perhaps no cliché is more widely accepted than "the most expensive words in the business are, it's different this time." In truth, it is usually different and the focus of investors and analysts alike is to find those few instances of similarity as we showed with financials.

We have summarized the results of both relative strength as well as troughs thereof in the graphs in Figures 14.16 and 14.17, but note that no one bull or bear market has ever had this sequence and that they are a composite of all those we have detailed.

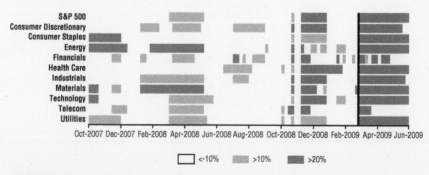

FIGURE 14.15 Market and Sector Filter: 2007 Bear Market and First Three Months of Bull Market

Source: Birinyi Associates, Inc.

TABLE 14.6   After a Strong Move in Financials and Technology

	Financials (11x) (Rallied more than 50%)		Technology (14x) (Rallied more than 50%)	
	Rally	Decline	Rally	Decline
Consumer Discretionary		1x		1x
Consumer Staples	1x	1x	1x	2x
Energy	4x		3x	
Financials	1x			2x
Healthcare			1x	2x
Industrials		1x	2x	
Materials	1x			2x
Technology	2x	3x		3x
Telecom	1x	2x	1x	
Utilities		2x		1x

Source: Birinyi Associates, Inc.

TABLE 14.7   Best and Worst Sector Performance After a 50 Percent Rally in Financial Sector

	Performance in the Next Three Months	
Financials 50% Rally Peak	**Best**	**Worst**
Sep-1964	Energy 5.14%	Technology −7.18%
Nov-1968	Materials −3.08%	Technology −10.81%
Jun-1981	Energy −0.55%	Industrials −20.28%
Nov-1982	Technology 13.10%	Staples −7.29%
Jul-1985	Energy 1.75%	Utilities −13.45%
May-1986	Utilities 20.30%	Technology −6.49%
Oct-1989	Staples 15.29%	Discretionary −5.44%
Apr-1993	Telecom 4.45%	Energy −3.81%
Mar-1997	Technology 12.75%	Utilities −1.56%
Mar-2004	Energy 0.13%	Telecom −8.57%
Mar-2009	Financials 26.93%	Telecom −1.93%

Source: Birinyi Associates, Inc.

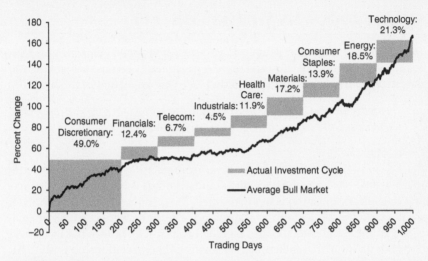

FIGURE 14.16 Actual Bull Market Investment Cycle (Based on Historic Norms)
Source: Birinyi Associates, Inc., Bloomberg.

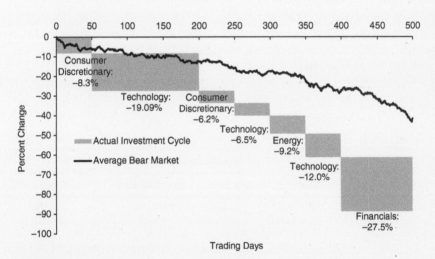

FIGURE 14.17 Actual Bear Market Investment Cycle (Based on Historic Norms)
Source: Birinyi Associates, Inc., Bloomberg.

SMALL STOCKS: ON AVERAGE, YES, BUT . . .

Two other cycles that merit analysis are small stocks and value/growth. Here again myth overtakes reality and there is a seemingly endless stream of opinions regarding small stocks (see Table 14.8). One being that of timing:

> . . . by the second years of most bull market rallies, shares of large, industry leading blue chips often start beating small-capitalization stocks.[3]

Really?

Some of the confusion might stem from classification. Since 1978, the Russell 2000 has been the accepted standard but it is rebalanced every year and thus its composition is not consistent. Prior to the start of the NASDAQ stock market in 1971, over the counter (OTC) stocks were considered small caps but until 1971 the OTC also included banks, which were not in the S&P until July 1976. With that in mind, we analyzed their relationship to the S&P.

Small stocks have extended periods of outperformance and extended periods where they underperform larger names. We found no technical, fundamental, or rationale basis to explain either. The relative strength of these names against the market even when we classify markets provides us with no real insights.

Thus, analysis of small stocks is another issue where the anecdotal reigns (see Table 14.9). They have historically provided a superior return, which seems to be evident in their performance. Over the past 10 bull markets, they have returned, on average, 187 percent versus 125 percent. Except for 1974 when that star is a bit less luminous.

Perhaps it is also surprising that they hold up as well as the S&P 500 during bear markets and recessions (see Tables 14.10 and 14.11).

TABLE 14.8 Small Stocks versus S&P 500 During Second Year of Bull Market

		Return Months 13–24		S&P 500—Small
Begin	End	S&P 500	Small Stocks	Stocks
6/26/1962	2/9/1966	17.00%	10.95%	6.05%
10/7/1966	11/26/1968	6.63	41.13	−34.50
5/26/1970	1/11/1973	10.91	13.51	−2.60
10/2/1974	11/28/1980	24.28	39.04	−14.76
8/12/1982	8/25/1987	2.01	−10.46	12.47
12/4/1987	7/16/1990	29.00	18.03	10.97
10/11/1990	7/17/1998	5.56	6.35	−0.79
8/31/1998	3/24/2000	13.80	24.43	−10.63
9/21/2001	1/4/2002	22.58	41.64	−19.06
10/9/2002	10/9/2007	8.03	10.42	−2.39

Source: Birinyi Associates, Inc.

TABLE 14.9 Performance During Bull Markets

Start	End	S&P 500	Small Stocks
Jun-1962	Feb-1966	79.78%	139.42%
Oct-1966	Nov-1968	48.05	191.95
May-1970	Jan-1973	73.53	51.20
May-1974	Nov-1980	125.63	636.06
Aug-1982	Aug-1987	228.81	183.98
Dec-1987	Jul-1990	64.77	51.82
Oct-1990	Jul-1998	301.66	276.58
Aug-1998	Mar-2000	59.52	69.85
Jul-2002	Oct-2007	132.35	92.21
Mar-2009	Apr-2013	135.52	175.89
	Average:	**124.96**	**186.90**

Source: Birinyi Associates, Inc.

TABLE 14.10 Performance During Bear Markets

Start	End	S&P 500	Small Stocks
Feb-1966	Oct-1966	−22.18%	−23.09%
Nov-1968	May-1970	−36.06	−46.57
Jan-1973	Oct-1974	−48.20	−52.80
Nov-1980	Aug-1982	−27.11	−21.71
Aug-1987	Dec-1987	−33.51	−35.39
Jul-1990	Oct-1990	−19.92	−27.21
Jul-1998	Aug-1998	−19.31	−26.91
Mar-2000	Jul-2002	−47.78	−36.59
Oct-2007	Mar-2009	−56.78	−59.41
	Average:	**−34.54**	**−36.63**

Source: Birinyi Associates, Inc.

TABLE 14.11 Performance During Recessions

Start	End	S&P 500	Small Stocks
Dec-1969	Nov-1970	−6.46%	−25.64%
Nov-1973	Mar-1975	−22.59	−11.99
Jan-1980	Jul-1980	12.72	15.96
Jul-1981	Nov-1982	6.76	7.89
Jul-1990	Mar-1991	4.36	−0.81
Mar-2001	Nov-2001	−8.20	−1.92
Dec-2007	Jun-2009	−37.56	−33.11
	Average:	**−7.28**	**−7.09**

Source: Birinyi Associates, Inc.

It should also be noted that "small stocks" is an applicable term. The value of the Russell 2,000 as of December 31, 2012 was $1.42 trillion while the S&P was $13.05 trillion. At that time, Apple alone was equal to 35 percent of the entire Russell 2000.

We are hesitant to provide significant investment advice regarding small stocks: the universe is inconsistent, and the results too disparate and random. Thus, the suggestion that small stocks do well early in a market or economic cycle is questionable and not one that we can endorse.

GROWTH VERSUS VALUE: ADVANTAGE GROWTH, BUT . . .

Growth vs. value is also a data issue. There are a number of indices that track these styles but Dow Jones' dates back only to 1992. S&P provides data back to 1977, but somewhat complicates issues by classifying one-third of the names as pure growth and one-third as pure value, with one-third being mixed.

Nevertheless, the results are presented in Table 14.12.

TABLE 14.12   U.S. Style Indices Yearly Returns

		S&P 500	
	S&P 500	**Pure Growth**	**Pure Value**
1996	20.26%	18.16%	13.37%
1997	31.01	29.30	30.52
1998	26.67	38.06	7.92
1999	19.53	59.12	−5.87
2000	−10.14	−8.47	9.30
2001	−13.04	−17.92	8.07
2002	−23.37	−32.12	−20.12
2003	26.38	41.55	37.31
2004	8.99	15.51	23.07
2005	3.00	6.54	10.85
2006	13.62	6.60	17.16
2007	3.53	5.84	−6.24
2008	−38.49	−39.59	−49.93
2009	23.45	49.42	50.26
2010	12.78	26.77	21.06
2011	0.00	0.06	−2.71
2012	13.41	14.22	23.07
Average	**6.92**	**12.53**	**9.83**
Median	**12.78**	**14.22**	**10.85**

Source: Bloomberg.

TABLE 14.13 Bull Markets

Start	End	S&P 500	Value	Growth
Jan-1977	Nov-1980	37.72%	29,01%	51.01%
Aug-1982	Aug-1987	197.56	200.35	193.60
Dec-1987	Jul-1990	55.46	47.29	68.21
Oct-1990	Jul-1998	287.76	239.23	337.63
Aug-1998	Mar-2000	59.56	37.08	80.77
Jul-2002	Oct-2007	96.21	116.16	72.12
	Average:	**122.38**	**111.52**	**133.89**

Source: Birinyi Associates, Inc.

Extending these to markets, it is perhaps not surprising that growth outperforms during bull markets and underperforms in bear markets. What might be disappointing is that value does not fare much better in declines (see Tables 14.13 and 14.14).

During the economic cycle, growth is consistently better during recessions and usually in expansions as well (see Tables 14.15 and 14.16).

When we "drill down" for intramarket rallies, there seems to be little information with regard to timing. In bear markets, value has had a slight advantage, although a marked one in the 2000 decline.

The contention that value does better in early stages of a bull or bear market or of a given economic cycle is unlikely to be profitable. It may be articulate, reasonable, and compelling, but in the final analysis we submit that many notions of bull and bear market characteristics are not sustainable.

This is also the case with many issues as well such as buybacks, insider activity, magazine covers, and the like. They are as likely to appear in up markets as well as down markets. To characterize them as bull or bear market ingredients or indicators is both misleading and superficial.

TABLE 14.14 Bear Markets

Start	End	S&P 500	Value	Growth
Nov-1980	Aug-1982	−23.79%	−21.03%	−27.87%
Aug-1987	Dec-1987	−27.73	−26.39	−29.54
Jul-1990	Oct-1990	−14.52	−14.37	−15.25
Jul-1998	Aug-1998	−19.34	−21.22	−17.60
Mar-2000	Jul-2002	−47.78	−37.01	−56.96
	Average:	**−26.63**	**−24.00**	**−29.44**

Source: Birinyi Associates, Inc.

TABLE 14.15 Expansions

Start	End	S&P 500	Value	Growth
Jan-1977	Dec-1979	5.79%	7.37%	5.42%
Aug-1980	Jun-1981	7.84	5.28	7.56
Dec-1982	Jul-1990	158.42	153.94	165.13
Mar-1991	Feb-2001	230.46	211.48	236.57
Dec-2001	Feb-2008	16.78	27.23	6.66
	Average:	**83.86**	**81.06**	**84.27**

Source: Birinyi Associates, Inc.

TABLE 14.16 Recessions

Start	End	S&P 500	Value	Growth
Jan-1980	Jul-1980	12.72%	11.53%	15.00%
Jul-1981	Nov-1982	5.59	3.62	9.62
Jul-1990	Mar-1991	4.80	1.74	7.40
Mar-2001	Nov-2001	−8.20	−11.65	−5.03
	Average:	**3.73**	**1.31**	**6.75**

Source: Birinyi Associates, Inc.

NOTES

1. Laura Washington, "What's the Stock Market Got to Do with the Production of Butter in Bangladesh?" *Money Magazine*, March 1, 1998.

2. "2012: The Cycle Continues," Birinyi Associates, Inc., January 2012.

3. "Now Entering Phase 2 of the Market's Comeback," *New York Times*, December 12, 2009.

CHAPTER 15

The Economy and the Federal Reserve Board

> *. . . the master-economist must possess a rare combination of gifts. He must be mathematician, historian, statesman, philosopher—in some degree. He must understand symbols and speak in words. He must contemplate the particular in terms of the general, and touch abstract and concrete in the same flight of thought. He must study the present in the light of the past for the purpose of the future.*
>
> —Robert Heilbroner

Two factors that should be incorporated into any investment process are the economy and Federal Reserve Board (FRB) policy. Integrating economic activity is somewhat difficult as the record of economists in determining the status thereof is, at best and charitably, poor. In 1980, the National Bureau of Economic Research (NBER) acknowledged that a recession had started just as it was ending. In 1991, the economy was found to be in a recession one month after it had ended (see Table 15.1).

The record is no better on expansions (see Table 15.2). The 11-month growth phase of August 1980 to June 1981 was declared in the twelfth month, and the expansion of 1991 ended in February 2001 but not until 21 months *after* it began were we told that it had begun!

Thus, while incorporating the economy into the process is important, we caution that the record of those forecasting it is less than scintillating.

Moreover, the relationship between the market and the economy is not a tight fit. Tradition and market lore have always been that stocks bottom six months before the economy. In reality, it is closer to 4½ months (see Table 15.3).

TABLE 15.1 Recessions

Start	End	Date Declared
April 1960	February 1961	—
December 1969	November 1970	—
November 1973	March 1975	—
January 1980	July 1980	6/3/1980
July 1981	November 1982	1/6/1982
July 1990	March 1991	4/25/1991
March 2001	November 2001	11/26/2001
December 2007	June 2009	12/1/2008

Source: Birinyi Associates, Inc.

The investment implication, what sectors one should buy in advance of the economy bottoming, are almost everything. As shown in Figure 15.1, the S&P gains just under 10 percent (in three months), with seven of the ten sectors providing market or near-market performance.

Going into a recession, the market is mixed with a negative bias, but the details are less evident. Defensive sectors do a bit better while energy and tech are down (see Figure 15.2).

GDP AND THE MARKET, NO SURPRISES HERE

Drilling down, GDP for each quarter for the last decade (back to 2002) was analyzed and sorted by performance (see Figure 15.3). Since 2002, there have been 14 (out of 45) quarters where GDP growth was equal to

TABLE 15.2 Expansions

Start	End	Date Declared
March 1961	November 1969	—
December 1970	October 1973	—
April 1975	December 1979	—
August 1980	June 1981	7/8/1981
December 1982	June 1990	7/8/1983
April 1991	February 2001	12/22/1992
December 2001	November 2007	7/17/2003
July 2009	March 2013	9/20/2010

Source: Birinyi Associates, Inc.

TABLE 15.3 S&P 500 Bottom versus Recession End

Recession End	S&P Bottom	Months Until End of Recession	Gain from Market Bottom to Recession End
February 1961	10/25/1960	4.20	21.30%
November 1970	5/26/1970	6.27	25.85
March 1975	10/3/1974	5.97	33.85
July 1980	3/27/1980	4.20	23.87
November 1982	8/12/1982	3.67	35.27
March 1991	10/11/1990	5.70	27.00
November 2001	9/21/2001	2.33	17.98
June 2009	3/9/2009	3.77	35.88
	Average	**4.51**	**27.63**

Source: Birinyi Associates, Inc.

or greater than 3 percent. The average S&P response was +5 percent but returns were clustered between 0 and 5 percent.

For the investor:

- Strong (GDP equal to or greater than 3 percent) growth is manifested primarily by energy, technology, industrials, and materials. In a word, cyclicals except consumer discretionary stocks. Defensive sectors (health care, staples) are underperformers.
- Moderate growth coincides with lackluster markets and limited sector insights.
- Subpar growth somewhat mirrors moderate growth: mixed markets, mixed sectors.
- Negative growth leads to negative results.

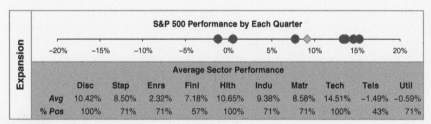

FIGURE 15.1 Market and Sector Performance Three Months Prior to the Beginning of an Expansion

Source: Birinyi Associates, Inc.

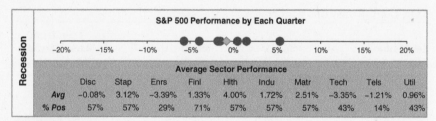

FIGURE 15.2 Market and Sector Performance Three Months Prior to the Beginning of a Recession

Source: Birinyi Associates, Inc.

While investors and analysts consider the economy, they are obsessed with the Fed and its members. Forecasting Fed policy and all of its nuances has always been a critical element for both the stock and bond markets. And it was, until 1994, the primary occupation of economists.

Historically, pre-February 1994, the results of the Fed's deliberations were not available until three months thereafter. In the intervening

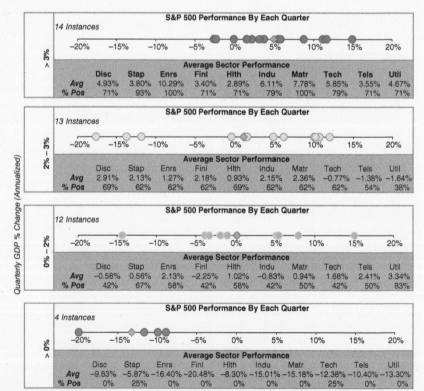

FIGURE 15.3 GDP Growth versus Market and Sector Performance

Source: Birinyi Associates, Inc.

period, economists sought to anticipate those deliberations and produce guidance regarding interest rates. In 1994, in one of those structural changes that had far-reaching impact, Chairman Greenspan changed procedure and immediately shared the conclusion. Not only did this create increased short-term volatility, it also altered the role of the economist.

Now, economists, being deprived of their previous primary function, turned to forecasting employment, retail sales, manufacturing, and other economic issues. Some even ventured into stock market commentary, resulting in more emphasis on the almost daily economic indicator about which they may or may not have been knowledgeable.

THE FED TIGHTENS: IT HURTS ONLY FOR A LITTLE WHILE

Equity market investors are, understandably, mostly concerned regarding shifts in the FRB's policy, both on a strategic and tactical response, if not in anticipation of those shifts. Detailing changes should be relatively simple, and we are all familiar with the graph that shows changes in the Discount Rate (to 1981) and, thereafter, changes in the Fed Funds Rate as shown in Figure 15.4.

We have shaded those areas that we consider to mark Fed tightening periods, which should make analysis simple. The key word is "should." Other analysts have considered the uptick in 1971 and 1997 as candidates, but since these were one-off increases we do not (see Figure 15.5).

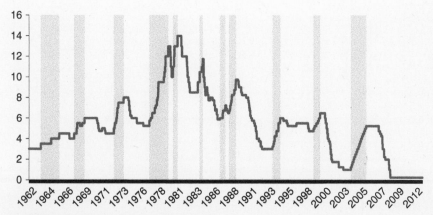

FIGURE 15.4 FRB Tightening Periods
Source: Birinyi Associates, Inc., FRB.

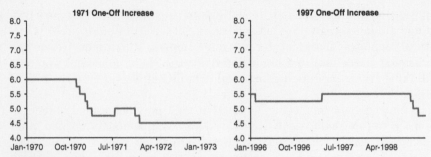

FIGURE 15.5   1971 and 1997 One-Off Increase

Source: Birinyi Associates, Inc., FRB.

Another source contends that the 1986 to 1987 tightening period actually began in 1987 and lasted just one increase. Although we think it is clear that the uptick began on December 16, 1986 and lasted until September 3, 1987, investors should be aware that other results may differ from our analysis (see Figure 15.6).[1]

Before the Fed changes policy, there is some market weakness, but it is inconsistent and despite our efforts to find some economic or market denominator that would explain or illuminate the difference between the periods of weakness and strength, we could not do so (see Figure 15.7).

Table 15.4 shows the S&P change on the day of the Fed announcement.

Although it is counterintuitive and surely contrary to most expectations, periods of rising interest rates are detrimental only in the short

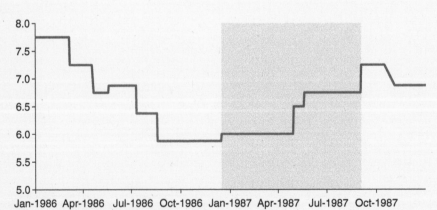

FIGURE 15.6   Differing FRB Tightening Periods

Source: Birinyi Associates, Inc., FRB.

TABLE 15.4 S&P 500 Change on Day of First Increase

				Rate		S&P 500
	Begin	**End**	**Length**	**Start**	**End**	**Event Day**
Discount Rate	7/17/1963	12/6/1965	873	3.00	4.50	−0.30%
	11/20/1967	4/4/1969	501	4.00	6.00	−1.26
	1/15/1973	4/25/1974	465	4.50	8.00	−0.72
	8/30/1977	2/15/1980	899	5.25	13.00	−0.56
	9/26/1980	5/5/1881	221	10.00	14.00	−1.84
Fed Funds	1/3/1984	8/21/1984	147	8.50	11.75	−0.54
	12/16/1986	9/3/1987	261	5.88	7.25	0.74
	3/29/1988	2/24/1989	332	6.50	9.75	0.78
	2/4/1994	2/1/1995	362	3.00	6.00	−2.27
	6/30/1999	5/16/2000	321	4.75	6.50	1.57
	6/30/2004	6/29/2006	729	1.00	5.25	0.41

Source: Birinyi Associates, Inc.

term, and even then not to the threshold of corrections (see Figure 15.8). (We would, however, disregard the average as it is unduly influenced by the 15 percent gain in 1986.)

During periods of rising interest rates, except for 1973, the stock market goes up. In both 1963 and 1986, it did so for a gain approximating 30 percent (see Figure 15.9). During those periods, investors should buy stocks, especially deep cyclicals, and avoid consumer and financial names.

We also asked if the degree of change in Fed rates had an influence on the performance of the S&P 500 (see Figure 15.10). At best, the correlation is weak.

It is, therefore, somewhat surprising to see the dread and concern in 2013 regarding the possibility of higher rates. Although it is readily

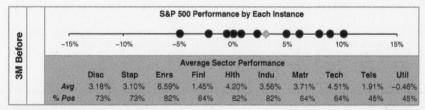

FIGURE 15.7 Market and Sector Performance Three Months Before First Tightening
Source: Birinyi Associates, Inc.

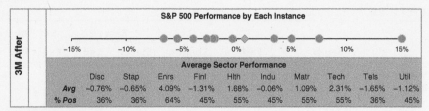

FIGURE 15.8   Market and Sector Performance Three Months After First Tightening
Source: Birinyi Associates, Inc.

agreed that policies such as QE3, and Operation Twist before it, were without precedent, it is also an apparent consensus that they will "end badly."

One strategist was quoted in a *Wall Street Journal* article advising investors to sell now as the market has "historically averaged an 8 percent drop in the six months before" Fed actions.

In another example of the lack of even superficial research, we calculate in the six months prior the average was plus 3.5 percent even with the 1988 result, which incorporated the '87 Crash (see Table 15.5). Removing 1988 the average was plus 5.8 percent, which is a light year from –8 percent.

TABLE 15.5   FRB Tightenings versus Six-Month Prior Performance

	S&P 500 . . . Months Before			
	12 Months	**6 Months**	**3 Months**	**Begin**
Discount Rate	21.40%	5.86%	5.81%	7/17/1963
	12.79	–0.46	–2.23	11/20/1967
	14.56	10.90	10.18	1/15/1973
	–5.57	–3.45	–0.57	8/30/1977
	14.64	28.64	8.92	9/26/1980
Fed Funds	18.58	–2.88	–1.06	1/3/1984
	17.93	1.59	7.92	12/16/1986
	–10.07	–19.53	4.93	3/29/1988
	4.50	4.84	2.23	2/4/1994
	21.07	10.54	6.11	6/30/1999
	16.14	2.81	0.77	6/30/2004
Average	**11.45**	**3.53**	**3.91**	

Source: Birinyi Associates, Inc.

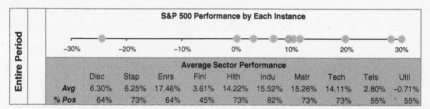

FIGURE 15.9 Market and Sector Performance during Entire Tightening Period
Source: Birinyi Associates, Inc.

1994: A LITTLE PERSPECTIVE, IF YOU PLEASE

Other reports have likewise warned and drawn parallels to 1994. The *Financial Times*, for example, devoted a full page to "The ghosts of '94", while *Bloomberg BusinessWeek* detailed the carnage in the markets that year; *Euromoney* (March 13) wrote about the threat of rising rates (". . . could be far worse than 1994").

1994 was a difficult year for markets but somewhat surprisingly given that investors seem to have been alerted. The *Financial Times* wrote in late January: "Why the Fed Should Tighten" and on January 31, Mr. Greenspan himself "strongly implied" that the Fed would raise rates, which he did several days later (February 4).

Bonds traded lower and it was to be a long year for fixed income as shown in Figure 15.11.

Stocks that were testing the 4,000 level on the DJIA and were up 5.7 percent before the Fed's February 4 increase (they lost 96 points that day) ended the year with a modest gain of 2.14 percent (see Figure 15.12). From January 31 to April 4 stocks fell 9.42 percent, which was not a correction, albeit barely. This despite the fact that the Fed continued to raise

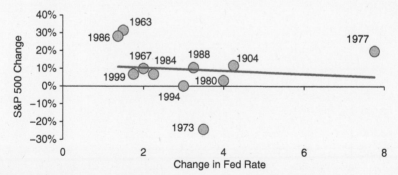

FIGURE 15.10 S&P 500 Change versus FRB Tightening Cycle
Source: Birinyi Associates, Inc., FRB.

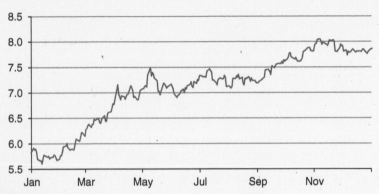

FIGURE 15.11   Yield on 10-Year Treasury Note: 1994
Source: Birinyi Associates, Inc., FRB.

rates including a 75 basis point increase (the largest since 1981) in mid-November.

1995: ECONOMISTS PREDICT BECAUSE THEY ARE ASKED, BUT WHY?

The concerns and fears articulated by the media were overwhelmed and negated by 1995, which was to be the best year of the last fifty, while bonds also participated and flummoxed economists. Only one of the fifty respondents in *BusinessWeek's* annual outlook survey anticipated a decline in the 30-year bond to 6 percent, with the majority expecting rates to rally (see Figures 15.13 to 15.15).

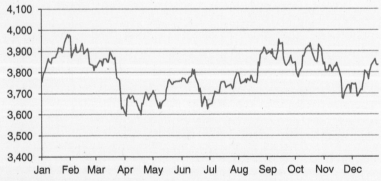

FIGURE 15.12   DJIA: 1994
Source: Birinyi Associates, Inc., Bloomberg.

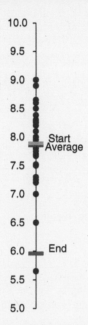

FIGURE 15.13 1995 Forecasted 30-Year T-Bond
Source: Birinyi Associates, Inc., *BusinessWeek.*

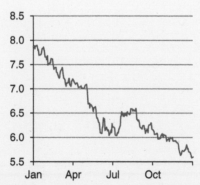

FIGURE 15.14 Yield on 10-Year Treasury Note: 1995
Source: Birinyi Associates, Inc.

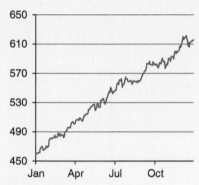

FIGURE 15.15   S&P 500: 1995

Source: Birinyi Associates, Inc., FRB, Bloomberg.

NOTE

1. This is especially disconcerting as it comes not only from a major brokerage firm, but also from an economic consulting firm.

CHAPTER 16

Picking Stocks

The smart investor must know the difference between what is temporarily undervalued and what is permanently undervalued.

—John Templeton

W hat to buy or sell is an increasingly difficult decision. Individual stocks have been joined by all manner of exchange-traded funds (ETFs), baskets, and other instruments. For the most part, we would advise against buying ETFs. ETFs are often variations of a theme. Rather than buy one retailer, one can buy them all either with Market Vectors Retail ETF (RTH) or the S&P Retail ETF (XRT).

That might be appealing after you have noticed how crowded your favorite store seems to be or how appealing the merchandise is at Target. But RTH is not just about Macy's and Target; it also includes AutoZone and Whole Foods. XRT is a group of 96 stocks including Tiffany & Co., Tractor Supply, and Lithia Motors. Do you really know what you are getting?

Another issue with ETFs is that they are regularly themes, and theme investing has a spotty record. Over time, we have seen an abundance of themes, none of which ever seemed to work out:

- There was the leisure theme as automation would give us more time for recreation and leisure. We seem to recall that bowling stocks were one manifestation of that idea.
- Another was the aging theme as the population lived longer and required more medical care. Nursing homes were at the core of that idea.
- And lest we forget, there was the alternative energy idea including solar power with First Solar (see Figure 16.1).

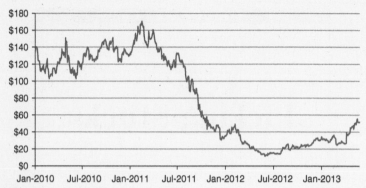

FIGURE 16.1   First Solar

Source: Birinyi Associates, Inc., Bloomberg.

Furthermore, ETFs regularly do not perform as they are intended. For instance, the United States Oil Fund (USO) is supposed to track the price change of West Texas crude oil. But, as shown in Figure 16.2, that has not happened.

For individuals, stock selection can be considerably more rewarding. Our newsletter limits itself to ten stocks in a growth portfolio and ten stocks in a conservative portfolio. While we hasten to add the familiar "past performance clause," we would like to think it exhibits diligence and discipline but it does not reflect commissions and the costs associated with trading (see Figure 16.3).

FIGURE 16.2   Oil ETF versus Actual Commodity

Source: Birinyi Associates, Inc., Bloomberg.

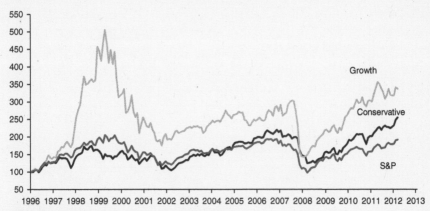

FIGURE 16.3 Reminiscences Performance

Source: Birinyi Associates, Inc.

So for an individual who has not delegated his or her portfolio to someone else, or for the professional who has the actual responsibility of managing and implementing the investment decision, it is both difficult and lonely, but also occasionally satisfying.

An often suggested approach is to buy what you know. Express your own experiences from products and services you yourself have tried. While this sometimes works, it sometimes does not. I once noticed that the teens of Fairfield County, Connecticut, had a strong preference for Gap Stores (see Figure 16.4). At that time—some years ago—they might have been alone, as the stock never responded.

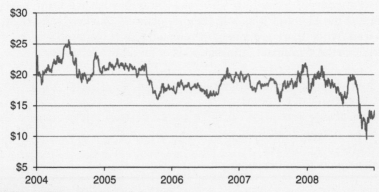

FIGURE 16.4 The Gap

Source: Birinyi Associates, Inc., Bloomberg.

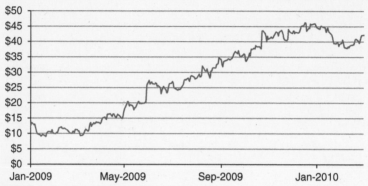

FIGURE 16.5 J.Crew Group

Source: Birinyi Associates, Inc., Bloomberg

When their tastes shifted or evolved to J.Crew, I knew better but like Mr. Twain's "cat having sat on a hot stove," I did not note that this stove was cold and only watched as J.Crew soared (see Figure 16.5).

On another occasion, we walked down Madison Avenue on a weekend and in amazement saw a queue at Deckers Outdoor as the store was limiting entrance to 5 or 10 customers at a time. This must surely be a sign of overwhelming demand. I painfully recall buying the stock at $100 and selling it around $80.

SEEDS: IDEAS TO GET YOU STARTED, PLANTING, AND HARVESTING COME LATER

To us the concept of *buying what you know* is what we term a *seed*. It generates the idea but it should then be planted, nurtured, and regularly reviewed. While there are a host of fundamental considerations, for most individuals the significant information is not readily available:

- Revenue source: domestic or international
- Consistency of earnings
- Critical suppliers
- Major competitors
- Wall Street opinions
- Comments from management

While these are important, they are not necessarily critical as they deal primarily with the *company* while most investors are buying the *stock*.

Furthermore, the fundamentals are, in our experience, overrated. One that is frequently discussed is the competence of management. Despite having had three courses with the Dean of all management consultants, Peter Drucker, I still have no good idea how one isolates and quantifies that characteristic. I recall only one detailed observation from him, which was that firms that are well managed are boring.

One of his favorite stories featured Alfred Sloan, the architect of General Motors, whose hearing aid had a talk or listen switch. During one Board meeting, the merits of a Mr. Smith were under consideration for a significant promotion. Mr. Smith had apparently expedited a shipment of axles for a given plant and at the eleventh hour settled a union dispute and so on.

Mr. Sloan, having heard enough, turned his hearing aid to talk at which point everyone else stopped. (It was, Drucker said, the only effective management tool he had ever seen.)

So, Mr. Sloan asked where was Mr. Smith when the schedule for axle shipments was drawn up and where was Mr. Smith when the union official first raised the issue and. . . . As Mr. Drucker said, "Mr. Smith was never heard from again." The professor's point was that good managers anticipate rather than react.[1]

For the moment, we will defer as to the next step and consider other seeds and their source.

Cross fertilization always merits attention. We regularly review recommendations and ideas from a variety of sources. Our interest is heightened when we find that a technical approach coincides with a fundamental view or a quantitative model. While we may not immediately buy into the idea, the fact that it is being analyzed from several different vantage points makes it interesting. But at this point it is only an idea.

While we insist that caution be exercised, we regularly read the end-of-year lists in the various publications and the names mentioned in surveys or reviews.

SPRAINED WRISTS EVENTUALLY HEAL (AND PROSPER)

Stocks with "sprained wrists" are also of interest, as opposed to stocks that are broken. Here we are suggesting that one should consider if an incident or development that is probably short-term in nature is being viewed as a long-term, significant problem. Which was, we thought, the case with News Corp in mid-2011 (see Figure 16.6).

That year, the company was found to have tapped phones and engaged in a variety of questionable practices at their London newspapers. Without making any moral judgments, we contended that this was a public relations

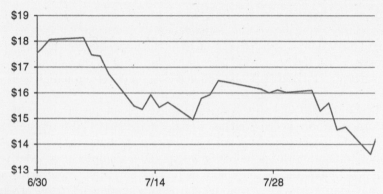

FIGURE 16.6 News Corp: 2011

Source: Birinyi Associates, Inc., Bloomberg.

issue. Fox would continue to produce television shows, the movie studio was still in business, and the *Wall Street Journal* would be delivered every morning (see Figure 16.7).

Several incidents in 2013 illustrated the same idea. In late April, Ralph Lauren was fined for bribing customs officials in Argentina and the news had an immediate, negative impact (see Figure 16.8). We considered this a temporary blip and more a function of a unique business circumstance, and by week's end we had made a handsome gain.

Or there was the case of Lululemon, which was not quite as clear (see Figure 16.9). It was discovered that at least one batch of their well-selling

FIGURE 16.7 News Corp

Source: Birinyi Associates, Inc., Bloomberg.

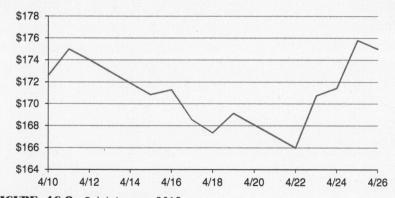

FIGURE 16.8 Ralph Lauren: 2013

Source: Birinyi Associates, Inc., Bloomberg.

yoga pants provided more than expected exposure. Here, one had to determine if this was temporary or had greater negative potential. We did not buy the stock but clearly should have.

In May 2012, JP Morgan stumbled badly when they announced that one of their traders in London had a $6.2 billion trading loss. The stock lost 25 percent over the ensuing month (see Figure 16.10). Here is a company we are very familiar with: we understand their business, and we were comfortable that this was a short-term issue and not a long-term fundamentally negative event. We used the weakness to buy and as of April 2013, we were quickly rewarded.

Our sprained-wrist theory is often found at earnings season. Is the gain or loss a one-time event, or does it suggest a significant change? Oracle

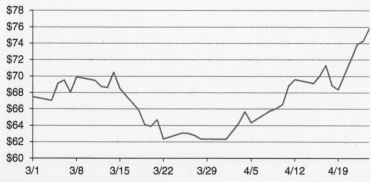

FIGURE 16.9 Lululemon: 2013

Source: Birinyi Associates, Inc., Bloomberg

FIGURE 16.10 JP Morgan

Source: Birinyi Associates, Inc., Bloomberg.

disappointed investors with its first quarter 2013 results, but said that it was a result of expansion; many new hires that had yet to gain experience and so forth (see Figure 16.11). We viewed this as temporary and nonrecurring, and therefore a chance to buy the stock at somewhat of a discount.

Situations like these can create either investment opportunities (News Corp) or trading ones (Ralph Lauren) and are one reason we always prefer to have some cash available.

It should also be a consideration in the other direction. Hurricane Sandy in late 2012 was truly a climatic event with a dramatic impact, including weeks long power outages. That in turn created a huge demand for generators. Generac Holdings, a company that made generators, saw its stock price spike (see Figure 16.12).

We considered this a temporary situation and realized that the immediate demand for generators could not be met, and while the company's

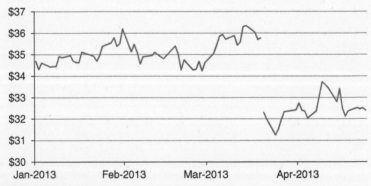

FIGURE 16.11 Oracle

Source: Birinyi Associates, Inc., Bloomberg.

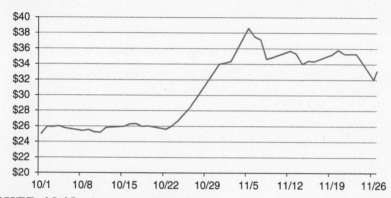

FIGURE 16.12 Generac Holdings: 2012

Source: Birinyi Associates, Inc., Bloomberg.

long-term prospects were probably improving, the $5 gain in the stock was unrealistic and we initiated a trade on the short side.

Consider stocks that "act well." Investors should regularly monitor a group of names that for whatever reason they would be comfortable buying, where they are aware of the business and have some knowledge of the company. By regularly monitoring, as we will discuss, investors should get a feel for the stock and some sense of its trading pattern.

Another candidate from 2013 was Boeing. The company bet the house on its new 787 Dreamliner. Shortly after delivery, the plane's batteries caught fire and the planes were grounded (as most people are well aware). Sensing an opportunity, we sold some stock, intending to buy it back at a lower price. As time went on, the planes stayed on the ground and solutions were not forthcoming. But the stock didn't go down and as the situation started to clear, the stock literally soared but without us on board (see Figure 16.13).

In the summer of 2012, Procter & Gamble cut forecasts reflecting softness in their European business (see Figure 16.14). Although the stock bent, it did not break and that, coupled with an oversold condition, allowed us to buy it in the very low 60s.

CAPITULATION: ANOTHER EXAMPLE OF THE ANECDOTAL PROCESS

Capitulation regularly creates opportunities. When monitoring a group of stocks, one will regularly find names in an unending downtrend. The bottom is regularly accompanied by *really* bad news.

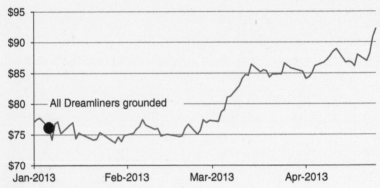

FIGURE 16.13 Boeing

Source: Birinyi Associates, Inc., Bloomberg.

Hewlett-Packard in November 2012 was such a stock and the bad news got worse when the company announced the $8 billion write-down of a 2011 acquisition, Autonomy. Sharks and sharp pens circled the stock and on 11/20/12, it traded to $11.71 on heavy (5x) volume (see Figure 16.15).

The combination of heavy selling, lower price, and it-can't-get-any-worse created an opportunity (see Figure 16.16).

The first quarter of 2013 report for Caterpillar might have been another example. For months, there was no good news and its 1Q results were likewise disappointing (see Figure 16.17).

Again heavy volume, drop in price, and bad news combined to make at least a tradable bottom.

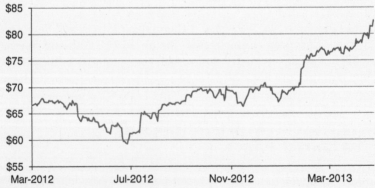

FIGURE 16.14 Procter & Gamble

Source: Birinyi Associates, Inc., Bloomberg.

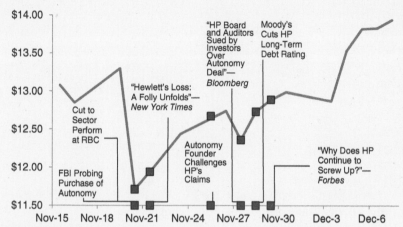

FIGURE 16.15 Hewlett-Packard: November 2012 through December 2012

Source: Birinyi Associates, Inc., Bloomberg.

TREND CHARTS: LATE IN, EARLY OUT, BUT PROFITABLE AND COMFORTABLE

We also find stocks by looking for exceptions and especially situations that are under the radar or scarcely mentioned. Some years back, we noticed that one of the blue chips in the Paris market was not in their index. Hermès, while familiar to many investors as an item of clothing or a pocketbook, was never considered as an investment (see Figure 16.18).

Since it was a well-known name, we considered first that it could be a possible addition to the CAC 40, the French equivalent to our Dow Jones

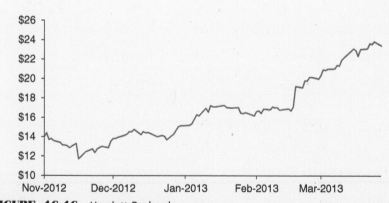

FIGURE 16.16 Hewlett-Packard

Source: Birinyi Associates, Inc., Bloomberg.

FIGURE 16.17 Caterpillar: February 2013 through May 2013

Source: Birinyi Associates, Inc., Bloomberg.

Industrial Average, which would create demand for the stock. It was later noted that while there were 20 analysts who covered and wrote about the company, it was somewhat unique as it was the most significant global company where there was not a single buy recommendation. While we are not contrarian per se, the combination of a strong brand, potential index inclusion, and potential upgrades was compelling and profitable. (Unfortunately, the stock trades only in Paris and therefore is subject to currency fluctuations.)

Having created some purchase candidates, our next step is to consider their circumstances. First we analyze the stock's technical circumstances using charts that show the direction and parameters of the stock. Some will readily object that given our thrashing and view of technicals, we are being

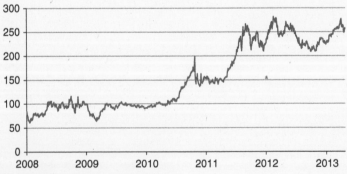

FIGURE 16.18 Hermès International

Source: Birinyi Associates, Inc., Bloomberg.

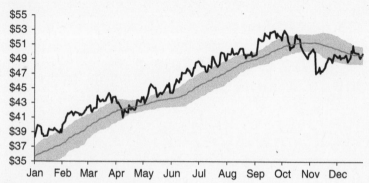

FIGURE 16.19 Disney: 2012

Source: Birinyi Associates, Inc., Bloomberg.

hypocritical. Not really, as we are not necessarily projecting, only implementing Newton's law that a body in motion will continue until. . . .

The charts we describe are illustrated by Disney in 2012, shown in Figure 16.19. Had we been interested at the time, we would have noted that the stock is in a well-defined uptrend. Yes, we would have been late; yes, it was already up; and unlike the chartist we have no idea how long or how high but we go with the trend.

The stock remains in the trend through the summer and hiccups somewhat in November when the company missed its earnings expectations. Had we bought the stock in January 2012 at $38 we would still have—after the earnings disappointment at $48—a 26 percent gain. And while the trend stalls, it does not break. At the end of April 2013, it is out of its trading parameters and vulnerable to bad news (see Figure 16.20). It may correct, it may consolidate (go sideways for some time), or it may go higher, but

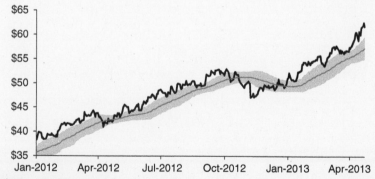

FIGURE 16.20 Disney

Source: Birinyi Associates, Inc., Bloomberg.

FIGURE 16.21 Disney 50-Day Average Spread (%)

Source: Birinyi Associates, Inc., Bloomberg.

at this point the stock is up 63 percent, a dilemma most investors would gladly entertain.

We might also create a chart that shows the spread between the stock's price and its average price over the last 50 days, as shown in Figure 16.21. *Every stock will have its own fingerprint and characteristics.* Disney seems to get 6 percent or so above its moving average and then consolidates. We are not suggesting that you sell at that point, only realize that from here gains will be labored.

At 8 percent *below* the stock is oversold and could go lower or present a buying opportunity. Chartists will insist on one or the other; we won't.

If we look more closely, the stock does get oversold in early November 2012 and trades through the lower end of the band (see Figure 16.22).

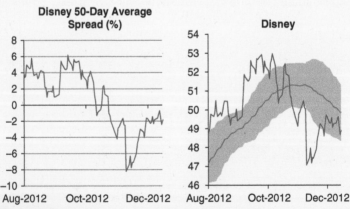

FIGURE 16.22 Disney

Source: Birinyi Associates, Inc., Bloomberg.

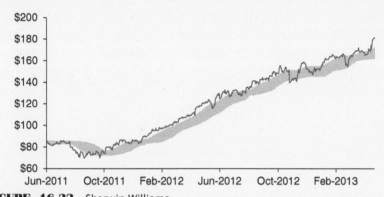

FIGURE 16.23 Sherwin-Williams

Source: Birinyi Associates, Inc., Bloomberg.

One might consider taking some significant profits but if we do some homework, we find that the depressed price was in response to lower sales and revenues. Few companies (Jack Welch's GE comes to mind as an exception) beat *every* quarter and we would be inclined—given what the stock has done—to stay the course. But we would understand if you trimmed or sold your position.

Tracking your names and names of interest at least on a weekly basis should result not only in better results, but also understanding.

A great stock in 2012 was Sherwin-Williams, whose trend was likewise in effect before January 1, 2012 (see Figure 16.23). We doubt that even the management could have expected the stock to gain over 70 percent that year and another 10 percent in 1Q 2013.

At some point, the trend will break and we would be late in selling the stock as this approach does not *anticipate*. It does, however, provide some help in the sentiment or psychology. As shown in Figure 16.24, Sherwin-Williams was trading above its range, in May 2013. A downgrade, a negative comment from management, or an earnings miss could have a more dramatic impact here than it had in April 2012. As of now, there is an abundance of happy holders who are more likely to be considering an exit than an entrance.

These charts can also help one understand the tactical circumstances. Disney and Sherwin-Williams were clearly buy and hold, or investments. IBM at the beginning of 2012 was in an uptrend, but it was not that well-defined and while we might have bought the stock in January at 186, by June that trend was broken, prompting us to sell at a small profit (see Figure 16.25).

Thereafter, it was clear that the stock was a *trading* name and subject to volatility, and added only 4 percent as a result.

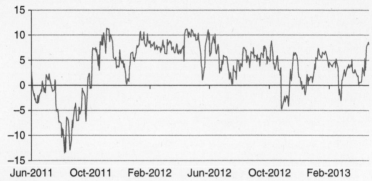

FIGURE 16.24   Sherwin-Williams 50-Day Average Spread (%)

Source: Birinyi Associates, Inc., Bloomberg.

Entering 2012, Best Buy was in a downtrend and for the investor was a proverbial "no brainer" (see Figure 16.26). One might guess at the possibilities and potentials and, yes, the stock had a nice gain at the start of 2013 as a result of a possible buyout, but in 2012 the stock was a no-no.

It is important, we think, to again note that one should undertake this analysis only after one is comfortable with the company. We would like to think we know Sherwin-Williams. Maybe not the financials nor their product mix or other interesting and trivial characteristics, but, as has often been said, "the most important fundamental is price."

Roland Grimm, former manager of the Yale Endowment, once said, "You have to be careful regarding the railroad analyst who knows how many ties there are between New York and Washington and not when to sell Penn Central."

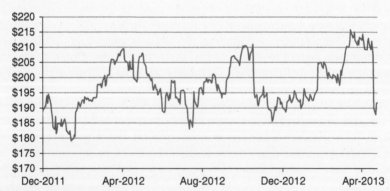

FIGURE 16.25   IBM

Source: Birinyi Associates, Inc., Bloomberg.

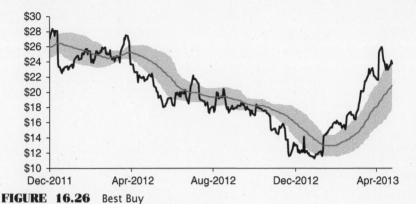

FIGURE 16.26 Best Buy

Source: Birinyi Associates, Inc., Bloomberg.

NOTE

1. The ultimate management story, however, comes from sports. Jim Murray, the decorated sports writer for *Sports Illustrated* and the *LA Times*, once stood near Arnold Palmer who was in a ditch, behind a tree, with his ball stuck in the mud.

   Palmer turned to him: "Murray, you are always talking about Hogan, what would he do in a situation like this?" Murray responded: "Hogan wouldn't *be* in a situation like this."

CHAPTER 17

The Trading Day

For the gods perceive things in the future, ordinary people think in the present, but the wise perceive things about to happen.

—Philostratus

There is an important issue that we have not addressed directly, which is that markets change, instruments change, investors change, as do regulations, fashions, and approaches. We recall that, not that many years ago, inflation was considered a positive for common stocks. The United States was a manufacturing economy; plants and equipment were expensive to build and implement. Hence, expanding or building a new auto plant or steel mill was costly.

Over time, the economy has transitioned into one of financial services and investors' views on inflation—especially after the 1970s—have taken a 180-degree turn (see Figure 17.1).

In the market itself, one of our favorite charts shows the relationship between technology and drugs. For many years they were highly correlated, as shown by the the chart in Figure 17.2.

Beginning in 1999, the drugs became more stable. They took on defensive characteristics and the correlation became undone. Over time, they have become considered more value than growth because of their cash flow and dividends (see Figure 17.3). Today, they are highly correlated with consumer non-durables such as foods and beverages.

The S&P itself has undergone a significant change, which should be a consideration in judging fund managers over time. As late as 1965, the largest component was AT&T, at 7.5 percent of the index. It and GM made up

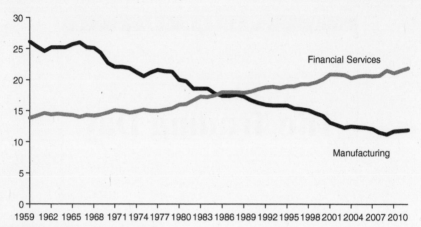

FIGURE 17.1   Percent of GDP

Source: Birinyi Associates, Inc.

almost 15 percent, while the top ten stocks accounted for over a third of the entire *500*. At the end of 2012, Apple at 3.8 percent was the stock with the greatest value; the 10 largest companies totaled only 20 percent of the index (see Table 17.1).

As a result, your grandfather's manager faced fewer decisions; his largest companies were more predictable, their business was more stable, and price-wise these companies were surely a lot less volatile.

Economists accommodate for change by seasonal adjustments, while statisticians use standard deviations and other adjustments to make comparisons equitable. It is our view that sometimes too much data is actually a handicap as it incorporates different circumstances. Risk measures, as one example, before the advent of options were a totally different environment.

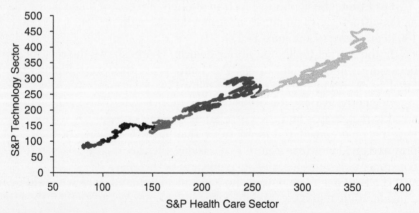

FIGURE 17.2   Health Care versus Technology: 1994 through 1998

Source: Birinyi Associates, Inc.

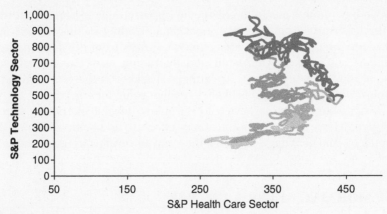

FIGURE 17.3 Health Care versus Technology: 1999 through 2012
Source: Birinyi Associates, Inc.

TABLE 17.1 Market Capitalization 1965 versus 2012

1965		
	Market Value ($, millions)	Weight (%)	Cumulative Weight (%)
AT&T	31,735	7.5	7.5
General Motors	29,503	7.0	14.5
IBM	17,537	4.1	18.6
Standard Oil-NJ	17,337	4.1	22.7
Kennecott	13,455	3.2	25.9
Dupont	11,007	2.6	28.5
General Electric	10,687	2.5	31.0
Sears-Roebuck	10,045	2.4	33.4
Gulf	6,013	1.4	34.8
Standard Oil-CA	5,847	1.4	36.2

2012		
	Market Value ($, millions)	Weight (%)	Cumulative Weight (%)
Apple	500,611	3.8	3.8
Exxon	394,611	3.2	7.1
IBM	216,439	1.9	9.0
General Electric	220,107	1.7	10.7
Chevron	211,650	1.7	12.4
Microsoft	224,801	1.6	14.0
Pfizer	184,648	1.6	15.5
AT&T	191,473	1.5	17.0
Procter & Gamble	185,627	1.5	18.5
Johnson & Johnson	194,265	1.5	20.0

Source: Birinyi Associates, Inc.

We have found portfolio enhancing opportunities in short-term trading by ignoring or omitting historical data. Trading in this decade, and especially the post financial crisis market, differs from previous markets, including bull markets. Our detail on daily trading, as well as the data supplied in the following chapters relating to markets, is therefore limited to the current experience and is likely to evolve going forward.

Despite our efforts, we have not been able to develop metrics for shorter periods and have no confidence in others' efforts to do so either. There is one exception—the next day—and even then only in certain circumstances.

THE MORNING AFTER A BIG DAY

We regularly publish a series, *The Trader's Handbook*, that details a variety of patterns and insights. The first being, the day after, or what we might expect after a significant day.

Table 17.2 summarizes the 92 days of 2 percent moves in the S&P after March 2009 through the first quarter of 2012, while Figure 17.4 illustrates a typical experience.

- The positive mood (there were 45 days of 2 percent gains) is seldom carried over. Futures the next morning are, on average, down 0.13 percent and on only two instances are they up more than 1 percent.
- Large moves are more likely to be negative; of the 11 days where there was a 1 percent move, it was negative in seven instances.

There were 47 days of 2 percent or greater declines, as shown in Table 17.3.

- Markets are more volatile following these declines than they are after similar advances: There were 12 days of subsequent 1 percent gains and nine declines of that magnitude.

TABLE 17.2 S&P 500: Day after Up 2 Percent

	Futures at 9:15	Gap	S&P 500 Change				
			Open to Close	10:00 to Close	Noon to Close	3:30 to Close	Day
Average	−0.13%	−0.13%	−0.02%	0.04%	−0.03%	−0.07%	−0.15%
Median	−0.13%	−0.11%	0.13%	0.15%	0.02%	−0.02%	0.04%
% Positive	43%	25%	59%	55%	51%	45%	51%

Source: Birinyi Associates, Inc.

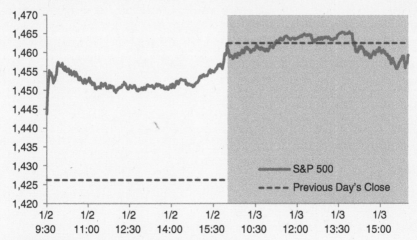

FIGURE 17.4 S&P 500: January 2 and 3, 2013

Source: Birinyi Associates, Inc., Bloomberg.

Days where the market moves 1 percent and closes at the high of the day are more common and account for 8.9 percent of all days since April 2009 (we have eliminated March 2009 given its volatility). The net result was totally random. We then segregated them by those that had a steady rise closing at or near the top, as was the case on December 18, 2012 (see Figure 17.5).

The next day's move was random. The opening was random as well (see Table 17.4).

Looking at days where the market went higher and traded lower, but was still up 1 percent by the close, was likewise not rewarding (see Figure 17.6).

Days following one percent moves—in either direction—provided no clues as to what might ensue the next day.

TABLE 17.3 S&P 500: Day after Down 3 Percent

| | Futures at 9:15 | Gap | S&P 500 Change | | | | |
			Open to Close	10:00 to Close	Noon to Close	3:30 to Close	Day
Average	−0.09%	−0.03%	0.25%	0.20%	0.14%	0.21%	0.21%
Median	0.20%	0.04%	0.19%	0.24%	0.10%	0.01%	0.37%
% Positive	56%	54%	54%	64%	64%	51%	58%

Source: Birinyi Associates, Inc.

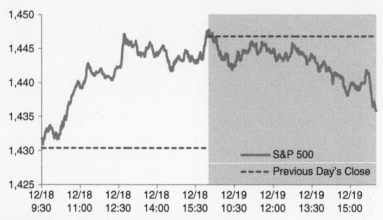

FIGURE 17.5   S&P 500: December 18 and 19, 2012

Source: Birinyi Associates, Inc., Bloomberg.

TABLE 17.4   S&P 500: Day after Up 1 Percent and Closes at High

| | Futures at 9:15 | S&P 500 Change | | | | | |
		Gap	Open to Close	10:00 to Close	Noon to Close	3:30 to Close	Day
Average	−0.07%	−0.09%	−0.09%	−0.08%	−0.07%	−0.05%	−0.18%
Median	−0.09%	−0.08%	0.04%	−0.04%	−0.03%	0.00%	−0.04%
% Positive	46%	35%	52%	47%	48%	48%	46%

Source: Birinyi Associates, Inc.

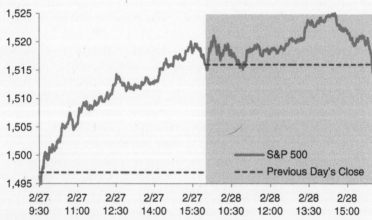

FIGURE 17.6   S&P 500: February 27 and 28, 2012

Source: Birinyi Associates, Inc., Bloomberg.

WHAT DO FUTURES TELL US?

Futures, however, do provide some guidance. On days when futures are up 1 percent, the market is likely to gain about 1 percent from the open to the close and it does so fairly consistently. Table 17.5 and Figure 17.7 illustrate this going back to the beginning of the bull market (March 9th, 2009).

TABLE 17.5 S&P 500: Futures Up 1 Percent

	S&P 500 Change				
	Open to Close	**10:00 to Close**	**Noon to Close**	**3:30 to Close**	**Day**
Average	1.06%	0.27%	0.17%	0.17%	1.86%
Median	1.06%	0.27%	0.05%	0.09%	1.74%
% Positive	78%	65%	51%	66%	90%

Source: Birinyi Associates, Inc.

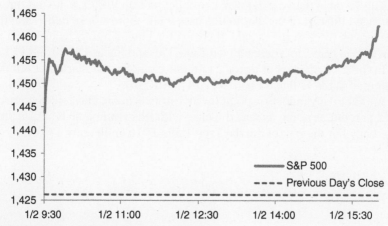

FIGURE 17.7 S&P 500: January 2, 2013
Source: Birinyi Associates, Inc., Bloomberg.

IT'S 10:00 A.M.: DO YOU KNOW WHERE YOUR STOCKS ARE GOING?

Intraday there are two critical junctures: 10:00 A.M. and noon. In the bull market that began in March 2009 there were (as of June 2013) 89 instances of the market being up 1 to 2 percent at 10:00 A.M. Thereafter, the market,

TABLE 17.6   S&P 500: Market Up 1 to 2 Percent at 10 A.M.

	S&P 500 Change			
	10:00 to Close	Noon to Close	3:30 to Close	Day
Average	0.03%	0.06%	0.14%	1.39%
Median	0.14%	0.01%	0.08%	1.45%
% Positive	61%	50%	67%	91%

Source: Birinyi Associates, Inc.

on average, makes little or no progress as also illustrated by the numbers for November 19, 2012 (see Table 17.6 and Figure 17.8).

Traders should, however, have a positive bias. More of those days will trade higher with the best individual day gaining 3.24 percent after 10:00 A.M. while the worst lost 2.89 percent (see Figure 17.9).

Markets which are stronger, up more than 2 percent at 10:00 A.M., will continue higher on a somewhat consistent basis (see Table 17.7 and Figures 17.10 to 17.11).

The 79 days that were down 1 to 2 percent at 10:00 A.M. netted out to unchanged the rest of the day. In this case while more stocks rallied and the large moves were to the upside, the case for buying into is as clear cut as when stocks gain 1 to 2 percent (see Table 17.8 and Figures 17.12 and 17.13).

In the 22 instances of down 2 percent or more, the market continues lower (see Table 17.9 and Figures 17.14 and 17.15).

Another daily inflection point for investors is noon. Markets that are up 1 to 2 percent at noon, as was the case with this reading at 10:00 A.M., are essentially flat the rest of the day (see Table 17.10 and Figure 17.16).

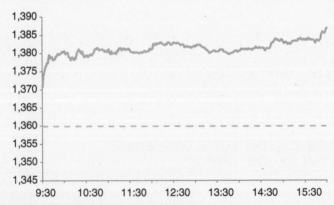

FIGURE 17.8   S&P 500: November 19, 2012
Source: Birinyi Associates, Inc., Bloomberg.

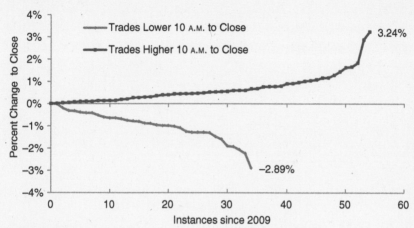

FIGURE 17.9   Market Trading after Up 1 to 2 Percent at 10 A.M.
Source: Birinyi Associates, Inc.

TABLE 17.7	S&P 500: Market Up More Than 2 Percent at 10 A.M.			
	S&P 500 Change			
	10:00 to Close	**Noon to Close**	**3:30 to Close**	**Day**
Average	0.86%	0.61%	0.33%	3.55%
Median	0.74%	0.51%	0.44%	2.98%
% Positive	82%	71%	71%	100%

Source: Birinyi Associates, Inc.

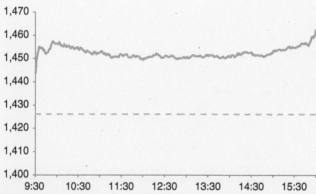

FIGURE 17.10   S&P 500: January 2, 2013
Source: Birinyi Associates, Inc.

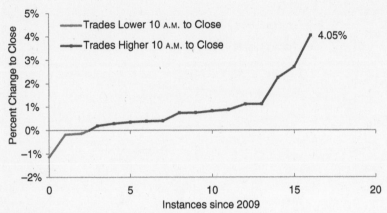

FIGURE 17.11 Market Trading after 2 Percent at 10 A.M.

Source: Birinyi Associates, Inc., Bloomberg.

TABLE 17.8 S&P 500: Market Down 1 to 2 Percent at 10 A.M.

	S&P 500 Change			
	10:00 to Close	**Noon to Close**	**3:30 to Close**	**Day**
Average	0.00%	0.03%	−0.02%	−1.41%
Median	0.05%	0.09%	−0.08%	−1.44%
% Positive	52%	54%	39%	10%

Source: Birinyi Associates, Inc.

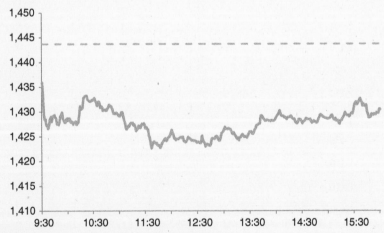

FIGURE 17.12 S&P 500: December 21, 2012

Source: Birinyi Associates, Inc., Bloomberg.

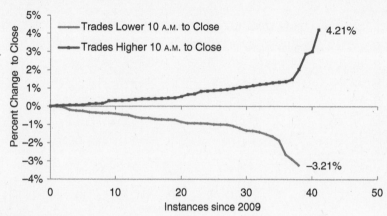

FIGURE 17.13 Market Trading after Down 1 to 2 Percent at 10 A.M.
Source: Birinyi Associates, Inc.

TABLE 17.9 S&P 500: Market Down More Than 2 Percent at 10 A.M.

	S&P 500 Change			
	10:00 to Close	Noon to Close	3:30 to Close	Day
Average	−0.51%	−0.52%	−0.23%	−3.07%
Median	−0.64%	−0.42%	−0.23%	−3.25%
% Positive	23%	27%	32%	9%

Source: Birinyi Associates, Inc.

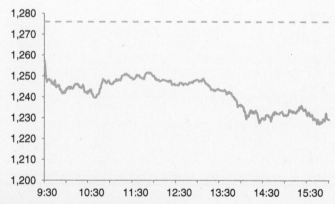

FIGURE 17.14 S&P 500: November 9, 2011
Source: Birinyi Associates, Inc., Bloomberg.

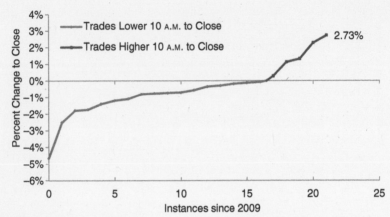

FIGURE 17.15 Market Trading after Down 2 Percent at 10 A.M.

Source: Birinyi Associates, Inc.

TABLE 17.10 S&P 500: Market Up 1 to 2 Percent at Noon

	S&P 500 Change		
	Noon to Close	**3:30 to Close**	**Day**
Average	0.09%	0.08%	1.46%
Median	0.07%	0.06%	1.45%
% Positive	57%	65%	95%

Source: Birinyi Associates, Inc.

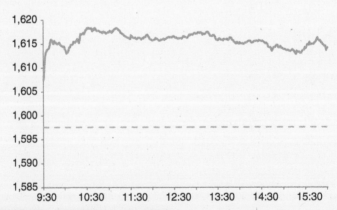

FIGURE 17.16 S&P 500: May 3, 2013

Source: Birinyi Associates, Inc., Bloomberg.

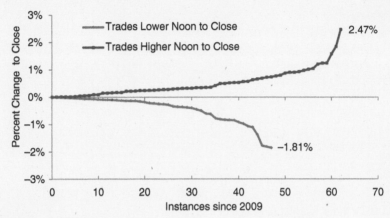

FIGURE 17.17 Market Trading after Up 1 to 2 Percent at Noon
Source: Birinyi Associates, Inc.

On balance, however, investors will tend to profit from buying, rather than selling (see Figure 17.17).

On stronger days (greater than 2 percent), the market continues higher, and only on September 27, 2011 was there a decline of 1 percent after noon while there were six days where the market gained another 1 percent (see Table 17.11 and Figures 17.18 and 17.19).

Negative instances at noon (1 to 2 percent) tread water the rest of the day (see Table 17.12 and Figure 17.20).

Buying on those occasions is more profitable than selling (see Figure 17.21).

Days that are down 2 percent or more at noon continue lower the rest of the day, but 85 percent of the entire day's loss has already occurred (see Table 17.13 and Figures 17.22 and 17.23).

TABLE 17.11 S&P 500: Market Up 2 Percent at Noon

	S&P 500 Change		
	Noon to Close	3:30 to Close	Day
Average	0.56%	0.28%	3.26%
Median	0.53%	0.28%	2.96%
% Positive	73%	70%	100%

Source: Birinyi Associates, Inc.

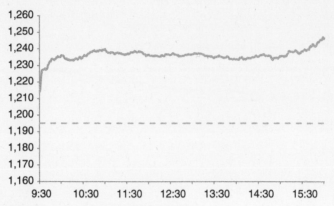

FIGURE 17.18   S&P 500: November 30, 2011

Source: Birinyi Associates, Inc., Bloomberg.

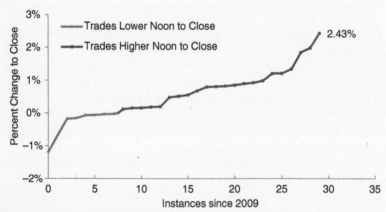

FIGURE 17.19   Market Trading after Up 2 Percent at Noon

Source: Birinyi Associates, Inc.

TABLE 17.12   S&P 500: Market Down 1 to 2 Percent at Noon

	S&P 500 Change		
	Noon to Close	**3:30 to Close**	**Day**
Average	0.00%	−0.05%	−1.39%
Median	0.08%	−0.07%	−1.40%
% Positive	53%	42%	4%

Source: Birinyi Associates, Inc.

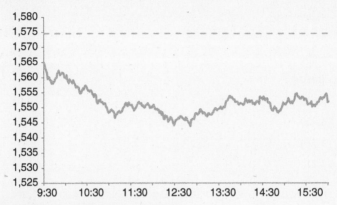

FIGURE 17.20 S&P 500: April 17, 2013

Source: Birinyi Associates, Inc., Bloomberg.

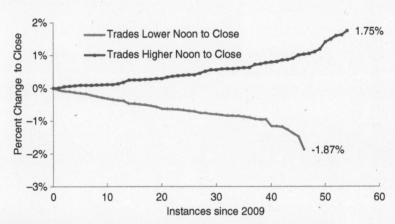

FIGURE 17.21 Market Trading after Down 1 to 2 Percent at Noon

Source: Birinyi Associates, Inc.

TABLE 17.13 S&P 500: Market Down 2 Percent at Noon

	S&P 500 Change		
	Noon to Close	**3:30 to Close**	**Day**
Average	−0.48%	−0.20%	−3.21%
Median	−0.64%	−0.17%	−3.11%
% Positive	26%	40%	3%

Source: Birinyi Associates, Inc.

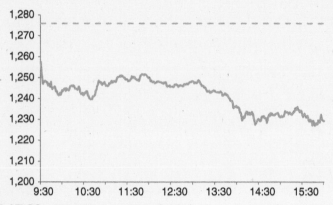

FIGURE 17.22   S&P 500: November 7, 2012
Source: Birinyi Associates, Inc., Bloomberg.

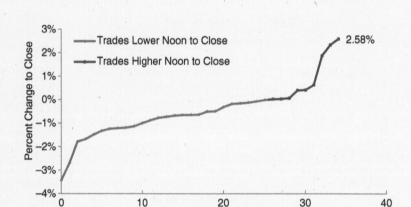

FIGURE 17.23   Market Trading after Down 2 Percent at Noon
Source: Birinyi Associates, Inc.

The following is a summary of the intraday results:

- Changes of 1 to 2 percent in either direction, at either 10:00 A.M. or noon, provide no opportunities.
- For whatever reason, larger changes tend to continue in the same direction (see Table 17.14).

TABLE 17.14 Number of Instances

		Number of Instances			Daily Average
		All	Positive	Negative	
10:00 AM					
	Up 1%–2%	88	54	34	0.03%
	Up 2%	17	14	3	0.86
	Down 1%–2%	79	41	38	0.00
	Down 2%	22	5	17	−0.51
Noon					
	Up 1%–2%	109	62	47	0.09%
	Up 2%	30	22	8	0.56
	Down 1%–2%	101	54	47	0.00
	Down 2%	35	9	26	−0.48

Source: Birinyi Associates, Inc.

CHAPTER 18

"Mind the Gap"

The gap between the rich and poor is widening fast.
—Richard Rogers

Large price changes, especially at the opening of the market, create one of the most difficult decisions that traders and managers face. Better than expected earnings, or some other development, may create a price gap. And the stock that closed last night at $42 is now quoted in the high 40s. This is both a trading and investing issue. Should one pay an extraordinary trading cost and, if so, what is the likelihood that the stock will appreciate further?

Market lore and legend says: "A gap must be closed . . . if it isn't closed in three days, it will be closed in three weeks, and if it isn't closed in three weeks, it will be closed in three months."

The greater majority of gaps today occur as a result of earnings, as in the case of Starbucks (SBUX). On July 26, 2012, SBUX reported earnings of $0.43 per share, missing the $0.45 estimate. As is the case with many NASDAQ stocks, the company reported after the normal 4:00 P.M. closing (see Figure 18.1).

As shown in Figure 18.2, the market took retribution and the stock went from $52.41 to $46.86, a decline of 10.5 percent, in trading to 6:00 P.M. In pre-trading the next morning (8:00 to 9:30 A.M.), the stock was basically unchanged but recovered somewhat during the regular trading session (up $0.57, 1.44 percent). The other 12 stocks exhibit the same characteristics: down after hours and little changed the next day.

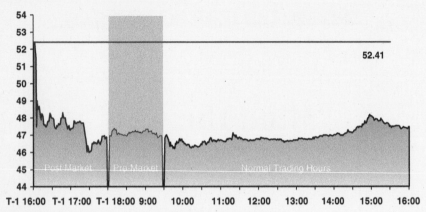

FIGURE 18.1   Starbucks Corp (SBUX): July 27, 2012
Source: Birinyi Associates, Inc., Bloomberg.

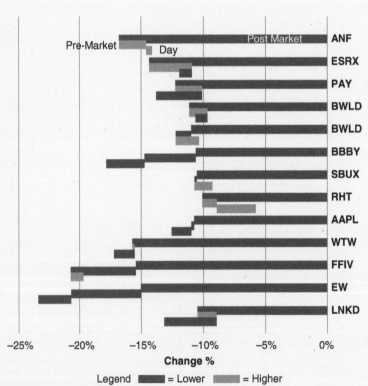

FIGURE 18.2   Post Market: Gap Down > 10 Percent
Source: Birinyi Associates, Inc.

AFTER THE POST-MARKET FALL . . . OR RALLY

Stocks that trade down 10 percent or more after hours are unlikely to move the next day. There is a tendency for them to trade a bit higher in pre-trading and then to lower during the regular session (see Figure 18.2).

Stocks that trade down only 5 to 10 percent in after-hours trading are likely to decline even more the next day with a loss approximating another 40 percent (of the total one-day move) or so. Thus if a stock drops $3 after hours, it should drop another $2 the next day (see Figure 18.3).

Good news has a slightly different reaction. Most stocks that gain during after-hours trading will continue higher the next day, regardless of the size of the gap. However, the gain is usually concentrated in the pre-trading session from 8:00 to 9:30. In only four of the twenty-one instances did the stock trade appreciably higher in the regular session (see Figure 18.4).

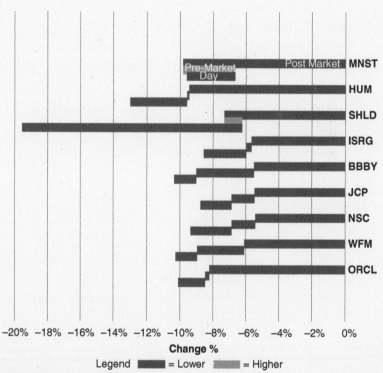

FIGURE 18.3 Post Market: Gap Down 5 to 10 Percent

Source: Birinyi Associates, Inc.

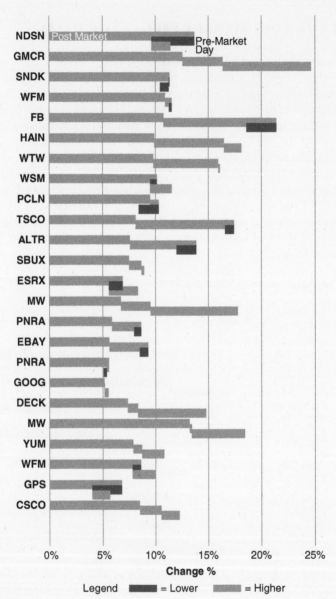

FIGURE 18.4 Post-Market Gap: Up

Source: Birinyi Associates, Inc.

In both of these scenarios, there is a positive bias going forward. Stocks that gap down will have a median return of 0.97 percent after one month and 5.2 percent after three (see Figure 18.5).

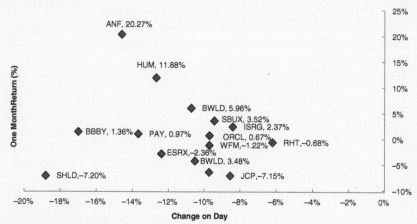

FIGURE 18.5 One-Month Returns Post-Market Gap Down

Source: Birinyi Associates, Inc.

Names that gap higher were a touch better: 1.48 percent after a month with a median of just over 3 percent, but only 2.17 percent after three months (2.73 percent median) (see Figure 18.6).

A second set of circumstances are stocks that report in the morning, before regular trading hours (that is before 9:30). Those that are lower, in the area of −5 to −10 percent, will *tend* to have their losses concentrated before 9:30. For most individual investors, the best opportunity to sell will have passed.

Three months out, they tend to be higher but with mixed results (see Table 18.1).

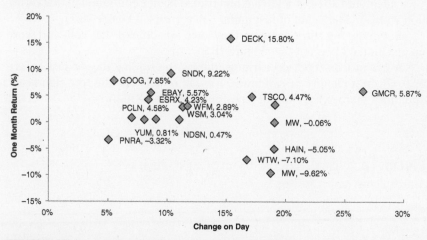

FIGURE 18.6 One-Month Returns Post-Market Gap Up

Source: Birinyi Associates, Inc.

TABLE 18.1 Pre-Market Gap Down

Ticker	Date	Pre	OP-CL	TD+30	TD+90
TFM	11/28/2012	−17.69%	6.41%	−9.72%	−10.57%
JOSB	1/28/2013	−17.44%	2.82%	6.77%	8.68%
FWLT	3/1/2013	−17.02%	1.28%	−0.79%	2.92%
ESI	7/26/2012	−11.84%	−2.80%	−28.14%	−42.09%
HUM	2/19/2013	−10.07%	4.31%	9.31%	0.66%
FOSL	11/6/2012	−9.93%	−0.59%	6.01%	20.91%
DRI	12/4/2012	−8.53%	−1.15%	−5.40%	−2.38%
BMY	8/2/2012	−7.30%	−1.45%	1.91%	2.24%
PXP	9/10/2012	−7.09%	−3.74%	0.50%	24.50%
TWC	1/31/2013	−6.55%	−6.26%	3.77%	4.71%
WHR	7/24/2012	−5.53%	−2.14%	18.95%	38.72%
FAST	6/5/2012	−5.42%	−4.58%	6.73%	12.11%
Average		**−10.37%**	**−0.66%**	**0.82%**	**5.03%**
Median		**−9.23%**	**−1.30%**	**2.84%**	**3.81%**

Source: Birinyi Associates, Inc.

GAPS PROVIDE OPPORTUNITIES AND HAVE *SOME* TENDENCIES, BUT NONE WRITTEN IN STONE

Good news is also absorbed quickly as most stocks will have made their move before the opening of regular trading. While the stocks will generally do better, the "easy money" will have been made (see Table 18.2).

One month after, stocks that had traded higher continued in that direction with a median gain of just under 5 percent (see Figure 18.7).

But going out three months, they gave up some of that gain and were up just under 3 percent (see Figure 18.8).

A few stocks reported earnings during the trading day or just before 9:30. Given a paucity of examples, we will merely list the few significant situations that we have found (see Tables 18.3. and 18.4):

−35% −30% −25% −20% −15% −10% −5% 0% 5% 10% 15%

FIGURE 18.7 Pre-Market: One-Month Gap Up Performance
Source: Birinyi Associates, Inc.

−40% −30% −20% −10% 0% 10% 20% 30% 40%

FIGURE 18.8 Pre-Market: Three-Month Gap Up Performance
Source: Birinyi Associates, Inc.

TABLE 18.2 Pre-Market Gap Up

Ticker	Date	Pre	OP-CL	TD+30	TD+90
ANF	11/14/2012	28.90%	4.25%	11.65%	21.48%
AOL	11/6/2012	25.38%	18.04%	−28.13%	−30.31%
KORS	8/14/2012	13.92%	2.15%	9.73%	2.52%
BHI	7/20/2012	12.05%	−2.54%	4.87%	3.30%
KORS	2/12/2013	11.93%	−3.43%	−9.13%	−13.79%
CSC	8/8/2012	11.79%	3.54%	11.85%	24.58%
APH	7/18/2012	11.45%	2.90%	5.93%	2.16%
CTSH	8/6/2012	10.98%	0.02%	−0.53%	2.82%
WAG	7/19/2012	10.85%	0.77%	4.18%	3.60%
MAT	7/17/2012	9.41%	0.27%	4.76%	4.02%
MJN	1/31/2013	8.94%	2.04%	−3.48%	6.26%
ORLY	2/7/2013	8.64%	−0.54%	3.22%	−0.56%
TXT	7/19/2012	8.81%	2.46%	2.91%	−5.85%
GPS	8/2/2012	8.32%	4.05%	7.96%	7.69%
ANF	8/15/2012	8.08%	0.86%	11.72%	−11.50%
EL	8/14/2012	7.96%	1.26%	0.78%	−4.46%
NFLX	10/8/2012	7.09%	3.13%	5.66%	34.93%
AOL	2/8/2013	6.31%	−0.82%	6.38%	11.59%
TIF	8/27/2012	5.78%	1.34%	−2.44%	1.00%
RL	2/6/2013	5.06%	−0.77%	−3.45%	−3.14%
	Average	**11.08%**	**1.95%**	**2.22%**	**2.82%**
	Median	**9.17%**	**1.30%**	**4.47%**	**2.67%**

Source: Birinyi Associates, Inc.

TABLE 18.3 Intraday Gap Down

Ticker	Date	OP-CL	TD+30	TD+90
STZ	1/31/2013	−17.23%	41.46%	48.76%
NVR	7/19/12	−14.03%	9.17%	17.61%
CMI	7/10/12	−9.96%	16.53%	6.02%
APOL	9/10/12	−7.09%	0.21%	−27.75%
BIDU	8/23/12	−5.74%	−1.66%	−18.99%
	Average	**−9.21%**	**6.07%**	**−5.78%**
	Median	**−8.52%**	**4.69%**	**−6.48%**

Source: Birinyi Associates, Inc.

TABLE 18.4 Intraday Gap Up

Ticker	Date	OP-CL	TD+30	TD+90
COG	6/27/2012	7.79%	1.92%	5.84%
GWW	7/18/2012	8.56%	−1.57%	−0.48%
	Average	**8.18%**	**0.17%**	**2.68%**
	Median	**8.18%**	**0.17%**	**2.68%**

Source: Birinyi Associates, Inc.

GAPS SQUARED

The price moves detailed in the previous pages are a regular and common feature of the stock market. There are, however, larger dislocations that we might term *spans*, *craters*, or even *gaps squared*. In these cases, the move is in excess of 20 percent and is more critical to investors than traders. While they are often related to earnings, they may also reflect a company's guidance or some other fundamental development. (We have not incorporated large price changes associated with mergers.)

In Table 18.5, we list six stocks that had a price gain in excess of 20 percent from the previous close. In all six instances, the stock traded a bit higher during the day. Only half were higher a week later and three months later, but the majority continued higher over the following month.

Upward moves of 15 to 20 percent are a mixed lot. There is a *tendency* for stocks to move higher over the next week, but a month afterwards, while mostly higher, much of that monthly gain had been achieved in the first week. In Table 18.6, all three measures (week, month, and three months) revert to trade date.

These stocks are notable, as three months later they are often characterized by sharp moves. As shown, over half of them have double-digit moves, although not always in the same direction.

TABLE 18.5   Gap Up 20 Percent

Gap Up 20%+		Prev. Close	Event Day Gap		Next Week	Next Month	Next Three Months
NFLX	1/24/2013	$103.11	$40.73	39%	12.4%	0.2%	0.5%
ANF	11/14/2012	31.23	8.89	29	4.3	11.6	21.6
NFLX	4/23/2013	174.43	41.20	24	−0.4	5.3	—
GMCR	2/2/2012	53.63	11.42	21	−3.3	1.6	−61.1
FOSL	8/7/2012	69.74	14.46	21	−7.9	−6.9	−8.5
EXPE	4/27/2012	32.63	6.50	20	0.8	11.4	35.0
	Average	—	—	26	1.0	3.9	−2.5
	Median	—	—	22	0.2	3.5	0.5
	Prob. Lower	—	—	—	50%	20%	40%

Source: Birinyi Associates, Inc.

TABLE 18.6 Gap Up 15 to 20 Percent

		Prev. Close	Event Day Gap		Next Week	Next Month	Next Three Months
NFLX	1/26/2012	$95.04	$18.86	20%	6.9%	−5.7%	−26.7%
OPEN	8/3/2012	34.14	6.66	20	10.1	8.6	13.7
GMCR	11/28/2012	28.95	5.60	19	11.7	9.5	32.7
TRIP	11/2/2012	29.41	5.60	19	−2.3	6.9	33.4
AKAM	7/26/2012	28.25	5.20	18	−1.0	5.9	3.1
TRIP	5/2/2012	36.53	6.72	18	−4.6	−3.8	−14.2
URBN	8/21/2012	31.27	5.63	18	0.1	5.1	1.0
EXPE	7/27/2012	45.71	7.90	17	3.7	−5.8	−7.4
WDC	7/26/2012	32.47	5.62	17	1.6	11.1	−14.0
GILD	4/19/2012	23.31	3.92	17	0.9	−4.4	2.9
JOSB	8/29/2012	41.63	6.37	15	5.2	2.2	−9.1
AKAM	10/27/2011	23.78	3.62	15	6.4	0.8	16.7
SHLD	2/23/2012	52.08	7.12	15	0.7	5.2	−17.3
ANN	8/17/2012	28.14	4.25	15	3.1	10.5	0.1
EXPE	10/26/2012	51.25	7.63	15	1.7	3.4	10.5
FSLR	8/2/2012	14.80	2.20	15	21.0	11.5	25.7
AMZN	4/27/2012	195.99	28.84	15	−1.3	−5.3	4.6
	Average			17	**3.8**	**3.3**	**3.3**
	Median			17	**1.7**	**5.1**	**2.9**
	Prob. Lower				**20%**	**30%**	**40%**

Source: Birinyi Associates, Inc.

OLD RULE: LARGE GAPS HAVE TO BE CLOSED—NEW RULE: ABOUT 25 PERCENT

The following addresses the issue of closing the gap. If it was the case, that the gap was closed, since they traded higher, the rule would require that they trade lower.

Expedia, the first entry on the graph in Figure 18.9, gapped up 20 percent and then rose another 35 percent over the subsequent three months. To close the gap it would have had to decline almost 38 percent.

As shown in Figure 18.9, some stocks (seven of thirty) did indeed do so, but the greater number did not.

On the downside, we detail only five large declines, all of which are higher three months out (see Table 18.7).

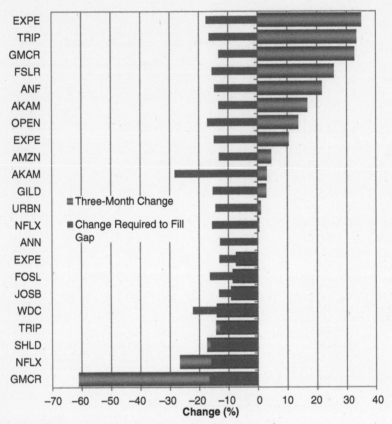

FIGURE 18.9 Change Three Months After Large Gap Up

Source: Birinyi Associates, Inc.

TABLE 18.7 Gap Down 20 Percent

		Prev. Close		Event Day Gap		
NFLX	10/25/2011	$118.8	−$43.9	−37%	3.5%	−11.5%	49.9%
GMCR	11/10/2011	67.0	−20.0	−30	26.4	38.2	59.9
FOSL	5/8/2012	125.8	−33.7	−27	−8.4	−5.3	16.9
ADSK	8/24/2012	35.7	−7.7	−22	3.1	9.3	6.0
NFLX	7/25/2012	80.4	−16.2	−20	−9.6	6.3	13.2
	Average	—	—	−27	3.0	7.4	29.2
	Median	—	—	−27	3.1	6.3	16.9
	Prob. Lower	—	—	—	0.4	0.4	0.0

Source: Birinyi Associates, Inc.

Stocks that trade down 15 to 20 percent tend to recover, and especially three months later, but 61 percent (the number that are up) is less than reassuring, and nearly half (15) of them have recovered their loss within three months. On average, it took 55 days to recover the loss (see Figure 18.10).

We conclude that investors should recognize that in the case of gaps, in either direction, there are no definite answers. There are tendencies, as we have outlined, but in a world of computerized trading, models, and other mechanized inputs, gaps may provide a significant opportunity for human judgment.

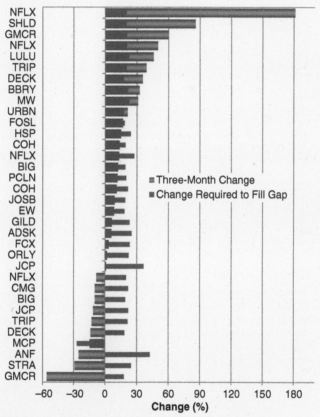

FIGURE 18.10 Change Three Months After Large Gap Down

Source: Birinyi Associates, Inc.

CHAPTER 19

You Must Remember This

It is not the strongest of the species that survives, nor the most intelligent that survives. It is the one that is most adaptable to change.

—Charles Darwin

Our experience and philosophy might be condensed into our market rules. They are unlikely to actually make you money, but our hope is that they will help you avoid some of the pitfalls that await both the casual and the consummate professional.

The Cyrano Principle comes to us via literature. You may remember that Mr. de Bergerac had the singular characteristic of a prominent nose. Our point is that if an issue is likewise prominent and pronounced, the stock market will be well aware of it.

Our principle implies that the stock market anticipates and therefore discounts the significant events or issues *before* they occur. Since 2009, one of the continuing bearish arguments has been that *this* quarter, earnings will disappoint. Okay, last quarter they were better than expected, but this quarter. . . .

Our response has just as consistently been the following: "and the market doesn't know this?" Earnings will be shy of expectations and *then* the market will go lower. In reality, that is not how the equity market—unlike the bond market—works. Like the old commercial about Mother Nature, it is not nice to surprise the stock market, and you aren't going to anyhow.

No, it does not discount acts of nature, or malfeasance, or revolutions, but the market's job is to collate, absorb, and digest information regarding earnings, the price of oil, interest rates, and the like.

This is not to suggest that the market will not react to bad news because there is always the marginal seller and the hesitant buyer; however, while it may bend, it won't break.

The principle has been most useful regarding corrections. When the market has a negative event and corrects, we ask "is this something the market should have anticipated?" More often than not, we respond in the affirmative and recognize that there will be some selling and interruption of the rally but it is only temporary. Our concern is when there are events we don't understand, declines that are not easily explained. (Even now, 26 years later we still debate the causes of the 1987 Crash.)

The bearish case is always more compelling, rationale, and articulate. The stock market anticipates, which is a cliché but not the reality for most investors, perhaps because they fail to complete the sentence that should be: The stock market anticipates *the future.* As we have seen with respect to money flows, the stock market regularly discounts events. Our experience with money flows is that roughly 20 percent of the stocks at any point will be in a discounting mode.

Most stocks—when money flows were viable—had patterns similar to the one shown in Figure 19.1.

That is, stocks went up on buying and down on selling. Furthermore, there was no price discovery and the investor or analyst who was forecasting a significant move (in either direction) was, in effect, saying that he or she knew something the market didn't know.

It is not just the stock market. For those who are skeptical regarding the efficiency of the market, we might suggest the experience known to all where our favorite football team is a 10-point underdog and they lose by eleven on a freak touchdown in the last 30 seconds.

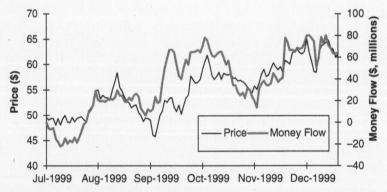

FIGURE 19.1   Colgate-Palmolive Money Flow
Source: Birinyi Associates Inc., Bloomberg.

Some may have participated in a weekly exercise where one is invited to pick the four games out of 20 or 30 college/professional games. Four, any four, and your "investment" of $10 returns $100. Everyone, of course, gets three of them right.

A cause of great frustration is that, unfortunately, the market does not articulate its positive insights while the negatives are front and center. We appreciate that it is disconcerting to read the morning paper regarding global strife, political corruption, man's inhumanity to man and nature, as well as the pettiness of politics, and still have an optimistic outlook. We will readily admit that had we entered a debate in March 2009, the bearish argument would have been judged the winner. But that is always the case because the negative is obvious; the future is opaque.

There is another issue here as well that was once articulated by Bill Miller in comments to his investors:

> *Being bearish or cautious always sounds smarter than being bullish. No one wants to be thought panglossian, in denial of evident problems and risks. Expressing concern, evincing skepticism, are signs of prudence and being prudent is what we have all been instructed to be since the courts held in 1830s.*

IT'S SMART TO BE BEARISH, BUT NOT NECESSARILY PROFITABLE

Forecast environments and not events. In a bull market, stock prices go higher. That may seem trite but one of the comments that we read regularly is the need for a catalyst or event to push prices higher. Analysts ask what will unglue the market or precipitate a rally.

That is the wrong question; one should really be asking if we are in a bull market or in a bear market. The instigator of the rally in March 2009 was an announcement by Citibank that they had made money in the previous quarter. Could we have anticipated that?

In 1982, Dr. Henry Kaufman's articulation of what the Fed was undertaking lit the fire, while in 1990, the market erupted when the first Gulf War began even though the conventional view was to *sell* into the rally and buy afterwards.

This also suggests that one avoid much of the day-to-day commentary and analysis in part because it is day-to-day and may be radically different tomorrow. It is often been said that market timing is not profitable. Our view is that it is very profitable—at the turns—but not on a week-to-week or month-to-month basis.

Most indicators are descriptive, not indicative. Sigmund Freud once commented on keeping things in perspective, something that we too often fail to do in the markets. We have already written that technical indicators are responsive; oscillators have to oscillate, trends have to be established before they are highlighted, and many stocks have to go up before we can declare that there is an abundance of new highs.

Over time, given our support by interns and trainees, we have probably analyzed more theories, approaches, and measures than anyone. One intern was sent to the Fashion Institute of Technology to see if there was any relationship to the idea that rising hemlines were really correlated to rising prices but found that the data was both inconsistent and insufficient. For those who scoff at these efforts or think them silly, we might direct them to the chapter in *The Money Game* entitled "Mr. Johnson's Reading List."

Our attitude largely stems from my experience on a trading desk. Traders faced with immediate decisions that regularly involve millions of dollars are not a tolerant lot. I tried vainly to find approaches, ideas, tools, but not until I designed my own systems could I provide profitable responses with tools that forecast or at least illuminated.

Discriminate between coincidental and causal. As illustrated earlier, in the example of butter production in Bangladesh, the fact that two events coincide does not mean that one is a function of the other.

In 1995, one strategist listed 8 or 10 reasons for optimism, including the fact that years ending in 5 had done well. That worked until it didn't, but our response was that this was a somewhat weak argument and especially for those who have a fiduciary responsibility.

S&P 500 Return in Years Ending in 5

	Return
2005	3.00%
1995	34.11
1985	26.33
1975	31.55
1965	9.06
1955	26.40
1945	30.72
1935	41.37

Source: Birinyi Associates, Inc. Bloomberg.

There is nothing more dangerous in business than an articulate incompetent. Most investing professionals have heard numerous, sad stories about individuals who bought a stock or gold bars because the seller was profound, well spoken, and convincing.

One need only watch almost any cable channel at 3:00 A.M. as evidence. Our advice has always been to directly act on investment advice only from a source where one has an economic relationship. Infrequently, our newsletter clients will find fault with our advice or recommendations to which our response is simply: Fire us.

That is not easily done if one responds to an ad or buys on the basis of a financial broadcast. *Everyone* on TV is articulate, knowledgeable, and compelling. That is why they are there. One money management operation of our acquaintance was headed by a prominent investor. The reality, however, was that he was the spokesman and the real brains and financial acumen never (or seldom) left the office.

Predicting rain doesn't count; building arks does. As I write this, we have received a publication "suggesting [health care] correction is possible." On most trading desks and in brokerage offices there are, to avoid confusion, two sets of tickets. One is for purchases and the other is for sales.

We know of no way to implement "possible." One of our guiding principles is that all reports should have a conclusion. When the market traded above our 1,600 target for the S&P in May 2013, we advised clients that the rally was still intact and going higher. At that time, we had not had the opportunity to review and update a target (which we do reluctantly) but did advise that we had taken a position in the December S&P 170 calls.

(At the beginning of the year when we forecast 1,600, we bought the Dec 160 calls, which doubled. We said then that the market would trade to that level *in the year.*)

We have not done so, but it might be an interesting exercise to track the number of recommendations that are actionable in some given week.

YOU CAN NEVER KNOW TOO MUCH ABOUT TOO MANY THINGS ON WALL STREET

Investing should be a profession; educate yourself. The first chapters of David Ogilvey's book, *Confession of an Advertising Man*, greatly impressed me with its emphasis on dedication, effort, and total immersion in the effort. Rather than collect stamps, he advised, as one example, collect old ads.

Gathering anecdotal data is sometimes a nuisance, for example, when an article is too large for our copy machine or the print is smudged. Interns suggest this was not why they took three finance courses, but once you have gathered six or more months of material, its value will become more and more apparent.

Everyone should be involved with his or her financial circumstances, but just as a 24-year-old is unlikely to spend too much time worrying about their health, a $25,000 nest egg is not a candidate for broad diversification.

Given that the focus of most individuals' goals is retirement upon 65 with more time available, individuals should be *more* involved and recognize the reality of their new status: There are no more paychecks and the $2,500 or whatever Social Security per month will not make up for an $8,000 loss.

Charlie Munger, Warren Buffett's less-known partner, is an outstanding investor and actually did better than Mr. Buffett in the years 1962 to 1975. In a speech at USC to students of the B-school he:

> *challenged [them] to broaden their vision . . . and see the market not as a separate discipline but as part of a larger body of knowledge, one that incorporates physics, social studies, psychology, philosophy, literature and mathematics.*

Years ago, we read but never documented, that a large number of the portfolio managers at that time were art history majors. Munger, in his talk, lamented the fact that today's managers often lack broad skills: "To a man with only a hammer, every problem looks pretty much like a nail."

Or as an ad for Drexel Burnham once read:

> *A good trader knows macro-economics, Fed watching, spread analysis and who's going to be MVP next year.*

To that end, we have always read a wide variety of publications, articles, and journals, and regularly scan at least the contents of new books. One summer, a trainee spent some time transcribing Eddie Murphy's comments from *Trading Places*:

> *Ok pork belly prices been dropping all morning. Which means everybody's sittin' in their offices waiting for them to hit rock bottom so that they can buy cheap and go long, except the people who own pork belly contracts are going batshit, we're losing all our damn money and Christmas is around the corner and I ain't got no money to buy my son the GI Joe with the kung fu grip.*

It might be somewhat of a stretch, but one of our experiences took us outside the normal financial-economic parameters. A friend recommended a book about trading, which was mildly interesting. But somewhere about page 15, or the beginning of Chapter 2, the writer compared a situation to Sherlock Holmes' dog, which didn't bark, from *The Hound of the Baskervilles*. I wasn't that academically diligent, but knew that what has been called the most famous incident in English literature was from a short story, *Silver Blaze*, not *The Hound of the Baskervilles*.

Perhaps I was too aggressive, but I took the view that if the writer had not done his homework regarding English lit, could I really be sure that his research on other matters was more reliable?

Those who regularly monitor the markets and are diligent in their efforts should develop a sense of reality. They will quickly recognize that in this game people do not bat .675, that few stocks double in any 12-month period, and that 5 percent fees provide significant hurdles.

Historically, and especially with our institutional clients, we have always suggested that our service not only provides useful historical insights and opportunities, but also that it does so efficiently. We dismiss the greater majority of reports and commentary because we know their agenda, we recognize tortured analysis, and we track commentators and their comments.

As in any profession, the first step is education, which we think should begin with Mr. Keynes' *General Theory*. More specifically, Chapter 12 of that book is probably the best thing ever written about the stock market and was the inspiration for another must-read, *The Money Game*.

Reminiscences of a Stock Operator, by Edwin Lefèvre, probably populates more financial bookshelves than any other book. Interestingly there are few practical ideas in it but it does present and amplify one critical issue: Pay attention to the market.

Then one might step back and read *Confusion de Confusiones* by Joseph De La Vega, written in 1688. The book discusses trading on the Amsterdam Stock Exchange (but not tulips) and, although stilted, shows that things change but markets are constant:

> *. . . take note and realize that there are three causes of a rise in prices on the exchange and three of a fall: the conditions in India, European politics, and opinion on the stock exchange itself. For this reason the news is often of little value.*

The *Tao Jones Averages*, by Bennett W. Goodspeed, is a practical guide to perspective clear thinking, while the *Go Go Years* by John Brooks is a fascinating history of an era somewhat similar to the dot-com bubble. *New Methods for Profit in the Stock Market* by Garfield Drew has some useful stories. Today we hear about the Super Bowl indicator; then it was the Gridiron Method of Forecasting, which involved taking the results of Harvard–Yale, California–Stanford, and Army–Yale: "Sell the year after California beats Stanford."

Nicolas Darvas' *How I Made $2,000,000* . . . is worth reading as it outlines a system that may or may not be applicable for all investors, but it does illustrate the value of discipline and having a process.

Others that we suggest include the following:

The Wisdom of Crowds by *The New Yorker*'s James Surowiecki
Keynes and the Market by Justyn Walsh
The Signal and the Noise by Nate Silver

We have overlooked other alleged classics such as *The Madness of Crowds* or some biographies, but think them of lesser importance with few tangible results.

In addition, there are several essays, beginning with "The Loser's Game" by Charles Ellis[1] and Richard Heilbroner's "Reflections: Economic Predictions,"[2] which we referenced earlier, as well as a study of Keynes' actual investing results, "Keynes the Stock Market Investor."[3]

NOTES

1. Charles Ellis, "The Loser's Game," *Financial Analysts Journal* 31, no. 4 (July/August 1975): 19–26.

2. Richard Heilbroner, "Reflections: Economic Predictions." *The New Yorker*, July 8, 1991.

3. David Chambers and Elroy Dimson, "Keynes the Stock Market Investor," September 6, 2012.

CHAPTER 20

Wall Street Week and Other Adventures

The critical issue is not the business cycle, it is the psychological cycle.

—Laszlo Birinyi

It might be a touch of hubris to quote one's self, but for years I cited the opening comment as the turning point in Keynes' results. Initially Keynes' investment results were mediocre, but later he did very well for himself and for those institutions he advised. I had always said the epiphany was when he realized the importance of sentiment and the fact that "investor psychology plays an integral role. . . ."

While reading Skidelsky's biography of Keynes,[1] I sought to find the context of the comment and could not. Upon further research, I found that neither Keynes nor anyone else was responsible. As a result, I will take credit even though I still contend that the comment is borrowed.

In any case, it has been a great ride, especially since it was not expected. I came to Wall Street only because of the paper-work backup in the late 1960s. People didn't work on Wall Street in those days and I recall on many social occasions or after playing ball in the park:

You work on Wall Street? Do you know Jack? He works on Wall Street. Tall guy, brown hair, super guy. Everybody knows Jack.

In those days, the market closed at 2:00 P.M. and, for a while, all day Wednesday. Not only was it impossible to get a cab after 4:00, there was virtually no place to eat aside from three-day-old hot dogs at the Staten Island Ferry or Chinatown. Despite NYU's business school being next door to the American Stock Exchange, few of us ever considered a career on Wall Street unless we knew somebody or had gone to Yale. (In the mid-1980s it was alleged that 20 percent of the Yale senior class applied to First Boston alone.)

Working 15-hour days with computers, which did less than today's smartphones, and making half of what traders and salesman made with their abbreviated workdays, put it in perspective. Getting a graduate degree was helpful, but in truth, playing poker the last two years at Chapel Hill was more helpful than all the finance courses at both the undergraduate and graduate level.

It required a 50 percent pay cut to start on a trading desk as a clerk/flunky, but when the opportunity came, there was no hesitation. At the time, trading was personal relationships and salesmanship; it was exciting, and it was not algorithms and computers. Walking onto the floor of the Exchange was a buzz not unlike entering the Bellagio or going to the Bronx for a World Series game.

Mitchell, Hutchins is gone now, taken over by PaineWebber (ending as a reverse takeover). Our head trader at the time, Jay Mangan, challenged us to come up with some ideas so we weren't just order takers and high-paid clerks. He hired me despite our prehiring final dinner conversation:

> *Okay, everything seems to be in place and we'd like to make you an offer.*
>
>   *What are you thinking?*
>
>   *Well I know I only have one year of experience but I am a quick learner, will work at my job and after checking around, think that $20,000 plus bonus would make me happy.*
>
>   *20 grand, hell, our clerks make 20 grand!*

As I recall we settled on $25,000 and when he asked me to come up with something that would keep my name in front of traders, I designed the first trading calendar. And in 1976, I introduced the Trading Calendar:

> *Mitchell, Hutchins Does Some Crystal Ball-Gazing in Latest Trading Research Products*
>
> *The most widely read Mitchell, Hutchins research product in the last few months hasn't been a report on a high-flying stock but something called the "Trading Calendar," the latest product of an ongoing effort by the firm to provide research specifically geared to traders.*
>
>   *As the calendar's author, trader Laszlo Birinyi Jr. explains, "We not only give people an idea of what's going to be happening that day, but also guidelines on what to expect, so they can react quickly."* [2]

There is an old story about a woman who sees *Hamlet* for the first time. Somehow, she had avoided reading the play and was unfamiliar with the script. When asked how she liked it she said the play was interesting, a bit long, with good acting, but "there were too many quotations."

The calendar was like that, in that it is hard to imagine that we weren't always aware of corporate developments or when economic announcements were scheduled. Borrowing an idea from an analyst who had provided an earnings preview for his stocks, I produced a sheet detailing upcoming earnings and those few economic indicators of the time. But even those few were often not a big deal. On one memorable occasion, I called the Commerce or Labor Department asking about the release of employment, or some other number: "On Friday, the fifteenth. No wait, Mary is out that day so it will be the next Friday."

In a small way, it was the beginning of a revolution, in that for the first time traders could anticipate rather than react. Before then, when a company released earnings or the CPI came out, we would wait until the analyst or economist digested the number, wrote a note, and then we might buy or sell.

The attitude of the time might be reflected in one broker's comment at the time:

> *These new guys are not interested in five-year forecasts; some of them want* quarterly *numbers!*

SALOMON BROTHERS: THE BAR WAS HIGH, EVEN FOR THE CHEF

Trading was exciting, rewarding, and gradually became more important to institutional investors who realized the impact that trading could have on their results. The trading calendar was the first of a number of ideas directed specifically toward traders and it was then suggested that I talk to firms that were more oriented toward trading than research and specifically Salomon Brothers.

A mutual friend made the contact and sometime in the spring of 1976 directed me to the 40th floor, One New York Plaza: "Ask for the head trader, Michael Bloomberg."

After a second breakfast the next day he offered me a position, which was a bit unnerving, as my role was to take my trading, sales, research, and other skills and "make something happen." Imagine joining the Yankees and being told you are on the team but you have to figure out where you are going to play.

It was the Salomon of legend and lore, perhaps captured in an early assignment where a major institution wanted a process automated and asked three firms for proposals that ended up in my lap.

We won the business and it was not only significant but would create revolving revenues so I duly expected congrats and kudos. Nothing; nada. When the orders starting coming, surely then I would be recognized. . . .

I finally realized that I was not going to get a pat on the back or even a "nice going." I was *expected* to get the business and had I not, then we might have had a conversation. Clearly, the Brothers was not a warm and fuzzy place, but having learned the culture of the firm, I absorbed it and prospered (or at least my pay increased).

Michael Lewis' *Liar's Poker* provides even more insights into the firm and the era but even before Lewis' day, it was unique. For one thing, management *managed* and even though I said hello to Mr. Bloomberg every day, we seldom conversed as I had certain responsibilities (including writing the firm's weekly market commentary). Interaction with management was often limited to their signing expense accounts and approving travel. In one memorable occasion, a senior partner tore up my first-class ticket to Paris and said "time is money, take the Concorde." (As I recall there were 12 people on the flight, 10 of whom checked in at the Plaza Athénée.)

Mr. Bloomberg, despite his responsibilities, did not have an office and, like Billy Salomon, sat on the trading floor. He called customers, put together trades, and held meetings, more likely than not, with two or three guys huddled in the corner. Mr. Salomon regularly walked around what was known on Wall Street as *The Room* and often stopped by to give me some grief.

At the time, I regularly ran around Central Park and often crossed his path as he ran up Fifth Avenue to the reservoir while I was running down. If on one of his tours I was indulging in a cigar, he would look at me and say, "I don't know how you can run and smoke those things."

The cigars were readily available in the private dining rooms. Years earlier, I had worked with a trader who was what we now term a *foodie*. Then he regaled us with stories of taking the desk from U.S. Trust to this place or two guys from Jennison to that new restaurant. Unfortunately, in the bear market of 1981 he lost his job and became a chef.

Sometime in 1985 or thereabouts, he reappeared as the head chef in Salomon Brothers' executive dining room—a former trader now cooking for other traders!

Leaving Salomon when it—understandably—became a corporation where department heads were expected to have budgets and write memos, led to the next fork in the road: *Wall Street Week* (*WSW*).

I had been on *WSW*, and after my second appearance suggested to the producer that they could use some new blood as the panelists were somewhat out of touch (retired) and unaware of the continued evolution of the market. He agreed and suggested that I might be interested in visiting Owings Mills, Maryland, on a regular basis.

It was a fascinating 10 years and, in truth, I never became close to Louis Rukeyser. In part, it was because I had no great desire to have a late dinner in Baltimore and get home midday Saturday. Furthermore, it was his show, his stage, and I was comfortable in the role that one panelist described to me:

Never forget, your job is to be a spear catcher.

As a result, I usually did only one show a quarter, and fortunately many of them were the year-end or mid-year show with the four panelists whose portfolios were leading the pack. I did, however, convince my lovely wife to finally accede to Lou's request to join him on one of his boat cruises.

I learned that since we were in people's living rooms every Friday night at 8:30, they considered themselves to be our intimates. Which was fine, but we couldn't really mingle (except when scheduled) or engage in most activities without drawing a crowd. As a result, the panelists had a private dinner with Lou every night and a number of excursions as well.

That was also the case at the annual Las Vegas get-together of 15,000 of his devoted fans. It was really remarkable, especially on Saturday afternoon when, for an additional fee, you could have your picture taken with him. Hundreds of people lined up in their best outfits for their ten-second photo op (move along please, no handshakes, sorry).

The show was also an interesting insight into the institutional money management business. For most professionals it was "amateur hour" and they paid scant attention to it. They did, however, lust after an opportunity to appear, so that Aunt Jan in Cleveland or Tulsa could see how far they had come or to show their ex what a mistake she had made.

Unfortunately, neither Lou nor *WSW* are still with us, nor is the market I knew. When I wrote the piece *The Next CRASH*, I suggested only half facetiously that 11 Wall Street might one day become an indoor mall complete with Starbucks and the Gap. Don't hold your breath, it still might happen or what would be the ultimate irony: an Apple store selling technology, which is what could ultimately lead to the NYSE's demise.

NOTES

1. Robert Skidelsky, *John Maynard Keynes: 1883–1946: Economist, Philosopher, Statesman*, (New York: Penguin, 2005).
2. *Wall Street Letter* 8, no. 19 (May 17, 1976).

Expansions/ Recessions and Bull/Bear Markets

Recession Data

Recession		Length (Months)	Date Declared	S&P 500 Change (%)	U.S. Long Bond Change (%)
Begin	End				
May-1937	Jun-1938	13		−29.6%	–
Feb-1945	Oct-1945	8		23.3	4.3%
Nov-1948	Oct-1949	11		−4.0	10.4
Jul-1953	May-1954	10		20.4	22.0
Aug-1957	Apr-1958	8		−9.1	15.8
Apr-1960	Feb-1961	10		14.5	5.0
Dec-1969	Nov-1970	11		−6.5	6.8
Nov-1973	Mar-1975	16		−22.6	−7.1
Jan-1980	Jul-1980	6	6/30/1980	12.7	−2.0
Jul-1981	Nov-1982	16	1/6/1982	6.8	19.2
Jul-1990	Mar-1991	8	4/25/1991	4.8	1.6
Mar-2001	Nov-2001	8	11/26/2001	−8.2	1.6
Dec-2007	Jun-2009	19	12/1/2008	−37.9	0.7
	Average	**11**		**−2.7**	**6.5**

Birinyi Associates, Inc., NBER.

Recession versus Bear Market

| Begin | | Bear Market |
Recession	Bear Market	Lead/Lag (M)
Apr-1960	12/12/1961	−21
	2/9/1966	
Dec-1969	11/29/1968	12
Nov-1973	1/11/1973	10
Jan-1980	11/28/1980	−11
Jul-1981	11/28/1980	7
	8/25/1987	
Jul-1990	7/16/1990	0
	7/17/1998	
Mar-2001	3/24/2000	11
	1/4/2002	
Dec-2007	10/9/2007	2

Bull/Bear Filter: S&P 500

Move	Begin	End	Start	Finish	Percent Change	Length (Days)
Bear	9/16/1929	11/13/1929	31.86	17.66	−44.57	58
Bull	11/13/1929	4/10/1930	17.66	25.92	46.77	148
Bear	4/10/1930	12/16/1930	25.92	14.44	−44.29	250
Bull	12/16/1930	2/24/1931	14.44	18.17	25.83	70
Bear	2/24/1931	6/2/1931	18.17	12.20	−32.86	98
Bull	6/2/1931	6/26/1931	12.20	15.35	25.82	24
Bear	6/26/1931	10/5/1931	15.35	8.82	−42.54	101
Bull	10/5/1931	11/9/1931	8.82	11.52	30.61	35
Bear	11/9/1931	6/1/1932	11.52	4.40	−61.81	205
Bull	6/1/1932	9/7/1932	4.40	9.31	111.59	98
Bear	9/7/1932	2/27/1933	9.31	5.53	−40.60	173
Bull	2/27/1933	7/18/1933	5.53	12.20	120.61	141
Bear	7/18/1933	10/19/1933	12.20	8.61	−29.43	93
Bull	10/19/1933	2/6/1934	8.61	11.82	37.28	110
Bear	2/6/1934	3/14/1935	11.82	8.06	−31.81	401
Bull	3/14/1935	3/10/1937	8.06	18.67	131.64	727
Bear	3/10/1937	3/31/1938	18.67	8.50	−54.47	386

Bull/Bear Filter: S&P 500 (*Continued*)

Move	Begin	End	Start	Finish	Percent Change	Length (Days)
Bull	3/31/1938	11/9/1938	8.50	13.79	62.24	223
Bear	11/9/1938	4/11/1939	13.79	10.42	−24.44	153
Bull	4/11/1939	10/25/1939	10.42	13.21	26.78	197
Bear	10/25/1939	6/10/1940	13.21	8.99	−31.95	229
Bull	6/10/1940	11/7/1940	8.99	11.39	26.70	150
Bear	11/7/1940	4/28/1942	11.39	7.47	−34.42	537
Bull	4/28/1942	5/29/1946	7.47	19.25	157.70	1,492
Bear	5/29/1946	5/19/1947	19.25	13.77	−28.47	355
Bull	5/19/1947	6/15/1948	13.77	17.06	23.89	393
Bear	6/15/1948	6/13/1949	17.06	13.55	−20.57	363
Bull	6/13/1949	8/2/1956	13.55	49.74	267.08	2,607
Bear	8/2/1956	10/22/1957	49.74	38.98	−21.63	446
Bull	10/22/1957	12/12/1961	38.98	72.64	86.35	1,512
Bear	12/12/1961	6/26/1962	72.64	52.32	−27.97	196
Bull	6/26/1962	2/9/1966	52.32	94.06	79.78	1,324
Bear	2/9/1966	10/7/1966	94.06	73.20	−22.18	240
Bull	10/7/1966	11/29/1968	73.20	108.37	48.05	784
Bear	11/29/1968	5/26/1970	108.37	69.29	−36.06	543
Bull	5/26/1970	1/11/1973	69.29	120.24	73.53	961
Bear	1/11/1973	10/3/1974	120.24	62.28	−48.20	630
Bull	10/3/1974	11/28/1980	62.28	140.52	125.63	2,248
Bear	11/28/1980	8/12/1982	140.52	102.42	−27.11	622
Bull	8/12/1982	8/25/1987	102.42	336.77	228.81	1,839
Bear	8/25/1987	12/4/1987	336.77	223.92	−33.51	101
Bull	12/4/1987	7/16/1990	223.92	368.95	64.77	955
Bear	7/16/1990	10/11/1990	368.95	295.46	−19.92	87
Bull	10/11/1990	7/17/1998	295.46	1,186.75	301.66	2,836
Bear	7/17/1998	8/31/1998	1,186.75	957.53	−19.31	45
Bull	8/31/1998	3/24/2000	957.28	1,527.46	59.52	571
Bear	3/24/2000	10/9/2002	1,527.46	776.76	−49.15	929
Bull	10/9/2002	10/9/2007	776.76	1,565.15	101.50	1,826
Bear	10/9/2007	3/9/2009	1,565.15	676.53	−56.78	517
Bull	3/9/2009	2/1/2013	676.53	1,513.17	123.67	1,425

Top-Performing Bull Markets: S&P 500

Move	Begin	End	Start	Finish	Percent Change	Length (Days)
Bull	10/11/1990	7/17/1998	295.46	1,186.75	301.66	2,836
Bull	6/13/1949	8/2/1956	13.55	49.74	267.08	2,607
Bull	8/12/1982	8/25/1987	102.42	336.77	228.81	1,839
Bull	4/28/1942	5/29/1946	7.47	19.25	157.70	1,492
Bull	3/14/1935	3/10/1937	8.06	18.67	131.64	727
Bull	10/3/1974	11/28/1980	62.28	140.52	125.63	2,248
Bull	3/9/2009	2/1/2013	676.53	1,513.17	123.67	1,425
Bull	2/27/1933	7/18/1933	5.53	12.20	120.61	141
Bull	6/1/1932	9/7/1932	4.40	9.31	111.59	98
Bull	10/9/2002	10/9/2007	776.76	1,565.15	101.50	1,826
Bull	10/22/1957	12/12/1961	38.98	72.64	86.35	1,512
Bull	6/26/1962	2/9/1966	52.32	94.06	79.78	1,324
Bull	12/30/1927	9/16/1929	17.76	31.86	79.39	626
Bull	5/26/1970	1/11/1973	69.29	120.24	73.53	961
Bull	12/4/1987	7/16/1990	223.92	368.95	64.77	955
Bull	3/31/1938	11/9/1938	8.50	13.79	62.24	223
Bull	8/31/1998	3/24/2000	957.28	1,527.46	59.52	571
Bull	10/7/1966	11/29/1968	73.20	108.37	48.05	784
Bull	11/13/1929	4/10/1930	17.66	25.92	46.77	148
Bull	10/19/1933	2/6/1934	8.61	11.82	37.28	110

Worst-Performing Bear Markets: S&P 500

Move	Begin	End	Start	Finish	Percent Change	Length (Days)
Bear	11/9/1931	6/1/1932	11.52	4.40	−61.81	205
Bear	10/9/2007	3/9/2009	1,565.15	676.53	−56.78	517
Bear	3/10/1937	3/31/1938	18.67	8.50	−54.47	386
Bear	3/24/2000	10/9/2002	1,527.46	776.76	−49.15	929
Bear	1/11/1973	10/3/1974	120.24	62.28	−48.20	630
Bear	9/16/1929	11/13/1929	31.86	17.66	−44.57	58
Bear	4/10/1930	12/16/1930	25.92	14.44	−44.29	250
Bear	6/26/1931	10/5/1931	15.35	8.82	−42.54	101
Bear	9/7/1932	2/27/1933	9.31	5.53	−40.60	173

Worst-Performing Bear Markets: S&P 500 (*Continued*)

Move	Begin	End	Start	Finish	Percent Change	Length (Days)
Bear	11/29/1968	5/26/1970	108.37	69.29	−36.06	543
Bear	11/7/1940	4/28/1942	11.39	7.47	−34.42	537
Bear	8/25/1987	12/4/1987	336.77	223.92	−33.51	101
Bear	2/24/1931	6/2/1931	18.17	12.20	−32.86	98
Bear	10/25/1939	6/10/1940	13.21	8.99	−31.95	229
Bear	2/6/1934	3/14/1935	11.82	8.06	−31.81	401
Bear	7/18/1933	10/19/1933	12.20	8.61	−29.43	93
Bear	5/29/1946	5/19/1947	19.25	13.77	−28.47	355
Bear	12/12/1961	6/26/1962	72.64	52.32	−27.97	196
Bear	11/28/1980	8/12/1982	140.52	102.42	−27.11	622
Bear	11/9/1938	4/11/1939	13.79	10.42	−24.44	153

Bull/Bear Filter: DJIA

Move	Begin	End	Start	Finish	Percent Change	Length (Days)
Bear	4/17/1930	12/16/1930	294.07	157.51	−46.44	243
Bull	12/16/1930	2/24/1931	157.51	194.36	23.40	70
Bear	2/24/1931	6/2/1931	194.36	121.70	−37.38	98
Bull	6/2/1931	7/3/1931	121.70	155.26	27.58	31
Bear	7/3/1931	10/5/1931	155.26	86.48	−44.30	94
Bull	10/5/1931	11/9/1931	86.48	116.79	35.05	35
Bear	11/9/1931	1/5/1932	116.79	71.24	−39.00	57
Bull	1/5/1932	3/8/1932	71.24	88.78	24.62	63
Bear	3/8/1932	7/8/1932	88.78	41.22	−53.57	122
Bull	7/8/1932	9/7/1932	41.22	79.93	93.91	61
Bear	9/7/1932	2/27/1933	79.93	50.16	−37.25	173
Bull	2/27/1933	7/18/1933	50.16	108.67	116.65	141
Bear	7/18/1933	10/19/1933	108.67	84.38	−22.35	93
Bull	10/19/1933	2/5/1934	84.38	110.74	31.24	109
Bear	2/5/1934	7/26/1934	110.74	85.51	−22.78	171
Bull	7/26/1934	3/10/1937	85.51	194.40	127.34	958
Bear	3/10/1937	3/31/1938	194.40	98.95	−49.10	386
Bull	3/31/1938	11/9/1938	98.95	158.08	59.76	223

(*continued*)

Bull/Bear Filter: DJIA (*Continued*)

Move	Begin	End	Start	Finish	Percent Change	Length (Days)
Bear	11/9/1938	4/11/1939	158.08	123.75	−21.72	153
Bull	4/11/1939	9/12/1939	123.75	155.92	26.00	154
Bear	9/12/1939	6/10/1940	155.92	111.84	−28.27	272
Bull	6/10/1940	11/7/1940	111.84	137.75	23.17	150
Bear	11/7/1940	4/28/1942	137.75	92.92	−32.54	537
Bull	4/28/1942	5/29/1946	92.92	212.50	128.69	1,492
Bear	5/29/1946	6/13/1949	212.50	161.60	−23.95	1,111
Bull	6/13/1949	12/13/1961	161.60	734.90	354.76	4,566
Bear	12/13/1961	6/26/1962	734.90	535.76	−27.10	195
Bull	6/26/1962	2/9/1966	535.76	995.14	85.74	1,324
Bear	2/9/1966	10/7/1966	995.14	744.31	−25.21	240
Bull	10/7/1966	12/3/1968	744.31	985.21	32.37	788
Bear	12/3/1968	5/26/1970	985.21	631.15	−35.94	539
Bull	5/26/1970	1/11/1973	631.15	1,051.69	66.63	961
Bear	1/11/1973	12/6/1974	1,051.69	577.60	−45.08	694
Bull	12/6/1974	9/21/1976	577.60	1,014.79	75.69	655
Bear	9/21/1976	2/28/1978	1,014.79	742.12	−26.87	525
Bull	2/28/1978	4/27/1981	742.12	1,024.05	37.99	1,154
Bear	4/27/1981	8/12/1982	1,024.05	776.92	−24.13	472
Bull	8/12/1982	8/25/1987	776.92	2,722.40	250.41	1,839
Bear	8/25/1987	10/19/1987	2,722.40	1,738.74	−36.13	55
Bull	10/19/1987	7/16/1990	1,738.74	2,999.75	72.52	1,001
Bear	7/16/1990	10/11/1990	2,999.75	2,365.10	−21.16	87
Bull	10/11/1990	1/14/2000	2,365.10	11,722.98	395.67	3,382
Bear	1/14/2000	3/22/2001	11,722.98	9,389.48	−19.91	433
Bull	3/22/2001	5/21/2001	9,389.48	11,337.92	20.75	60
Bear	5/21/2001	9/21/2001	11,337.92	8,235.81	−27.36	123
Bull	9/21/2001	3/19/2002	8,235.81	10,635.25	29.13	179
Bear	3/19/2002	10/9/2002	10,635.25	7,286.27	−31.49	204
Bull	10/9/2002	10/9/2007	7,286.27	14,164.53	94.40	1,826
Bear	10/9/2007	3/9/2009	14,164.53	6,547.05	−53.78	517
Bull	3/9/2009	2/1/2013	6,547.05	14,009.79	113.99	1,425

Top-Performing Bull Markets: DJIA

Move	Begin	End	Start	Finish	Percent Change	Length (Days)
Bull	8/24/1921	9/3/1929	63.90	381.17	496.51	2,932
Bull	10/11/1990	1/14/2000	2,365.10	11,722.98	395.67	3,382
Bull	6/13/1949	12/13/1961	161.60	734.90	354.76	4,566
Bull	8/12/1982	8/25/1987	776.92	2,722.40	250.41	1,839
Bull	11/9/2003	1/19/2006	42.15	103.00	144.37	802
Bull	4/28/1942	5/29/1946	92.92	212.50	128.69	1,492
Bull	7/26/1934	3/10/1937	85.51	194.40	127.34	958
Bull	2/27/1933	7/18/1933	50.16	108.67	116.65	141
Bull	3/9/2009	2/1/2013	6,547.05	14,009.79	113.99	1,425
Bull	12/24/1914	11/21/1916	53.17	110.15	107.17	698
Bull	10/9/2002	10/9/2007	7,286.27	14,164.53	94.40	1,826
Bull	7/8/1932	9/7/1932	41.22	79.93	93.91	61
Bull	11/15/2007	11/19/2009	53.00	100.53	89.68	735
Bull	6/26/1962	2/9/1966	535.76	995.14	85.74	1,324
Bull	12/19/1917	11/3/1919	65.95	119.62	81.38	684
Bull	12/6/1974	9/21/1976	577.60	1,014.79	75.69	655
Bull	10/19/1987	7/16/1990	1,738.74	2,999.75	72.52	1,001
Bull	5/26/1970	1/11/1973	631.15	1,051.69	66.63	961
Bull	3/31/1938	11/9/1938	98.95	158.08	59.76	223
Bull	11/13/1929	4/17/1930	198.69	294.07	48.00	155

Worst-Performing Bear Markets: DJIA

Move	Begin	End	Start	Finish	Percent Change	Length (Days)
Bear	10/9/2007	3/9/2009	14,164.53	6,547.05	−53.78	517
Bear	3/8/1932	7/8/1932	88.78	41.22	−53.57	122
Bear	3/10/1937	3/31/1938	194.40	98.95	−49.10	386
Bear	1/19/2006	11/15/2007	103.00	53.00	−48.54	665
Bear	9/3/1929	11/13/1929	381.17	198.69	−47.87	71
Bear	11/3/1919	8/24/1921	119.62	63.90	−46.58	660
Bear	4/17/1930	12/16/1930	294.07	157.51	−46.44	243
Bear	6/17/2001	11/9/2003	78.26	42.15	−46.14	875
Bear	1/11/1973	12/6/1974	1,051.69	577.60	−45.08	694

(continued)

Worst-Performing Bear Markets: DJIA (*Continued*)

Move	Begin	End	Start	Finish	Percent Change	Length (Days)
Bear	7/3/1931	10/5/1931	155.26	86.48	−44.30	94
Bear	9/30/1912	12/24/1914	94.15	53.17	−43.53	815
Bear	11/21/1916	12/19/1917	110.15	65.95	−40.13	393
Bear	11/9/1931	1/5/1932	116.79	71.24	−39.00	57
Bear	2/24/1931	6/2/1931	194.36	121.70	−37.38	98
Bear	9/7/1932	2/27/1933	79.93	50.16	−37.25	173
Bear	8/25/1987	10/19/1987	2,722.40	1,738.74	−36.13	55
Bear	12/3/1968	5/26/1970	985.21	631.15	−35.94	539
Bear	11/7/1940	4/28/1942	137.75	92.92	−32.54	537
Bear	3/19/2002	10/9/2002	10,635.25	7,286.27	−31.49	204
Bear	9/12/1939	6/10/1940	155.92	111.84	−28.27	272

Yearly Returns

Year	DJIA	DJTA	DJUA	S&P	Nasdaq	Long Bond	EAFE
2012	7.26%	5.72%	−2.49%	13.41%	15.91%	2.69%	13.55%
2011	5.53	−1.70	14.74	0.00	−1.80	35.31	−14.82
2010	11.02	24.57	1.75	12.78	16.91	9.15	4.9
2009	18.82	15.90	7.35	23.45	43.89	−25.91	27.75
2008	−33.84	−22.61	−30.38	−38.49	−40.54	41.85	−46.09
2007	6.43	0.23	16.59	3.53	9.81	10.71	8.62
2006	16.29	8.68	12.75	13.62	9.52	−1.16	23.47
2005	−0.61	10.48	20.95	3.00	1.37	9.31	10.86
2004	3.15	26.30	25.50	8.99	8.59	8.86	17.59
2003	25.32	30.18	24.04	26.38	50.01	0.77	35.28
2002	−16.76	−12.50	−26.79	−23.37	−31.53	16.17	−17.52
2001	−7.10	−10.30	−28.68	−13.04	−21.05	4.21	−22.61
2000	−6.18	−1.02	45.45	−10.14	−39.29	20.22	−15.21
1999	25.22	−5.47	−9.27	19.53	85.59	−14.78	25.27
1998	16.10	−3.29	14.37	26.67	39.63	17.06	18.23
1997	22.64	44.37	17.43	31.01	21.64	15.03	0.24
1996	26.01	13.87	3.16	20.26	22.71	−4.32	4.40
1995	33.45	36.15	24.17	34.11	39.92	34.14	9.42
1994	2.14	−17.44	−20.84	−1.54	−3.20	−11.99	6.24

Yearly Returns (*Continued*)

Year	DJIA	DJTA	DJUA	S&P	Nasdaq	Long Bond	EAFE
1993	14.60	21.61	3.75	7.10	14.75	20.01	30.49
1992	4.17	6.72	−2.27	4.50	18.45	6.71	−13.89
1991	20.32	49.19	7.84	26.31	56.84	17.32	10.19
1990	−4.34	−22.72	−10.78	−6.56	−17.80	4.39	−24.71
1989	26.96	21.44	26.18	27.25	19.26	20.07	9.22
1988	11.85	29.51	6.40	12.40	15.41	7.70	26.66
1987	2.26	−7.22	−15.01	2.03	−5.26	−6.29	23.18
1986	22.58	13.97	17.85	14.62	7.36	25.99	66.80
1985	27.66	26.89	16.91	26.33	31.36	34.30	52.97
1984	−3.74	−6.76	13.42	1.40	−11.22	17.11	5.02
1983	20.27	33.50	10.35	17.27	19.87	−0.46	20.91
1982	19.61	17.90	9.59	14.76	18.67	40.94	−4.63
1981	−9.23	−4.47	−4.73	−9.73	−3.21	2.97	−4.85
1980	14.93	57.73	7.34	25.77	33.88	−1.39	19.01
1979	4.19	22.19	8.52	12.31	25.11	−0.15	1.82
1978	−3.15	−4.89	−11.73	1.06	12.31	0.65	28.91
1977	−17.27	−8.37	2.68	−11.50	7.33	−0.33	14.61
1976	17.00	37.29	29.56	19.15	26.10	19.16	
1975	39.35	20.36	21.66	31.55	29.76	9.58	
1974	−27.57	−26.89	−23.06	−29.72	−35.11	0.12	
1973	−16.58	−13.64	−25.21	−17.37	−31.06	−1.10	
1972	14.58	−6.79	1.49	15.63	17.18	5.70	
1971	6.11	41.94	−3.36	10.79	14.12	13.20	
1970	4.82	−2.73	10.68	0.10		12.10	
1969	−15.19	−35.07	−19.75	−11.36		−5.10	
1968	4.27	16.45	7.24	7.66		−0.30	
1967	15.20	14.91	−6.07	20.09		−9.20	
1966	−18.94	−17.99	−10.78	−13.09		3.70	
1965	10.88	20.52	−1.64	9.06		0.70	
1964	14.57	15.01	11.64	12.97		3.50	
1963	17.00	26.59	7.55	18.89		1.20	
1962	−10.81	−1.95	0.05	−11.81		6.90	
1961	18.71	9.93	29.13	23.13		1.00	

(*continued*)

Yearly Returns (*Continued*)

Year	DJIA	DJTA	DJUA	S&P	Nasdaq	Long Bond	EAFE
1960	−9.34	−15.06	13.88	−2.97		13.80	
1959	16.40	−2.28	−3.48	8.48		−2.30	
1958	33.96	62.59	32.69	38.06		−6.10	
1957	−12.77	−36.72	0.06	−14.31		7.50	
1956	2.27	−6.16	6.83	2.62		−5.60	
1955	20.78	11.95	2.71	26.40		−1.30	
1954	43.96	55.12	20.04	45.02		7.20	
1953	−3.77	−15.49	−1.06	−6.62		3.60	
1952	8.42	36.19	11.39	11.78		1.20	
1951	14.37		15.23	16.35		−3.90	
1950	17.41		−0.75	21.68		0.10	
1949	13.09		23.07	10.46		6.40	
1948	−2.13		0.45	−0.65		3.40	
1947	2.23		−10.38	0.00		−2.60	
1946	−8.14		−2.26	−11.87		−0.10	
1945	26.97		44.60	30.72		10.70	
1944	11.80		20.58	13.80		2.80	
1943	13.81		50.41	19.45		2.10	
1942	7.61		3.71	12.43		3.20	
1941	−15.38		−29.37	−17.86		0.90	
1940	−12.57		−22.40	−15.09		6.10	
1939	−2.83		11.12	−5.18		5.90	
1938	27.73		13.12	24.55		5.50	
1937	−32.82		−41.57	−38.59		0.20	
1936	24.82		17.87	27.92		7.50	
1935	38.53		66.01	41.37		5.00	
1934	5.44		−23.57	−4.71		10.00	
1933	63.74		−15.31	44.08		−0.10	
1932	−22.64		−12.45	−14.78		16.80	
1931	−52.67		−48.34	−47.07		−5.30	
1930	−31.73		−31.12	−28.48		4.70	
1929	−18.70			−11.91		3.40	
1928	47.74			37.88		0.10	

Yearly Returns (*Continued*)

Year	DJIA	DJTA	DJUA	S&P	Nasdaq	Long Bond	EAFE
1927	27.67					8.90	
1926	4.05					7.80	
1925	25.37						
1924	26.16						
1923	-2.70						
1922	21.50						
1921	12.30						
1920	-32.90						
1919	30.45						
1918	10.51						
1917	-21.71						
1916	-4.19						
1915	78.84						

Cost of Timing the Market

Cost of Timing the Market: DJIA 1900 through 2012

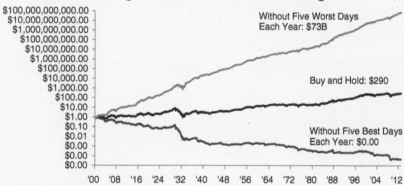

Without Five Worst Days Each Year: $73B

Buy and Hold: $290

Without Five Best Days Each Year: $0.00

DOW JONES RETURN

Annual changes in the Dow Jones under the three "$1.00 invested" scenarios:

Year	Annual Change	Without Five Best Days	Without Five Worst Days	Year	Annual Change	Without Five Best Days	Without Five Worst Days
1900	3.79	−11.98	20.18	1957	−12.77	−22.96	−0.93
1901	−8.70	−24.74	18.74	1958	33.96	24.62	45.50
1902	−0.42	−11.72	17.90	1959	16.40	8.41	27.93
1903	−23.61	−36.28	−4.58	1960	−9.34	−16.62	−0.22
1904	42.64	26.24	73.57	1961	18.71	9.48	31.42

(continued)

Year	Annual Change	Without Five Best Days	Without Five Worst Days	Year	Annual Change	Without Five Best Days	Without Five Worst Days
1905	37.84	19.03	65.06	1962	−10.81	−24.33	6.21
1906	−2.29	−13.40	15.01	1963	17.00	6.31	27.25
1907	−37.73	−49.69	−14.94	1964	14.57	9.02	22.15
1908	46.64	27.20	69.13	1965	10.88	4.17	20.80
1909	14.97	4.55	34.47	1966	−18.94	−26.20	−9.61
1910	−17.81	−28.34	−1.97	1967	15.20	6.08	25.23
1911	0.21	−10.97	13.50	1968	4.27	−4.26	13.12
1912	7.71	0.43	20.28	1969	−15.19	−21.85	−7.14
1913	−10.34	−18.84	4.03	1970	4.82	−10.36	20.81
1914	−5.14	−16.33	12.10	1971	6.11	−5.03	17.07
1915	73.88	42.99	110.62	1972	14.58	7.05	23.64
1916	10.42	−14.74	45.07	1973	−16.58	−28.04	−1.43
1917	−21.71	−34.52	1.36	1974	−27.57	−40.36	−13.77
1918	10.51	−2.82	28.70	1975	38.32	20.28	57.98
1919	30.45	10.86	65.18	1976	17.86	7.13	30.67
1920	−32.90	−43.85	−16.27	1977	−17.27	−23.08	−8.87
1921	12.30	−0.74	28.74	1978	−3.15	−15.20	9.97
1922	21.50	10.40	39.77	1979	4.19	−5.44	16.99
1923	−2.70	−13.01	13.25	1980	14.93	0.85	32.69
1924	26.16	15.68	45.82	1981	−9.23	−18.67	2.75
1925	30.00	18.93	56.25	1982	19.60	−2.19	37.40
1926	0.34	−12.43	20.67	1983	20.27	6.98	34.54
1927	27.67	15.25	45.31	1984	−3.74	−16.13	7.11
1928	49.48	29.79	78.64	1985	27.66	15.52	37.63
1929	−17.17	−43.08	46.60	1986	22.58	9.78	46.30
1930	−33.77	−46.67	−8.09	1987	2.26	−21.81	69.82
1931	−52.67	−71.08	−29.49	1988	11.85	−4.50	39.24
1932	−22.64	−50.89	20.70	1989	26.96	13.08	50.07
1933	63.74	7.00	144.05	1990	−4.34	−16.26	14.05
1934	5.44	−11.38	32.37	1991	20.32	3.47	38.07
1935	38.53	22.63	60.05	1992	4.17	−4.35	14.40
1936	24.82	12.28	48.96	1993	13.72	5.57	24.10
1937	−32.82	−45.47	−6.42	1994	2.14	−6.32	15.18
1938	27.73	3.66	67.24	1995	33.45	24.11	45.14
1939	−2.83	−21.52	21.22	1996	26.01	15.16	43.68
1940	−12.57	−26.55	18.96	1997	22.64	4.33	50.00
1941	−15.38	−23.76	−2.15	1998	16.10	−3.41	46.75
1942	7.61	−1.73	22.00	1999	25.22	10.92	43.84
1943	13.81	4.89	30.99	2000	−6.18	−20.48	16.91
1944	11.80	5.67	19.54	2001	−7.10	−22.58	19.47

Year	Annual Change	Without Five Best Days	Without Five Worst Days	Year	Annual Change	Without Five Best Days	Without Five Worst Days
1945	26.97	15.91	41.24	2002	−16.76	−34.98	3.85
1946	−8.14	−20.91	16.40	2003	25.32	7.21	45.67
1947	2.23	−6.00	18.14	2004	3.15	−4.77	12.87
1948	−2.13	−10.60	15.58	2005	−0.61	−8.37	8.59
1949	13.10	5.35	25.79	2006	16.29	6.14	28.69
1950	17.39	6.21	42.34	2007	6.43	−5.27	25.52
1951	14.37	4.91	26.95	2008	−33.84	−54.96	1.36
1952	8.42	1.60	16.56	2009	18.82	−4.99	52.31
1953	−3.77	−9.27	6.49	2010	11.02	−4.11	32.93
1954	43.96	33.88	56.46	2011	5.53	−11.66	36.08
1955	20.78	10.06	45.90	2012	7.26	−2.67	20.57
1956	2.27	−5.76	11.84				

History of Regulation

Date	Event
1983	Nasdaq starts NQDS: Level II (Market Depth) data made available to the public.
Jan 1988	In response to the 1987 crash, the SEC and NASD Board of Governors approved amendments to the Rules of Practice and Procedures for the Small Order Execution System (SOES) to better handle small orders for individuals.
Nov 1988	Insider Trading and Securities Fraud Enforcement Act of 1988: Added harsher penalties for violations of the Securities Act of 1934 to further discourage insider trading.
Jan 1993	State Street Global Advisors introduces SPDR ETF (SPY).
Aug 1993	President Clinton limits deduction for pay to $1 million but exempts options. The FASB wants to deduct value from earnings, Silicon Valley objects, it doesn't happen. Joseph Stiglitz details it in *The Roaring Nineties.*
May 1994	Nasdaq sued for price-fixing, forced to integrate ECN's into system to increase competition.
Jul 1994	FINRA adopts Rule 5320 (Manning Rule): Firms must place client's interest ahead of their own.
Dec 1995	Congress passes the Private Securities Litigation Reform Act: tightening requirements for filing lawsuits against companies, executives, and accounting firms.
Jan 1997	SEC implements Order Execution Obligations: demands that market makers and specialists act competitively and honestly in the market.
May 1997	Common Cents Stock Pricing Act, HR 1053: removes legal barriers to pricing in decimals.

(continued)

Date	Event
Jun 1997	NYSE announces stock quotes change from eighths to sixteenths and decimals by the year 2000.
Aug 1997	Direct market access given to small investors: Online brokerages can give real-time pricing.
Apr 1998	SEC revises circuit-breaker rules: NYSE can halt at 10, 20, and 30 percent drops rather than point-limit drops.
Dec 1998	Regulation of Exchanges and Alternative Trading Systems (Reg ATS): SEC seeks to protect investors and fix concerns about Alternative Trading Systems; gives ATSs option to register as exchanges; HFTs allowed in market.
Nov 1999	Portions of the Banking Act of 1933 (Glass-Steagall Act) repealed by Financial Services Modernization Act of 1999 (Gramm-Leach-Bliley Act).
May 2000	SEC rescinds Rule 390: exchange-listed securities can now be freely traded off the exchanges.
Jun 2000	SEC orders exchanges to submit plans for converting to decimal trading of stocks and some options by September 5, 2000.
Aug 2000	Regulation Fair Disclosure (Reg FD): SEC requires companies to release material information to all investors at the same time.
Nov 2000	Disclosure of Order Execution and Order Routing Practices: SEC requires broker-dealers to make routing locations of customer orders public.
Dec 2000	Commodity Futures Modernization Act: deregulates OTC derivatives market.
Feb 2001	SEC approves FINRA Rule 2520: defines and sets rules/restrictions for a "Pattern Day Trader" classification to protect against risk.
Apr 2001	NYSE launches Direct+: system automatically matches orders by bypassing specialists.
Jul 2002	Nasdaq goes public: capitalizes on revenue generation from trading services.
Jul 2002	Sarbanes-Oxley Act: imposes higher standards for public companies after Enron and Tyco scandals.
Jul 2005	Regulation National Market System (Reg NMS): SEC requires prices to be listed on all exchanges and creates trade-through rule.
Mar 2006	NYSE acquires Archipelago: NYSE moves toward HFT.
Jul 2007	Regulation SHO and Rule 10a-1: SEC eliminates Uptick Rule; traders can now short stocks while price declines.
Oct 2008	Exchange Rule 107B: SEC approves NYSE pilot program designating "Supplemental Liquidity Providers" and allowing for rebates for provided liquity.

Date	Event
Oct 2008	"Naked" Short Selling Antifraud Rule: SEC imposes to "further evidence the liability of short sellers."
Oct 2008	SEC approves the NYSE "New Model": phasing out specialists in favor of Designated Market Maker structure.
Nov 2008	BATS becomes an exchange: After SEC approval, the former ECN can compete directly with Nasdaq and NYSE.
Jun 2009	Nasdaq and BATS introduce flash orders: allows traders to see actionable indicators of interest (market price).
Jul 2009	NYSE introduces Super Display Book System: cuts trade execution time from 105 to 5 milliseconds.
Oct 2009	Clearly Erroneous Trade Rule: SEC approves consistent standard across exchanges for breaking trades.
Feb 2010	SEC amends Reg SHO: restricts short selling at or below National Best Bid if stock is down 10 percent intraday (new uptick rule).
May 2010	Flash Crash: DJIA loses 1,000 points in five minutes after HFTs magnify mistake.
Jun 2010	New circuit-breaker rule: SEC adopts new five-minute trading halt for S&P 500 stocks that change 10 percent in five-minute period in response to flash crash.
Jul 2010	Dodd-Frank Wall Street Reform and Consumer Protection Act: passed in reaction to and in an attempt to avoid another financial crisis.
Nov 2010	Risk Management Controls for Brokers or Dealers with Market Access: SEC requires controls to prevent overexposure of any market participant, ensures regulatory compliance with regard to market access, and to prevent clearly erroneous orders ("fat fingers," "stub quotes").
Jul 2011	Large Trader Reporting requirements: greater scrutiny on large trader activity after May 2010 flash crash.
Apr 2012	Jumpstart Our Business Startups Act (JOBS Act): eases requirements for potential/new public companies and restrictions on marketing some private placements.
Jul 2012	Retail Liquidity Program: NYSE initiative to open up dark pools to competition by allowing market makers to offer retail stock orders a fraction of a penny better than National Best Offer.
Sep 2012	NYSE charged for Improper Distribution of Market Data: information selectively shared with some customers.
Apr 2013	LULD (Limit Up Limit Down) pilot program goes into effect. No Limits 9:30–9:45 and 3:30–4:00.

Glossary

Advance/Decline Line (A/D): An index that measures the net number of stocks rising each day compared to the number that fell. Using the S&P 500 as an example, if on a day 300 stocks rose and 200 fell, the Advance/Decline Index would be +100 (300–200). Today's net number is then added to the previous day's cumulative A/D.

backtesting: The testing of an investment strategy using historical data to determine its profitability. Not run using real money or real-time data.

basis point: One hundredth of 1 percent (.01%). Indicated by "bps." 1% = 100 bps.

bear market: A decline of at least 20 percent from the previous high.

benchmark: Is a "yardstick" by which investment performance is measured.

beta: Measures an investment's risk relative to a given benchmark. A number greater than 1 means an investment had more risk than the benchmark, while less than 1 is less risky. For example, a stock with a beta of 1.2 means that the stock will be 20 percent more volatile than the market as a whole.

bond vigilantes: An individual who is concerned that a country's current fiscal and or monetary policy will hurt that country's sovereign debt. (See also hawk.)

bull market: An advance of at least 20 percent from the previous low.

buy-side: The part of the investment community that is managing money (mutual funds, hedge funds) and using investment products supplied by their counterpart on the sell-side. (See also sell-side.)

capitulation: When an investor or group of investors finally gives up after a long decline or rally and sells (buys) their risky investments. Associated with high volume and a market low (top).

capitalization-weighted index: An index where the members' weights are determined by the value of each company. The value of each company is determined by multiplying the shares outstanding of each company by its current share price. The S&P 500 is an example of such an index.

consumer discretionary: Stocks, such as clothing retailers, that are influenced by the prevailing economic conditions.

consumer staples: Sells products that make up a core of one's daily activity, such as food. These products are less likely to see a decline in sales during an economic slowdown.

correction: A decline of between 10 and 20 percent from a recent high.

cost basis: The original cost of one's investment.

cyclical trend: An advance or decline that is both shorter and opposite in nature than the prevailing secular trend.

death cross: When a shorter-term moving average, such as the 50-day, breaks below a security's longer-term moving average like the 200-day moving average. (See also golden cross.)

dove: Those who argue for lower interest rates. The opposite of a hawk. (See also hawk.)

Dow Theory: A technical indicator that says that a move in the Dow Jones Industrial Average must be confirmed by the Dow Jones Transportation Average.

downtick: A trade at a lower price than the previous price. (See also uptick.)

drawdown: The maximum amount an investment falls from peak to trough before recovering to its prior peak.

earnings per share: A company's total net earnings adjusted for the number of shares outstanding.

ERISA: Employee Retirement Income Security Act of 1974. Implemented rules that protect the retirement assets of Americans. Managers of retirement assets are now held personally responsible for the mismanagement of retirement assets.

fungible: A unit of one investment is equivalent to another unit of the same good of the same quality at the same time and place. For example, a 10-dollar bill is fungible for two 5-dollar bills or 10 1-dollar bills.

golden cross: When a shorter-term moving average, such as the 50-day, breaks above a security's longer-term moving average like the 200-day moving average. (See also death cross.)

hawk: Those who argue for higher interest rates out of fear that low rates will cause an undesired increase in inflation. The opposite of a dove. (See also dove.)

high-frequency trading: Firms that, using sophisticated software and direct links to exchanges, trade thousands of times a day often for just a few pennies profit per share.

high-water mark: The highest cumulative return a fund has achieved, as of the most recent year end, and a level that must be exceeded before an incentive fee can be paid. Most often associated with hedge funds.

incentive fee: A percentage of profits that is paid to the investment manager at the end of each year, if the manager has made money and is above the fund's high water mark. Typically associated with hedge funds and, while the percentage varies widely, the central tendency is 20 percent. (See also high-water mark.)

leverage: Using borrowed money to increase the potential return of an investment. It likewise increases the risk of that investment.

long: To own an investment.

moving average: The average price of a security or index for the previous x trading days. For example, a 50-day average includes the price today and the previous 49 trading days.

overbought: A technical analysis term indicating that many stocks have done well over a recent period. The use of the word indicates the possibility of a correction or at least a pause in the advance. (See also oversold.)

oversold: A term associated with technical analysis. Most often used to generalize that many stocks have done poorly recently and a rally is imminent. (See also overbought.)

overweight: When one owns a greater weighting of an investment than one's benchmark. (See also underweight.)

price-weighted index: An index whose member weights are determined by the current price of its members. For example, if an index consists of two stocks where one is $100 and the other is $50, the $100 stock will have a weight two times greater than the $50 stock. The most popular example is the Dow Jones Industrial Average (DJIA).

relative strength: The comparison of one asset's performance with another asset's performance. Typically, a graph is drawn to visually display the relationship between the two assets. A rising line indicates the outperformance of an asset.

risk on/risk off: The response to supposed risk in the global investment climate. When investors perceive less risk in global financial markets, they will increase their net exposure and are said to be "risk on." When the perceived risk increases, investors sell their investments, which is deemed to be "risk off."

secular trend: A prolonged advance or decline.

sell-side: The part of the investment community whose primary responsibility is executing orders given to them by the buy-side. They are interested in selling investment services. (See also buy-side.)

short: Selling an investment that one does not own in the hopes of profiting from a decline in its price.

tail risk: The risk that an investment will experience an abnormally large loss, or gain, above what would normally be expected, given known risks.

thinly traded: Indicates a stock that trades low volume and infrequently. Most often, the stock will have large changes in price even with small buy or sell transactions.

total return: The periodic return of an asset including price appreciation and all dividends collected during the holding period.

trendline: A line drawn on a securities price chart connecting either the highs or the lows to better determine the directional trend of the security.

underweight: When one owns a smaller weighting of an investment than one's benchmark. (See benchmark.)

uptick: A trade at a higher price than the then previous transaction. (See also downtick.)

About the Author

Laszlo Birinyi is founder and president of Birinyi Associates Inc., a research and asset management firm based in Westport, Connecticut. A graduate of the University of North Carolina and New York University, Graduate School of Business Administration, he began his career as a sales trader. At Mitchell, Hutchins, he introduced the first trading calendar so that the trading desk could respond more quickly to earnings and other indicators.

In 1976, he was hired by Salomon Brothers where he wrote the firm's first stock market letter and created the first Block Monitor, which later became known as Money Flows. He was responsible for a variety of market studies including studies on trading costs and volatility, while his trading manual, *The Equity Desk*, was cited in Michael Lewis' *Liar's Poker*.

In 1989, he left Salomon and formed his own firm while consulting for what is now Bloomberg, LP, where he became their first third-party provider. From 1990 through 1999 he was a panelist on *Louis Rukeyser's Wall Street Week*. In 1999 he was inducted into that show's Hall of Fame, with Rukeyser calling him simply "the world's number one stock picker."

About the Website

In addition to the material contained in Chapter 5 on money flows, the author provides further reading and background on money flows and its origins, calculations, and record on the website. Available only online, the material allows the reader to better understand the significance of money flows.

The author also provides a spreadsheet that, when updated by the reader, will calculate two of the author's favorite overbought/oversold indicators and allows the reader to better determine the technical status of the market.

To access the companion website, please go to http://www.wiley.com/go/mastertrader. When prompted for a password, please enter "birinyi."

Index